I0836732

FAITH WORKING BY LOVE:

AS EXEMPLIFIED IN

THE LIFE OF FIDELIA FISKE.

BY

D. T. FISKE.

WRITTEN FOR THE CONGREGATIONAL SABBATH SCHOOL AND
PUBLISHING SOCIETY, AND APPROVED BY THE
COMMITTEE OF PUBLICATION.

BOSTON:
Congregational Sabbath School and Publishing Society,
NO. 13 CORNHILL.

PREFACE.

THEODORE PARKER, having read Wayland's "Life of Dr. Judson," wrote thus in his journal: "What a man! What a character! Had the whole missionary work resulted in nothing more than the building up of such a man, it would be worth all it has cost."

If such a man could use such language, may not the friends of missions say that the missionary work in Persia would be worth all it has cost, if it had simply furnished to the world such a specimen of true Christian womanhood as is seen in the life and character of FIDELIA FISKE?

In these days, when so many are earnestly discussing the question of "woman's rights" and "woman's sphere," it may be well to turn attention to the example of one, of whom Rev. Dr. Anderson says, "In the structure and working of her whole nature, she seemed to me the nearest approach I ever saw, in man or woman, to my ideal of our blessed Saviour, as he appeared on the earth."

Those contributions to biographical literature, which have been made by foreign missions, during the last half century, are invaluable. They constitute a part of the priceless heritage of the church. They illustrate and augment the power of Christianity in the world, and in many ways help forward the great missionary enterprise.

Soon after the death of Miss Fiske, a strong desire was felt by those who knew her best that some record of her life might be given to the public. I was urged to undertake the work, but could not consent to do so, until, after long delay, it seemed to be providentially laid upon me as a duty. I regret exceedingly that it was not committed to some one who could have given to it immediate and continuous attention. My task has been a humble but laborious one; — that of an editor rather than of an author. I have aimed, as far as possible, to let Miss Fiske tell the story of her own life. From the superabundant materials, I have endeavored to select such as would give a just and truthful impression of one whose piety was so suggestive of "The Cross and the Crown," and so illustrative of that Faith that works by Love.

If any of the friends, who have so kindly furnished letters and other materials for this volume, are disappointed at the omission of so much that is valuable, they will readily discover the reason for the omission in the present size of the volume.

In the preparation of these pages, it has been pleasant and profitable to hold intimate communion with so choice a spirit; and in the perusal of them I trust others may find a like pleasure and profit.

If this imperfect record of Miss Fiske's life and labors shall serve to kindle in other hearts the flame of Christian love that burned so brightly and steadily in her own, and shall help advance the cause of missions, to which she so cheerfully gave herself for Jesus' sake, my highest wish in regard to it will be realized.

NEWBURYPORT, December, 1868.

CONTENTS.

CHAPTER I.

ANCESTORS.

CHAPTER II.

BIRTHPLACE.

CHAPTER III.

EARLY DAYS.

CHAPTER IV.

LIFE AT MT. HOLYOKE SEMINARY.

CHAPTER V.

DECISION TO BE A MISSIONARY.

CHAPTER VI.

EMBARKATION, VOYAGE, LAND JOURNEY, ARRIVAL.

CHAPTER VII.

STATE OF THE NESTORIAN MISSION IN 1843. — FIRST IMPRESSIONS AND FIRST LABORS.

CHAPTER VIII.

OCTOBER, 1843, TO JUNE, 1844.

CHAPTER IX.

JUNE, 1844, TO JUNE, 1845.

CHAPTER X.

JUNE, 1845, TO JUNE, 1846.

CHAPTER XI.

JUNE, 1846, TO JUNE, 1847.

CHAPTER XII.

JUNE, 1847, TO SEPTEMBER, 1848.

CHAPTER XIII.

SEPTEMBER, 1848, TO JUNE, 1849.

CHAPTER XIV.

JUNE, 1849, TO JUNE, 1850.

CHAPTER XV.

JUNE, 1850, TO JULY, 1851.

CHAPTER XVI.

JULY, 1851, TO JUNE, 1852.

CHAPTER XVII.

JUNE, 1852, TO JUNE, 1853.

CHAPTER XVIII.

JUNE, 1853, TO JUNE, 1854.

CHAPTER XIX.

JUNE, 1854, TO JULY, 1855.

CHAPTER XX.

JULY, 1855, TO JUNE, 1856.

CHAPTER XXI.

JUNE, 1856, TO JUNE, 1857.

CHAPTER XXII.

LAST YEAR IN PERSIA.

CHAPTER XXIII.

JANUARY, 1859, TO DECEMBER, 1860.

CHAPTER XXIV.

JANUARY, 1861, TO DECEMBER, 1862.

CHAPTER XXV.

1863.

CHAPTER XXVI.

LAST LABORS AT SOUTH HADLEY.

CHAPTER XXVII.

LAST SICKNESS.

CHAPTER XXVIII.

TESTIMONIALS.

FAITH WORKING BY LOVE.

CHAPTER I.

ANCESTORS.

To be either proud or ashamed of our lineage is a sign of weakness and folly. To be grateful for a worthy ancestry is both reasonable and Christian. To recognize a close connection between the piety of parents and the piety of children, and of children's children, is what none will refuse to do who believe in the reality and perpetuity of the covenant which God of old established between himself and his chosen people and their seed after them in their generations.

FIDELIA FISKE* was a child of the covenant. She could look back through many generations along an unbroken line of godly ancestors. This fact belongs to the record of her life; nor will it seem out of place in this opening chapter to glance at those hereditary influences under which that life began.

In 1637, WILLIAM FISKE, with his elder brother Rev. John Fiske, emigrated from the County of Suffolk, England, to this country, settling first in Salem, Massachusetts, and subsequently in the adjoining town

* The branch of the family to which Miss Fiske belonged have generally omitted the final *e* from the name. It is retained in this volume because it was adopted universally by the early settlers in this country; and because Miss Fiske, during the latter part of her life, returned to the more ancient orthography, and expressed her decided preference for it.

of Wenham. According to the testimony of Cotton Mather,—who places the name of "Mr. John Fiske" on his list of "reverend, learned, and holy divines by whose Evangelical ministry the churches of New England have been illuminated,"—they were children "of pious and worthy parents, yea, of grandparents, and great-grandparents, eminent for zeal in the true religion."

William Fiske was a man of intelligence, energy, and Christian integrity. He took a leading part in public affairs; enjoyed the confidence and esteem of his townsmen, holding at different times all the important offices of trust which were at their disposal, being their Representative to the General Court for six successive years. From him the subject of this memoir was descended. The intervening genealogical links were five in number.

William Fiske, Jr., was the eldest son of the above William; was born, lived, and died in Wenham. He inherited largely his father's abilities and virtues, was deacon of the church, and, like his father, held various offices of public trust and honor, representing his town for six years in the General Court.

Ebenezer Fiske, son of William, Jr., was born in 1679; resided in Wenham, was deacon of the church, and died at the age of ninety-two.

Ebenezer Fiske, Jr., son of Ebenezer, was born at Wenham, July 2, 1716. Leaving his early home, he resided in different places, removing at length to Shelburne in 1761, where he was one of the earliest settlers. He was a man who had great influence in shaping the civil and ecclesiastical affairs of this new town. Athletic, resolute, fearless, and spirited, with a high sense of personal honor and independence, and of inflexible religious principles, he exerted great influence in the growing community.

His wife, Dorcas Tyler, of Upton, was a woman well fitted, by her native good sense, tact, energy, and eminent piety, to be the companion of the sturdy pioneer. Burdened with the cares of a numerous family, she yet walked with God; and through her daily life there breathed a serene, cheerful, saintly spirit. She was accustomed to spend much time in prayer, and frequently set apart whole days for this purpose. Her last days were days of almost continuous praying; and the burden of her prayers then was, as it had previously been, that her posterity might be a godly seed even to the latest generation. The family traditions of this godly woman were familiar to Fidelia in her early years, and inspired her with a profound and tender veneration for her memory.

She makes this touching allusion to her in a letter to a cousin, in 1858:—

"It must have been a mournful pleasure to you to visit the old burying-ground. How many, many times have I been there, to remember that I was mortal! I used to love to stand by the grave of our great-grandmother, and feel that her prayers for me would be answered. Do you know what a praying soul she had? Have you heard your father tell how she used to pray for her descendants to the end of time? How, in her dying hour, she laid her hand on the head of many a grandchild, and prayed that he or she might be the Lord's? Grandpa used to love to tell us, when little girls, about it, and would almost always add, 'I wish Fidelia's name had been Dorcas, she looks so much like her.' I wish I might be so like her as to receive the white stone on which is written the new name. We do not know how much we are indebted to the good woman's prayers for our hopes in Jesus."

Again, alluding to the ascertained fact that more than three hundred of the descendants of this praying ancestor were members of Christ's church, she thus writes to her mother, in 1857 : —

"Is it not in answer to that good great-grandmother's prayers, — to her prayers on her dying-bed? I remember well what you used to tell me of her when I was a little girl, and sat in the little yellow-bottomed chair by your side. I often think that I may be receiving blessings in answer to her prayers ; for I know that she prayed for her children's children for all coming time. I sometimes wish that you had given me her good name, Dorcas Tyler, as grandpa wished you to do. But it would not have made me like her. Let me wear my Saviour's name and be content."

EBENEZER FISKE, son of Ebenezer and Dorcas, was twelve years of age when his father removed to Shelburne. In him the strong qualities of the father reappeared, though somewhat softened and toned by the gentler qualities of the mother. He enjoyed the universal respect and confidence of those who knew him. In form and bearing he is said to have resembled Washington. There was something peculiarly venerable and saintly in his appearance and manners when an old man. The writer never recalls his noble form and benignant face without reviving those early impressions which associated him with the patriarchs of the Bible. After a serene and cheerful old age, followed by a period of helpless and blank dotage, he passed away in 1841, closing a life of ninety-two years.

His wife's maiden name was Sarah Barnard, of Shutesbury, whose rare domestic virtues, gentle spirit, and affectionate manner are all fresh in the memory of many still living. She died in 1816, at the age of sixty-two, while her son Pliny was yet revolving the question of becoming a missionary to the heathen, and just two weeks before the birth of that grand-daughter whose missionary life will find a partial record in this volume.

Of these grandparents Fidelia thus writes in 1852: "Living on the old place, and with our good grandfather, I was familiar with everything that pertained to each uncle and aunt. Our 'grandpa' used to hold us many long hours on his knee, and tell us of Uncle Levi, and Uncle Pliny, and Uncle John, till we seemed to see each one as he trod those hills and engaged in his daily labors. And many and many a time have I been incited to diligence by the articles of our good grandmother's industry, presented by that dear grandfather. He used to tell us how she spun and wove, and used her skilful needle when others would be sleeping. I have seen that beautiful pair of linen stockings which she kept in your father's cradle, and knit upon when she was nursing him. I have heard grandpa tell how beautifully those stockings fitted to the good old breeches; and then he would take from the upper drawer of 'the high case of drawers' the silver buckle which he hardly thought graced the knee so much as did grandma's handiwork."

RUFUS FISKE, the eldest child of Ebenezer and Sarah, and the father of Fidelia, was born March 22, 1781. He lived upon the ancestral farm, and in his character exhibited a happy combination of the ancestral virtues. To the vocation of a farmer he united that of a cooper, as his forefathers had done for several generations. He was a man of marked candor, and of "large, roundabout common sense." His opinion had great weight with his neighbors and townsmen, who often referred their difficulties and disputes to his decision, and among whom he was deservedly called "the peacemaker." He was a devout and exemplary Christian, sound in doctrine, firm in principle, and of a meek, quiet, benevolent spirit. In family government he was strict, yet mild, blending "goodness and severity" after the divine pattern. His word was law, but law in which authority was largely mingled with love. He ruled well his own house, yet put himself on terms of great freedom and familiarity with his children. He governed them, and yet was their companion and confidant. He died in 1840.

HANNAH WOODWARD, his wife, and the mother of Fidelia, was a native of Taunton, but, at the time of her marriage, a resident of Buckland. She was a woman of gentle spirit, of an equable temperament, quietly active and efficient, filling well the sphere of a Christian wife and mother. She lived to enjoy a serene old age, surviving the missionary daughter, whom, in a few months, she followed to the better land.

CHAPTER II.

EARLY DAYS.

Birthplace and Early Home.—Shelburne.—Character of the People.—Natural Scenery.

LOCAL as well as ancestral influences are among the determining forces of every life and character. There are felicities and infelicities of birthplace as marked as those of parentage. The surroundings of childhood, outside the family, leave their indelible impress on the plastic nature. Natural scenery, climate, and social customs and institutions are to be ranked among the educators of youth.

The town of Shelburne, in which the first twenty years of the life of Fidelia Fiske were chiefly spent, is situated in the central part of Franklin County, Massachusetts. It is a "hill town," lying upon one of the spurs that break up the eastern slope of the southern portion of the Green Mountains. The territory comprising it was included in the township of Deerfield, till 1768, when it was incorporated as a distinct town, and named after Lord Shelburne, of England, who acknowledged the compliment by sending over a large and valuable bell as a present to the town; which, however, never reached its destination, being captured, as tradition says, in Boston harbor, by the British, on the breaking out of the Revolutionary War.

Till quite recently the population of Shelburne scarcely exceeded a thousand souls. There is no village in the town except that of Shelburne Falls in the south-west corner. The people generally are devoted to agricultural pursuits, and are frugal, industrious, of simple habits, having among them but few representatives of either extreme of social life, — the poor or the rich.

The most marked physical feature of the town is Ball Mountain, a high and rugged elevation, extending from north to south nearly across the entire township; westward it descends precipitously to the valley of the Deerfield River and its tributaries; its eastern slope is more gradual and extensive, broken up by a succession of hills which subside at length into the rich meadows that form the basin of the Connecticut River. On nearly the highest point of this mountain the great-grandfather of Fidelia Fiske, in 1761, took up his residence, erecting there a rude dwelling, near the spot where after him dwelt his children and children's children, and where Fidelia was born.

The pioneer farmer, in selecting this high and rocky locality for his home, had an eye, perhaps, more to exemption from early and late frosts and the attacks of Indians than to the beauties of nature. And yet, to a lover of natural scenery, a more charming spot could hardly have been chosen, even in that mountainous region, where one cannot travel far in any direction without coming upon views in which the grand and the beautiful are wondrously blended. To the eastward the valley of the Connecticut lies spread out before the eye in all its peculiar loveliness, with its rich mosaic of meadow, forest, and mountain, farm-house, and village; while the course of the river is distinctly traceable, on many a summer morning, by the silvery bank of fog that lies upon its bosom. Beyond, in the distance, rise the highlands, which mark the central part of the State, — Wachusett being clearly distinguishable by its pre-eminence, — while to the north-east appears Mount Monadnock in New Hampshire, and to the south-east, the Holyoke range, with its beautifully serrated crest, flanked by those two noble institutions, which will forever associate that region, not only with the cause of education, but, scarcely less, with the cause of foreign missions, — Amherst College on the right, and Mount Holyoke Female Seminary on the left.

While the youthful eye of Fidelia looked out daily upon this broad and lovely landscape, we cannot doubt that she was there silently and unconsciously drinking in those elevating and expanding influences, which helped to train her mind and heart for her great life-work. A few minutes' walk westward from her home brings one to the Great Ledge, on the very brow of the mountain, whence is obtained a view, quite different in its main features from that already described, less extensive, but not less charming. Almost beneath one's feet lies the thriving village of Shelburne Falls, two miles distant, while, directly in front, the Deerfield River winds gracefully away through a narrow valley till lost from sight among the hills, a few miles from the spot where the Hoosac Tunnel penetrates the Green Mountains. To the right, a lesser stream leads the eye up along its tortuous course till one is puzzled to know how it ever could have found its way through such a region, where the hills are mountains, and the mountains seem like an impenetrable barricade of nature. To the left is another succession of scarcely less mountainous towns, some of which have given to the world names that are immortal,—Buckland, the birthplace of Mary Lyon; Hawley, the birthplace of Jonas King, and Cummington, the birthplace of William Cullen Bryant.

Fidelia's attachment to her native place and to her mountain home was deep and lasting; and the strength and the beauty of those scenes amid which her childhood was spent were transfused and happily blended in the character she bore thence. The pictures, which she there, in her early communings with nature, hung up in her "chambers of imagery," remained undimmed, and were invested with a new and tender interest, when, in after years, she hung beside them companion pictures, found in her missionary tours among the mountains of Koordistan.

CHAPTER III.

Birth. — Early Home. — First School. — Thoroughness and Self-reliance in Study. — Reads "Mather's Magnalia" and "Dwight's Theology." — Parental Authority. — Filial Obedience. — Confidential Relations between Father and Daughter. — Study of the Bible. — Early Religious Impressions. — Conversion. — Unites with the Church. — Miss Webster's School. — Teaches School. — A Pupil at Franklin Academy and at Conway.

Of the six children — all daughters — of Rufus and Hannah Fiske, Fidelia was the fourth, and was born May 1, 1816. Two of the six died in infancy before the birth of Fidelia. The two younger than herself preceded her to the eternal world; the eldest alone surviving her.

The early home of Fidelia was a plain one-story farm-house, the most important apartment in it being the large family-room which served as kitchen, nursery, dining and sitting room. Here the principal affairs of the household life, domestic, social, and religious, were quietly carried on. Here, around the immense fireplace, with its huge pile of blazing logs, the little circle gathered every evening, while sewing, knitting, reading, and studying, enlivened with grandsire's stories of the olden times, filled up pleasantly and profitably the swift hours, till at length the great Bible was brought forth, a chapter read, and fervent prayer offered, and presently the house was still until the early dawn summoned its inmates to a renewal of their peaceful pursuits. The life led in that mountain home was quiet and simple, though by no means dull and monotonous. Unreached by the numberless novelties and artificial excitements of the city and the village, it had an even and healthful flow. What it lost in present intensity it gained in silently accumulating forces. What it lacked of thrilling incident was supplied by the ceaseless and ever-varying voices of nature, and by the stimulating influences of those great religious truths inwrought from the beginning.

As a child, Fidelia was unusually thoughtful and observing. Nothing seemed to escape her notice. She was an interested listener when others were conversing, and was quick alike to detect mistakes and to treasure up new and important facts.

When about four years of age she began to attend the district school, in the little school-house a few rods from her father's dwelling. Here, for the next ten or twelve years, much of her time was spent in pursuing the studies usually taught in country schools. Though by no means a prodigy, she yet learned with great facility, easily outstripping others of the same age, and winning the place of honor in her class. She early manifested a disposition to learn *thoroughly* whatever was assigned her. However difficult the lesson, she could not rest until she felt sure that she had completely mastered it. This early habit of thoroughness in her studies was the germ of a valuable trait of character, afterwards so conspicuous. As a teacher and missionary, it was ever a maxim with her to do well whatever she undertook.

And coupled with this early habit of thoroughness was another equally valuable, — that of *self-reliance*. Most young children are only too glad to be helped over the hard places in their studies. They like to be told how to do the difficult example much better than to find out how to do it by patient thinking. Fidelia wished no such help. She was unwilling to get her lessons by proxy. She preferred to do her own thinking, and found more pleasure in conquering difficulties herself than in having them removed for her by others. This quiet, self-reliant spirit of the child reappeared conspicuously in the woman, as multitudes can testify who wondered how one so frail could undertake and accomplish so much. In mastering without help the difficult task of the school-room she was unconsciously girding herself for successfully meeting the more difficult tasks of after life. Many still remember how the promptness, quiet self-possession, and invariable accuracy of the delicately formed little girl, in her recitations, awakened an approving smile in the spectators; and how, at the public examinations, the hardest questions seemed, almost as a matter of course, to fall to her.

At a very tender age she evinced a great fondness for reading, and for reading of such a character as children seldom are interested in. Most of the books in the family were treatises upon religious subjects. These she read and re-read as eagerly as the young of the present day devour the exciting romance.

Writing, in 1852, to a young niece in regard to cultivating a taste for careful reading, she says:—

"It is not so much to have read many books as to have read a few well. I cannot tell you how much I value having read all my father's books many times when a child. Your grandmamma will tell you how I used to read the 'Missionary Heralds' to her; also the 'Life of Thomas Spencer,' 'Memoir of Martyn,' etc."

Nor was her reading at this time confined to her father's little library. There was established in Shelburne about this time a "Social Library," owned in shares, each proprietor being allowed to draw out a certain number of books for a definite time. Fidelia's father was a proprietor, and had one or more books from the library at his house most of the time. These were selected with reference to his own taste and wants; but he soon found that whatever he cared to read was read with even greater avidity by his little daughters. Fidelia, especially, though having barely acquired the rudiments of the language, could allow no library book to be returned until she had made herself acquainted with its contents. Among the first books thus read by her was Mather's "Magnalia." No one was aware that she was reading it till it was nearly completed. She would steal away unobserved into the parlor, where the work was kept, and there hour after hour was she absorbed over the pages of those volumes, almost too large for her to handle. This was when she was only six years of age. The reading of this work deeply affected her. Some portions of it wrought powerfully upon her tender nature, and for a time gave an unhealthy excitement to her imagination. She suddenly became very timid, and was afraid to be alone, or to go into any unoccupied room after dark. When asked the reason her reply was, that she was afraid of the witches. Her father made such explanations as satisfied her, and in a great measure allayed her fears, although it was a long time before she could wholly rid herself of the idea that possibly the witchcraft scenes which Mather described might be repeated. Indeed, she used to say that her mind was not wholly disenchanted of that early spell till she re-read the "Magnalia" at the age of sixteen. Another of the works from the library which she read with great interest was "Dwight's Theology." This she read entirely through twice when she was eight years old. Dwight surely was strong meat for babes; but this babe seems to have well digested it. The writer has heard her say that she felt through life greatly indebted to that early reading of those volumes of theology, and that she always retained a distinct remembrance of the manner in which many of the doctrines were there discussed.

With this great mental activity, moral qualities were not slow in developing. As a child, she was not all sweetness and docility. The common depravity of our nature clearly asserted itself in the early unfoldings of her character. She had a strong will, which was sometimes decidedly rebellious, and she had to learn obedience by the things she suffered. When only two or three years old, a fit of wilfulness called for somewhat severe and protracted punishment. This her mother administered, with a firm hand, until the child yielded. The discipline was salutary in its influence. Fidelia never forgot it, and used in after life to thank her mother, saying that she always loved her better for it, and believed that it was her first lesson in true submission. But, if it was her first, it was not her last lesson of that kind. Parental authority was represented in her parents, especially in her father, in a mild but decided form. It was not harsh and arbitrary, but it was as unyielding as the rocks. The word gently spoken was a law that could not be disregarded with impunity. The command, though uttered in softest tones, it was well understood, must be obeyed. And so wisely was this authority exercised, and so blended was it with kindness, that a wilful and rebellious spirit could not long live under it. Fidelia became so thoroughly submissive and obedient, and had such a deep and reverent love for her father, that, in after years, she used to say that, when yet a child, she often wished that he would command her to do something difficult or disagreeable, that she might have the privilege of obeying him, and that there was a positive pleasure in obedience. This early submission to parental authority doubtless prepared the way for that sweet, unhesitating submission to the will of her heavenly Father, which marked her whole Christian life.

Her relations to her father as she advanced in years were more like those which usually exist between a daughter and her mother. He was her companion, her confidant, and her counsellor. He wisely encouraged and directed her love of knowledge, and advised as to her studies and reading. She freely carried to him all her little troubles and cares, and it was one of the peculiar trials of her later years that she could not go to him for counsel in her seasons of perplexity. She often did this in her dreams. When after her perilous tour among the Koordish Mountains, in 1856, in which she had some narrow escapes, she used to dream over her dangers at night, and in her dreams would seem to see the form of her father, beckoning to her and saying: "This way, my child, —this way, and you will be safe." She was largely indebted to her father for that remarkable familiarity with the Bible, which often surprised and delighted her friends. With him it was emphatically the Book of books. Fond of general reading, it was his special delight to consult the lively oracles. He fully adopted the great Protestant principle, that the Holy Scriptures are a perfect rule of faith and practice for every person. He honored the Bible in the family, making it the great text-book of religious instruction. When his children manifested a distaste for their lessons in the Catechism he permitted them to substitute the inspired for the uninspired word. He believed it quite as safe for them to drink at the fountain-head as at the stream. When Fidelia, on a certain occasion, informed her missionary associates that she never learned the Assembly's Catechism, they were almost as much amazed as if she had avowed heresy. But they had to confess that they could detect no deficiency or unsoundness in her theological views. If they could distance her in the Catechism, they were sometimes mortified at her superior knowledge of the Bible. It was not her father's practice, in conducting the biblical instruction of his children, to assign them stated tasks of study or reading. He conversed much and familiarly with them about Bible characters and events, and by various devices sought to awaken an interest which should make them love to search the Scriptures. He was fond of the Socratic method, and his pertinent questions greatly stimulated their curiosity and research. He was wont to turn little daily incidents into the means of increasing their biblical knowledge. For instance, one day his little daughters petitioned him to purchase a new French bedstead. He replied, "Well, I will see about it; but I have read in a certain book about a king who had an iron bedstead; did you ever read about it, and can you tell me the name of that king?" They well understood what that "certain book" was, and were soon busily turning over the leaves of their Bibles, and from that day were familiar with the history of the king with an iron bedstead. Thus trained, Fidelia early became exceedingly fond of the Bible. It had a peculiar charm for her, which lasted and increased through life. She was equally at home in the Pentateuch, and the Gospels, the Prophets, and the Epistles, the Psalms, and the Revelation. And her deep, reverent love for the sacred volume, and her great familiarity with it, were owing principally to the example and wise instruction of that excellent father.

There are probably few children who are devoted to God in the baptismal covenant, and breathe the atmosphere of a truly Christian home, who are not, at a very early age, the subjects of deep religious impressions. Fidelia could not remember the time when her mind was not impressed by religious truth, and seriously exercised about the question of her personal salvation. She read with avidity all religious books that fell in her way, and was an attentive and thoughtful hearer of the Word. But she was naturally reserved on the subject, as most children are; and shrank from being called upon to make a disclosure of her feelings. On one occasion, a clergyman from a neighboring town, being at her father's house, was conversing with different members of the family about their religious state, when, fearing that he would speak to her, Fidelia left the room; but so desirous was she to hear what was said, that she soon returned. The gentleman, in her appearance and movements, read her state of mind, and wisely said nothing to her personally. But when he rose to take his leave he approached her, and, taking her by the hand, for a moment looked kindly into her face, and then turning to her mother said, "Mrs. Fiske, I think salvation will soon come to this house." These words deeply affected the already agitated and burdened heart of the child. She used afterwards to remark that probably he could have said nothing to her that would have moved her so much. She went away to weep and to wish more earnestly than ever that salvation would speedily come to her troubled soul.

In 1825, when eleven years of age, her elder sister, while attending Miss Lyon's school in Buckland, was, with many others, hopefully converted. The event made an indelible impression on Fidelia's mind. Late in life she thus alludes to it. Having spoken of the joy caused in the homes of many of Miss Lyon's pupils that winter by the intelligence of their conversion, she says, "In writing, a tender scene in one of those homes comes up vividly. A letter was handed to a father; he read and wept; it was given to the mother, and her tears flowed as soon as her eye fell upon the first line. The little children knew that the letter had come from Buckland. They looked on and were sad, not having yet learned that there are tears of joy as well as of sorrow. 'What is it, mamma?' said the eldest one. The letter was passed to the child and she read; 'Your daughter has a trembling hope that she is a Christian. God is with us. Pray for us.' Then the child wept with the parents, and there arose in her young heart the desire to know her sister's God, and she had no rest till she was numbered with the chosen people of God."*

Two years later her Sabbath school teacher,—a daughter of her pastor,—having one day faithfully addressed her class on the importance of personal religion, requested all who were willing to try to become Christians immediately, to raise their hands. Instantly the hand of every pupil but one went up. That one was Fidelia; the only one of them all, probably, who at that time was feeling any special religious interest. She went from the class in a state of great mental distress. The thought that she had refused to express a willingness to try to be a Christian troubled her exceedingly. The refusal itself seemed to her to be very sinful and to indicate the great sinfulness of her heart. That night she lay on her bed wakeful and tearful, as she reflected on what she had done, and on her sad and exposed condition. Still she told no one her feelings. The little heart carried its burden in secret for many months. At length her anxiety became too great to be longer concealed. Her mother, one day, suspecting the true state of the case, and alluding to the fact that something seemed to be troubling her, kindly inquired, "What is it, my child?" The full heart instantly overflowed with the long pent-up feeling as she said, "Mother, I am a lost sinner." She soon found peace in believing, and began to cherish that Chris-

* Recollections of Mary Lyon, p. 63.

tian hope which ever after was "an anchor to her soul, sure and steadfast." When her pious grandfather was informed of her conversion he said, in substance, "It must be that God is about to do a great work here, for he generally brings great results from small beginnings." In a double sense did his words prove true. By the instrumentality of that converted grand-daughter, God had a great work to accomplish in a distant land many years after the good man had gone to his rest; and her conversion was the first fruits of an extensive revival of religion in that place. Sometimes, when a missionary, in urging her pupils to be willing to begin the Christian life alone, and not to feel that they must wait for others to be interested, or for a season of general revival, she used to allude to her own experience, and say that when she heeded the special call of God's Spirit, she did not know that there was another soul in town longing to find the way of life. She soon had the joy, however, of knowing that the same Divine Spirit, who had wrought such a wondrous change in her heart, was in like manner working in the hearts of many of her friends and acquaintances.

The following extract from a letter to her uncle, Hon. Levi Fiske, of Byron, New York, contains the only record of her feelings at this time, which has been preserved: —

"SHELBURNE, May 30, 1838.

"DEAR UNCLE: — Well do I recollect the last words you spoke to me at our last interview. As you pressed my hand within yours and bade me adieu, these words fell from your lips: 'Oh that you might be enabled to remember your Creator in the days of your youth!' The petition which you then put up to Heaven for me has, I trust, been answered. I have, as I hope, been enabled to remember my Creator; but, oh, what were my feelings when I first began to think about him! He appeared to me like a cruel and unjust God, and gladly would I have dethroned him had it been in my power. Thus did I continue in opposition to God, till he was, as I hope, in his infinite mercy, pleased to humble my proud heart, and make me willing to accept the terms of mercy. Although I have since that time lived at too great a distance from my God, yet I trust I can say that he is precious to my soul. My situation in life is now truly interesting, and what renders it so is that the Spirit of God is in the school of which I am a member. There have been three hopeful conversions, and a number of others appear to be anxiously inquiring what they shall do to be saved. A general solemnity pervades the school. When you hear of this, dear uncle, will you not offer one fervent prayer to the God of heaven that he will continue to pour out his Spirit upon us till every soul shall be converted?"

On the 12th of July, 1831, Fidelia Fiske, with nineteen others, made a public profession of her faith in Christ, and became a member of the Congregational Church at Shelburne.

The school referred to in the above extract was a "select school," taught at the centre of the town, during portions of the years 1831 and 1832, by Miss Caroline Webster, of Newburyport, Massachusetts, subsequently the wife of Rev. J. R. Barnes. This was the first school Fidelia attended, except the small district school near her home. The superior advantages here enjoyed she fully appreciated, and turned them to good account. She made rapid progress in her studies, and became a great favorite in the school, both with teacher and pupils. The second year she was an assistant teacher, and in this capacity had her first experience in that employment in which she became eminently successful, and in which the larger part of her life was spent.

Mrs. Barnes thus writes of her in 1865: "I think of Miss Fiske as beyond her years in capabilities of mind and heart; as gentle in natural disposition, ever wearing a sweet, winning smile; as scrupulously observant of all school regulations; as ever seeking the spiritual welfare of her companions; aiming at the culture in her own heart of a missionary spirit. To illustrate: after the morning Bible lesson, she would be seen quietly moving about, with her arm around a companion, and, with earnest countenance and subdued tone, pressing home the truths to which all had just listened."

From the time of her conversion Fidelia took a deep and active interest in the spiritual welfare of others. Many of her youthful friends could bear testimony to her faithful and affectionate pleadings with them to seek the Saviour whom she had found. She soon became a teacher in the Sabbath school, and here found a most congenial sphere of usefulness. Her interest in her pupils was not confined to the hour spent with them on the Sabbath. She sought in various ways to win them to Christ, often calling the pen to her aid.

From 1833 to 1839 Miss Fiske was most of the time engaged in teaching in the common or district schools of her native town. Her services were in great demand, and that was deemed the fortunate district that secured them. She won the universal love of her pupils, and, by her affectionate spirit, winning ways, and good sense, was able easily to govern schools which others found turbulent and unmanageable. And she was as great a favorite out of the school-room as in it. The custom of "boarding round" made her for a few days an inmate of all the families whose children attended the school. In none of those families was the boarding of the teacher deemed a burden which they were anxious to have reduced to its minimum. Parents felt it a privilege to have her with them and with their children in their homes. In the summer of 1838, she taught one term in the neighboring town of Bernardston, where her memory is still fragrant among those who were her pupils.

During this period of teaching she twice exchanged, for a short time, the position of teacher for that of pupil. The winter of 1834 found her a member of "Franklin Academy," at Shelburne Falls, — a flourishing institution, then under the care of Rev. John Alden. In the spring of 1837, she attended, for a few weeks, a "select school" in Conway, taught by Deacon John Clary, who says of her, "I remember her as strictly conscientious in the discharge of every duty, as industrious and successful in her studies, and as exhibiting a deportment at all times fully deserving the unqualified approbation of her teachers and associates."

CHAPTER IV.

LIFE AT MT. HOLYOKE SEMINARY.

Enters the Middle Class. — Early love for Miss Lyon. — Scholarship. — Revival of Religion. — Letters to Parents and Sister. — Sickness. — Supposed Death. — Death of her Father and Sister. — Teaches. — Visits Miss Lyon. — Returns to the Seminary. — Graduation. — Appointed Teacher in the Seminary.

In the autumn of 1839, Miss Fiske became a member of the Middle Class in Mt. Holyoke Seminary, at South Hadley; an institution which, from the day of her first connection with it, to the day of her death, occupied a large place in her thoughts and affections, her last earthly labors being devoted to its welfare.

Her elder sister had been a pupil of Miss Lyon, in Buckland; her pastor, Rev. Dr. Packard, was one of Miss Lyon's confidential advisers in regard to the founding of the seminary; while her father, from the first, had felt a lively interest in the enterprise and a strong confidence in its success. It was not strange, therefore, that Fidelia should be favorably disposed toward the new institution, and should desire to avail herself of the advantages it offered, so much superior to those previously within the reach of most of the young ladies in that region. The seminary had already been in operation two years, and its complete success could no longer be regarded doubtful. The high literary and religious character, which its founder impressed upon it at the outset, had become widely known; and the Lord had set his seal upon it, in the form of one of that series of precious revivals of religion, with which, throughout its entire history, the institution has been so remarkably blessed. It was with eager and delightful anticipations that Fidelia found the way opening for her to pursue a more extended and thorough course of study, and in a place where she believed intellectual and spiritual culture could go hand in hand.

Her anticipations were more than met at South Hadley. She found herself in a thoroughly congenial element. The very atmosphere of the seminary was exhilarating to her intellectual and spiritual nature. The diligence and thoroughness in study there required, and the almost rigid order and system which prevailed throughout the establishment, suited her mental habits. The prominence given to religious instruction and religious duties happily met the wants of her rapidly developing religious life. She felt the quickening influence of contact with so many other minds whose general aims and sympathies accorded with her own. Especially did she feel and respond to the rare influence of that imperial mind which originated, and presided over, the institution. She early conceived a profound and reverent attachment for Miss Lyon, which time only intensified, and this attachment was in no small measure reciprocated. It was a wise providence that brought two such natures together, — fit teacher for fit pupil. We can but recognize a moral beauty in the circumstances which associate, intimately and forever, the name of Fidelia Fiske with the name of Mary Lyon.

It is much to be regretted that the record of Miss

Fiske's life at the seminary cannot be furnished by her own pen. Her home letters during this period were numerous, but few of them can be found. It is supposed that during the last year of her life she destroyed these and many other of her youthful productions. Though they may have possessed no great literary excellence, yet they would have given us a better insight into her school life, and would have enabled us to trace more distinctly the growth of her character. The first year of her life at South Hadley was a busy but a happy one. She enjoyed it to the full, and, notwithstanding her quiet and modest manner, her real worth began early to be recognized both by pupils and by teachers. To say that she was among the foremost in her class is no disparagement to others. Her recitations bore witness to the same habit of thoroughness in her studies which she evinced when a little child. Her scholarship won the respect, as her gentle, cheerful, and affectionate disposition won the love, of all in the school. She entered heartily into everything which related to the general welfare of the institution, and especially into all plans and measures for promoting the spiritual interests of its members. The following extracts from the only two letters written during this year, which have been preserved, may be fitly introduced in this connection: —

"MT. HOLYOKE SEMINARY, Feb. 26, 1840.

"MY DEAR PARENTS: — When I remember that four weeks have gone by since I left you, I feel almost ashamed of my neglect in not writing before this. But these weeks, like those of the earlier part of the year, have been crowded with employment. Our engagements are such that they seem designed to allow us to pay no moment but in purchase of its worth. . . . Strangers to the turmoil and excitement of the surrounding world, our days pass most pleasantly, and I hope profitably. I often ask myself, 'What return shall my heavenly Father receive for the numberless privileges he bestows upon me?' Oh, that a diligent improvement of them may fit me for usefulness while I dwell in this vale of tears. To-morrow, as you are aware, is the day of annual fasting for colleges and other literary institutions. The anticipation of it brings to the minds of many of the members of this seminary most interesting and hallowed associations. They remember how, the last year, their Father met them at this season, and brought to himself many wandering souls. Oh, that the Spirit of God might be with us, to lead both saints and sinners to the proper place!

"*February* 29. — Our day of prayer, to which we had looked forward with so many anxious feelings, has passed, and its report has gone to heaven. It was a solemn season. I felt it one of the most solemn I had ever known. The morning's light found some few assembled for prayer. Then we had a precious season as we sought the direction of our Father in the duties of the day. Instead of going down to breakfast, many were found in their chambers, holding communion with their own hearts. As soon as it was light, we were assembled in the hall for family devotions. Miss Lyon then made some remarks on the manner of spending the day; and we separated, each to go to her own room and employ the time in heart-searchings. At eleven o'clock, A.M., we met in the seminary hall for prayer, and in the afternoon attended public services at the church. In the evening a prayer-meeting was held in the hall half an hour, — all indulging hope being invited. At the expiration of this time the impenitent were invited, who wished for the prayers of Christians. All came, and we felt that it was indeed a solemn place. Several prayers were offered, during which the half-suppressed sigh could be heard in different parts of the room. At eight o'clock, all who were determined to seek the Saviour were requested to meet in Miss Lyon's room, while Christians, in small circles, prayed for them. Some, we hope, sought and found heavenly peace. The judgment-day alone can tell the influence of the day on immortal souls. To-day (Saturday) has not been less interesting to us. Our meetings have been very solemn. Oh, may we not grieve the Spirit of God from us!"

These tokens of increasing religious interest about her caused her heart to turn with tender solicitude to her youngest sister, still unconverted, to whom she thus writes: —

"MY VERY DEAR SISTER H.: — A few moments of this evening are left me, and to whom shall I devote them? Perhaps none have better claims than yourself. My thoughts have often been with you during the last few days. As I have seen some of my dear companions, who felt that they were in the broad road to death, kneel again and again, that prayer might be offered for them, I have thought, 'Have I not a sister dear to my heart, who has no friend in heaven?' And, as I have seen those who long have felt deeply, and still refuse to come to Jesus for the pardon of their sins, I have thought, and in sadness thought, 'My dear sister stands on the same ground.' And is it thus? And shall it be that days and weeks roll by, and still no heavenly hope light her soul? O Heaven forbid! If, at last, your unworthy sister shall be found among those who have no part nor lot in heaven, may you be saved! That this may be the case, shall be my prayer, morning and evening, as I bend the knee in the closet. Sometimes, as rising day meets your eye, oh, remember that you have a sister who feels it a privilege then to agonize in prayer for you. Let not the neglect of others, oh, let not the unfaithfulness of her who now writes you, keep you from giving to your soul your most serious attention. The list of the redeemed is fast filling; you are invited to join this numerous company. Oh, will you not? May I be permitted, with affectionate tenderness, to bring the subject home, and ask you to give it your present attention?"

The religious interest in the seminary rapidly increased from that day of prayer, and continued until all the pupils were indulging the Christian hope. The number of hopeful conversions was about thirty, —nearly the same as during the previous year. Amid the delightful scenes of such a revival, Miss Fiske was taking practical lessons which were to be invaluable to her in similar scenes, on missionary ground, in which she was to bear so important a part.

When she entered the seminary she was uncertain how long she would be able to continue there. Her plans, however, were soon definitely formed to remain and complete the course, which she hoped to do in two years. But these plans were unexpectedly interrupted. Just at the close of her first year, a malignant form of typhoid fever appeared among the pupils, particularly among the members of her own class. There were forty cases in all, nine of which proved fatal. In some instances, the young ladies were attacked by the disease almost immediately after reaching their homes for vacation. Miss Fiske was one of this number. She reached her friends apparently in perfect health, but in two days was prostrated by the same fever with which so many of her companions were suffering and dying. For many days she lay at the very gate of death, and all hope of her recovery was given up. Friends took leave of her, and watched about her bed, momentarily expecting the silver cord to be loosed. At one time she seemed to them, and even to herself, to have left the world, and to have actually passed within the veil. But their outbursting grief was speedily checked by signs of reanimation. The tide of life that had been so long ebbing turned, and she began gradually to come back, and take hold again upon the things of earth, which she seemed to have given up forever. Her recovery was very slow, and weeks passed before she could leave her sick-bed, or feel confident that she was to be spared to resume the work of life.

Her experience during that season of sickness she ever regarded as invaluable. She used to say that she then, for the first time, learned the real feelings and wants of the sick and dying, and how to care for them. This, among other things she learned, — that we should never presume that our friends, when delirious, or when apparently dying, are insensible to, or unaffected by, what is said and done in their presence. She also gained vivid impressions in regard to the reality of the invisible world, which never grew dim. Of that peculiar experience when she thought herself dying, she seldom spoke, but when she did speak of it with intimate friends, it was with great tenderness of feeling and in subdued tones, as if it were something sacred. She could hardly persuade herself that she did not really pass the line which separates the visible from the invisible world. She felt that she knew what it was to die, and that the Saviour had truly met her and spoken to her, assuring her of his love. Ever afterwards death wore for her a new and pleasing aspect. Dying was but the coming of Jesus, according to his promise, to take his own to be with him where he is.

For many years she could contemplate the final change without fear or shrinking. Death had ceased to be the "King of terrors." But after having witnessed, in 1857, instances of death in the missionary circle to which she belonged, which were peculiarly painful, her feelings were somewhat changed. She would no longer say, "I have no dread of death," but only, "I can look beyond."

In 1862, in a letter of sympathy to a recently bereaved friend, she thus alludes to that affecting passage in her own personal history: —

"It is sweet to feel that Jesus wills that all his should be with him where he is, and that he comes for them *himself*. I love to dwell upon those hours when I supposed he had come for me in 1840. I could not tell others of it; but it was such sweet peace to know that he was there, and that he would do all. Since that hour I can never think of the dying Christian as being at all alone. Death is swallowed up in victory; and why should it not be? Jesus is there; his presence is a blessed reality; the spirit can go with him."

Miss Fiske's own severe sickness was not her only trial during that memorable autumn. Another bitter cup was given her to drink. While she was slowly recovering, the destroying angel smote once and again the household over which he had seemed hovering so long. The malady which had so nearly proved fatal in her case was communicated to other members of the family, and quickly bore two of the number away. Her loved and honored father, who had stood by her bed and so tenderly taken, as he supposed, his final leave of her, now himself passed out of sight through that same gate that seemed to have opened for her, — she being still unable to leave her bed, or witness the parting scenes. A few days previously, that beloved youngest sister, for whose conversion she had felt so deeply and prayed so fervently, — and not, we trust, in vain, — had been attacked by the same disease, and quickly followed her father into the spirit world.

Thus, instead of returning to the quiet retreat and delightful studies of her loved seminary, she was, in the severe school of affliction, taking lessons which the great Teacher saw were needful to complete her education and prepare her for the work to which he had appointed her.

It was not deemed prudent for Miss Fiske to return to the seminary that year. Months elapsed before she regained her full measure of health. But she could not be content to be needlessly idle, and during a portion of the year she resumed her favorite employment of teaching in her native town.

In the course of this year Miss Lyon was deeply afflicted in the death of her mother. Soon after that event she thus wrote to Miss Fiske: —

"Can you not come and stay with me a few days? I am not able to go out of my room much, and it would be a great comfort to me to have you with me. Dear one! I have felt for you most tenderly in your trials. They have been mine, and my feelings have been such that, in my present state of health, I have hardly dared to trust myself to write you. I want to talk with you of your loss, and of our nine dear pupils who have gone to be with Christ, of mother and sister, and of your own plans for the future. Do not try to do too much. Rest, and rest here with me, if you can leave your mother. Arms of love wait to receive you."

The kind invitation could not be accepted immediately; but some months later, when teacher and pupil met, the latter felt that there were none other than "arms of love thrown around her," and she thus wrote of that meeting: "I can never forget how fast those tear-drops fell, as she silently laid her head on my shoulder for a few brief minutes, and then broke the silence by saying, 'How I do thank God that he could spare you to come back to life! I know you would have been glad to go at once to heaven; but will you not also be happy in laboring a little longer for Christ?' There was to me a new view of the preciousness of laboring for Christ, as I looked upon that countenance where smiles and tears so met." *

The autumn of 1841 found her again at the Mount Holyoke Seminary, a member of the senior class, — not the class she originally joined, that having graduated during her absence. The year passed pleasantly away. An interesting record of it doubtless could be made if her home letters had been preserved. From one written at this time, which has come to light, the following extracts are made: —

TO MRS. L. F. S.

"SOUTH HADLEY, Nov. 5, 1841.

"MY DEAR MRS. S.: — I have not forgotten my promise to write you, and, since I have heard of your very severe affliction, I have felt my obligations to you stronger than before. I remember with deepest gratitude the tender sympathy you manifested for our family in the season of our deep affliction, and now, that like waves of sorrow are rolling over you, I would fain mingle my tears with yours, and in all your griefs bear a sympathizing part. . . . .

"But, my dear friend, amid all these trying scenes, is it not to you a source of richest consolation that they are directed by your kind Father's hand, — the hand of One who feels for you with all the constancy and tenderness which a parent can feel for a child? Yes, He who wept on earth over the remains of a loved friend has felt for you as you have watched over your dear Sarah's dying bed. Has he

* Recollections of Mary Lyon, p. 138.

not given you much consolation in the hope that, as she was taken from a mother's arms, she was placed in her Saviour's bosom? I shall ever be grateful for the privilege of seeing her the Sabbath before I left Shelburne, and hearing from her own lips expressions of her feelings in view of the last great conflict. I could but hope that by divine grace she was prepared for the change that seemed fast coming over her. . . Will you not be thankful that you have been permitted to train an immortal mind to add to the notes of praise to our God? And while the privilege of educating her and fitting her for usefulness is denied you, may you be comforted by the thought that One who loves her better than any earthly parent can love, is instructing her in those things which are heavenly and divine. Near the throne, we hope, she dwells rejoicing with those who encircle it. And it may be that her seraph spirit shall come to her widowed mother on errands full of love. . . . It will be but a little while, my dear friend, before we shall have done with all the things of earth. And, if indeed the children of God, we shall rest where tears are wiped from every eye, and sorrow is unknown. Surely, when drinking deep of the fount of eternal love, we shall not regret any sacrifice which in the days of our flesh we make for the Saviour's cause. We make sacrifices for earthly friends; shall we fail to be willing to do it for him whom we profess to love better than any other? No; rather let us willingly return each gift for which our Father calls. He ever knows what is best, and will ever do what is right. Let us implicitly trust him in life, and in death he will be our Friend, and our portion through a blissful eternity. . . . .

"I am very pleasantly situated. Our family consists of about two hundred. Three-fourths of them are hopefully pious. Our seasons of prayer and religious conversation are deeply interesting, and we hope the Spirit of God is indeed in the midst of us. Yet we see not that prevailing spirit of prayer, and that deep concern for immortal souls, which their worth demands. May we not be left to grieve the gentle messenger from our family!"

Immediately upon graduating she was appointed a teacher in the seminary. With what feelings she accepted the appointment, and contemplated the new and interesting sphere of usefulness thus opened to her, the following extract from a letter will indicate.

"SHELBURNE, Sept. 9, 1842.

"I think I have not written you since our aged grandfather's decease. He died the next June after father died. Thus in the short space of nine months half of our family were called to their eternal home. Our house is indeed left unto us desolate; but our Father hath done it, and we will not complain. . . . I have spent the last year at Mount Holyoke Seminary; came home in August, having finished the course of study. I now expect to return in October, to teach for a year. I look forward with pleasure, yet with a feeling of deep responsibility, to my labors. Our school is large, and embraces a most interesting circle of young ladies, upon whose education we feel much is depending. Remember me in your prayers, that I may do just what God would have me do. Last year about forty, who came among us strangers to God, were, we hope, numbered among the dear followers of the Lamb before they left us. We enjoyed many precious seasons, which I doubt not will be remembered during the ages of eternity with deepest joy by many redeemed souls."

As was anticipated, Miss Fiske proved a valuable addition to the excellent corps of teachers under whose able and wise management the seminary was rapidly conquering popular prejudices and winning golden opinions, even from those who had at first looked coldly or frowningly upon the enterprise. But she was permitted to retain this position only a few months before she heard the Master's voice calling her away to her great life-work in a foreign land.

We have now reached the great crisis in her history. With peculiar interest we proceed to trace the inception and maturing of that decision which made her a missionary to the heathen.

CHAPTER V.

DECISION TO BE A MISSIONARY.

Early Missionary Interest. — Dr. King. — Missionaries Visit the Seminary. — Miss Lyon's Missionary Prayer-Meeting at Norwich. — Dr. Perkins' Application for Missionary Teachers. — Miss Fiske offers to go. — Friends Object. — Visits Shelburne with Miss Lyon. — Decides to go to Persia. — Farewell Meetings. — Missionary Instruction given at Andover. — Letter. — A Mother's Consecration of Children to the Missionary Cause.

THE great decisive purposes of life, though often, in one sense, formed suddenly, are yet in another sense always of slow growth. They are the ripe fruit of all our previous training and culture. The seeds of them are often planted in the nursery. They have, moreover, a divine as well as a human side. They are the eternal thoughts of God, not less than the free acts of his creatures, and we can sometimes distinctly trace the working of those thoughts, and see how they preintimate the great decision in which they are to culminate, long before that decision is actually made. When Fidelia Fiske received a definite proposition to become a missionary to the heathen, the subject was one with which her mind had long been familiar. Her missionary interest dates back to her early childhood. She was three years old when her uncle, Rev. Pliny Fiske, left the country to become a missionary in the Holy Land. She retained a very vivid impression of the affecting scenes connected with his departure. From that time foreign missions was an almost daily topic of conversation in her father's family, and Fidelia must have had the thought deeply impressed on her tender mind that it was a high and sacred calling to be the bearer of the glad tidings of salvation to distant pagan lands. She shared in the interest awakened in the family by the reception and reading of letters from the missionary uncle; and she shared also in the deep grief caused by the news of his early death. When a very little girl she used often to play being a missionary, making sometimes an amusing use of what she had learned from her uncle's letters. One day she came into the house eagerly exclaiming, "Ma, I have been to Jerusalem in the wheelbarrow." "Been to Jerusalem in the wheelbarrow, my child?" the mother replied. "Yes, ma, I went up to Jerusalem in the wheelbarrow, I did."

As soon as she was able to read, she seized eagerly upon every item of missionary intelligence that fell under her eye; and no member of the family waited more impatiently than she for the coming of the "Missionary Herald," which she always read through, often aloud to her mother. And it is still remembered with what eagerness the little girl used to climb up to the high case of drawers and take down the back volumes of the "Herald" and the "Panoplist."

When she was eleven years of age, Rev. Jonas King, missionary to Greece, then in this country, was one day visiting at her father's, and, after rehearsing his missionary experience, he placed his hand on Fidelia's head and told her she must go out as her Uncle Pliny did, and teach the heathen the gospel;

and added, "I wish you were old enough to go with me to Greece." She never forgot those words, and the pressure of that hand, and reminded the good man of them the next time she met him, which was at Smyrna, when on her way to Persia.

After her conversion, her missionary interests became more definite and decided, and she soon began to revolve the question of personal duty in the matter. During her senior year at South Hadley, she had for a room-mate a daughter of one of the early missionaries to the Sandwich Islands, of whom she writes: "From her society, I feel in a measure introduced into the interior of a missionary family. I have elicited much from her that I consider valuable, and which I shall carefully store." Under date of September 9, 1842, soon after she graduated, she writes: "I have, the last year, had my interest considerably increased in the cause of missions. Several missionaries have visited us, among whom were Mr. Parker, from China, Mr. Thurston, from the Sandwich Islands, Mrs. Butler, from the Choctaws, Mr. Perkins, accompanied by Mar. Yohannan (the Nestorian bishop), from Persia. The last two were present at our late examination. The bishop addressed us most affectingly. In closing, he slowly said, 'While you go on to improve, oh, remember us, *so dark! so dark!*' My heart responded, 'My brother, thy people I will remember, and gladly would I be spent for their salvation.'"

A few weeks later, while looking over, with one of her associate teachers at South Hadley, Dr. Perkins' volume, "Eight Years' Residence in Persia," she exclaimed, "How I should love to teach those little children! It would be just such employment as I should like, to go out into the streets and pick them up, and comb their hair, and wash their faces. But, if we cannot go in person to the heathen, we can wash the feet of those who do go, and wipe them with the hairs of our head."

This was before Dr. Perkins had made any request at the seminary for one to go back with him as a missionary teacher.

We thus see how the Lord was, for years, specially preparing the mind and heart of Miss Fiske to accept cheerfully the work to which his own purpose had designated her. Already, indeed, had that work been secretly accepted by her, provided she should be called to it. When actually engaged in it she she thus writes: "For years" (elsewhere she says from "the time of her conversion"), "with the exception of some months following my severe sickness of 1840, I felt almost sure that my home was to be on missionary ground. At the period to which I have alluded, I felt that my physical energies were so impaired that I must give up the cherished expectation. Subsequently to that, while happy in my Holyoke retreat, I seemed to feel that it was not my abiding-place. Why I should thus have felt, I know not. I hope I was not deluded in the belief that my Father had a work for me among the benighted souls of another land, and that I heard his voice calling on me to depart thence and to come hither."

How much this secretly cherished hope of being a missionary had to do with the reasons which led her to decline a proposal to become the wife of a New England pastor, it is scarcely pertinent to inquire. Certain it is that the want of an eligible offer of marriage was not among the motives that predisposed her to a missionary life. We now come to the immediate circumstances which led to the great decision.

At the meeting of the American Board at Norwich, Connecticut, in the autumn of 1842, Miss Lyon was deeply impressed with the thought that her beloved seminary should be more thoroughly pervaded with the missionary spirit. She immediately sought to impart this impression to her teachers and pupils. Calling a meeting of those present, she told them that the institution was founded to advance the missionary cause, and that "she sometimes felt that its walls had been built from the funds of missionary boards." At that meeting the seminary was consecrated anew to the cause of missions. "The Lord," writes Miss Fiske, "accepted the offering, but, in so doing, asked not only that they should give gold and silver, but that one-half of the twelve teachers who were with her that year, should, sooner or later, go in person to the heathen. Miss Lyon was often heard to say in subsequent years, 'I little knew how much that prayer-meeting would cost me.'" And Miss Fiske little knew how much it would cost her. While she and others were earnestly pleading for the heathen and for an increase of the missionary spirit in their own hearts, the Lord's messenger was approaching with a call to her to become a missionary herself. The manner in which that call was given will be described, for the most part, in the words of Rev. Dr. Perkins, in his funeral sermon, preached soon after the intelligence of Miss Fiske's death reached Persia: —

"On the sixteenth of January, 1843, near the close of my first visit to America, I went to South Hadley to obtain teachers for our female seminary, having failed in my many applications elsewhere. I called on the pastor of the place (Rev. Mr. Condit), and stated my object; and he soon waited on Miss Lyon, the principal of the seminary, and laid the case before her. On returning he reported that Miss Lyon would see me at 7 P. M., and in the mean time take some measures 'in her own peculiar way' to facilitate the business. I called at the seminary at the hour appointed, when Miss Lyon informed me that at evening prayers she had stated to her school that I wished two teachers to to go with us to Persia; and she had requested that any young ladies who would like to go, or who felt a deep interest in the subject, might address to her each a note, and deposit it in a place designated; that we would then examine the cases of those who should address her and make a selection; but that it should not be known who besides the elected ones had written to her. In accordance with this arrangement forty notes had been received in the course of an hour. Two of the trustees (Deacon Porter, and Rev. Mr. Hawks), happening to be present, joined us in our deliberations. Miss Fiske, then an assistant teacher, having but recently graduated, was one of the applicants, and she evidently stood far above all the rest as the most suitable candidate, in the estimation of Miss Lyon and the trustees present. Indeed, it was a serious question whether they could give up Miss Fiske, as a teacher in the seminary, even to become a missionary. But, on my reminding them that in making the sacrifice they would only fulfil the highest object of their seminary, the point was soon yielded. While some of the notes were quite long, Miss Fiske merely wrote, 'If counted worthy, I should be willing to go.' She was the only person who raised a question as to her worthiness.

"Miss Lyon's description of Miss Fiske, whom she knew thoroughly and loved devotedly, was so commendatory, that I could then accept it only as the prompting of her partiality and love for her pupil, though from the lips of so cautious and discriminating a judge of character. To my cool remark that Miss Fiske seemed to me to possess much stability, Miss Lyon replied, 'Yes, but not less versatility.' But how soon I had ample reason to feel that the half, nay, the tithe, had not been told me!

"Miss Lyon and Miss Fiske were to select a second teacher from the many candidates after my departure. Miss Fiske, however, on laying the subject before her widowed mother, found her so strongly averse to giving up her daughter, that she was compelled to a negative decision."

The following letters will indicate the state of her mind both before and after this decision was reached, and also show that she was influenced by the advice of Christian friends whom she consulted, as well as by the pleadings of maternal affection.

"South Hadley, Jan. 17, 1843.

"My dearly beloved Mother: — Whenever separated from you I feel a deep interest in your welfare, and the knowledge that I have been and still am a sharer in your tender love, sympathies, and prayers, does but bind you still more strongly to my heart day by day. And when I feel these glowings of love within, and know that they are reciprocated by a tender mother, thankfulness always fills my heart that it is a *Christian* mother who loves me; yes, and more than this, that I am the child of a sainted father. Oh, it is a precious privilege to be consecrated by believing parents to the Lord in the early dawn of infancy! And, more than this, to have this consecration often renewed as years roll away. Oh, it does lead one to feel, and strongly feel, that one is not one's own! You, my dear mother, together with my dear father, have, I believe, thus often consecrated your children; not only in a sick, and, as you supposed, dying hour, but in days of health and prosperity. That you were sincere in this consecration I doubt not for a moment. I have had evidence of your sincerity in your efforts to promote my usefulness, and willingness ever to have me go where Providence directed. And now, my mother, one more opportunity presents itself to renew this consecration before you leave this vale of tears. Shall I tell you how? I almost shrink from it. But why should I? Why fear to ask the Christian mother to do what perhaps she loves to do? I will not. No; I will tell you what my Father has presented to me, which I must present to you. The question is this: Are you willing that Fidelia should leave you to dwell the rest of life in a foreign land? to spend the rest of her days in pointing heathen souls to the Lamb of God? These questions have been, this week, proposed to me. The ground is Persia; my employment to be teaching. For further particulars I refer you to uncle, to whom I wrote yesterday, as the mail goes in a few minutes.

"And now, my dear mother, the subject lies before you. You will decide in regard to it, I trust, guided by Heaven. I shall anxiously wait a reply. My sisters, you, too, have a right and the privilege to express your feelings, and I desire that you should do so. And from Uncle and Aunt B. I also desire an expression of feeling. I cannot say another word, for my letter must now go.

"Your affectionate daughter,

"FIDELIA."

"SOUTH HADLEY, Jan. 18, 1843.

"MY DEAR COUSIN: — In accordance with the freedom I have long used in laying open to you my plans and prospects, I write you a few lines at this time. I have had reason to believe that I have shared in your prayers and sympathies in the trying scenes of life; and now, when called to decide one of the most trying questions ever brought before me, may I hope for the same tender sympathies, accompanied by your prayers and counsels? The question is, whether or not I will, or rather, whether it is my duty to, engage in the work of Foreign Missions. It is proposed to me to return, in company with another young lady, with Mr. Perkins, to Persia. The question must be decided in a *very few days*. In about two months Mr. P. leaves, and, if I decide to go, I must in that time make preparations for a long voyage and a life among the heathen. Have you not, dear cousin, one word to say to me on the subject? I should value your thoughts exceedingly. My friends in the seminary, among whom are Miss Lyon and others of the teachers, wish me carefully to consider my duty in regard to leaving my field of usefulness here. Some of the trustees present express the same wish. I value every suggestion from Christian friends, and I certainly should be influenced by them, for I feel, and deeply feel, that I know not what I ought to do. Oh for grace to direct! I do appreciate the unspeakable privilege of committing my way to Almighty God. If he directs, all will be right; and I would rejoice to follow in the path pointed out, be it in my own or another land. I have often looked at the subject of personal consecration to the work of missions with a deep interest. It is no stranger to my heart. But, when brought so near as at the present time, it assumes many new forms. A thousand questions come up, before unasked; a thousand fears, lest wrong motives may influence me in a decision. Were I deciding for myself alone, it would seem a matter of comparatively little consequence. My own sufferings and trials are truly of little weight when compared with the promotion of Christ's kingdom. I would desire this more than anything and all things else, be I where I may.

"I want very much to see you. Is there a time during the days of the week when you are at liberty for a few hours? If so, I wish very much you would call and see me. This week is our vacation. I remain here. Write me, if you find it inconvenient to call and see me, and speak with all the freedom that you would to a sister. Should my decision be to go, I shall hope to see you for some little time before that time comes. Perhaps I may be at home the time of your next vacation. Please write to me very soon, if I may not see you, and remember me unceasingly in your prayers, that I may honor my blessed Redeemer in all my ways.

"Affectionately yours,

"Fidelia Fiske."

"South Hadley, Jan. 26, 1843.

"My dear Cousin: — You ask me to write you as soon as the question of my going to Persia is settled. I gladly comply with your request. You seem to believe that a '*secret decision*' was formed when I wrote you. It was so, as far as my own feelings were concerned, if I should be led to see it my duty to go, and no further. I felt that I needed the advice of Christian friends, and I have sought it. I yesterday received letters from Shelburne. Among others Mr. Packard wrote me. He seems decided that it is not my duty to go; or, at least, he cannot see it to be. He gives the same reasons which you gave, with some additional ones. The opinion of other friends at home seems to coincide with his. Much as I had desired to spend my life in laboring for heathen souls, I dare not decide contrary to the advice of the wise and good. Had it seemed best, I would most gladly have gone; but as it is, I cheerfully remain, hoping this trial may make me more faithful in duty, and lead me better to improve the many opportunities for usefulness which are thickly strown around my path. Oh, it is *how* we live, more than *where* we live! I hope and pray that I may feel a deeper interest in the cause of missions than I have ever yet done, and that I may throw a stronger influence in favor of it around these dear young ladies with whom I am associated.

"I wrote Mr. Perkins this morning what would probably be the final decision. We received a letter from him yesterday, in which he says, 'I do hope Miss Fiske will decide to go and help plant "a Holyoke" in Oroomiah. We shall justly consider it the loveliest plant of the East, — "The rose of Sharon."' He adds, to Miss Lyon: 'And I believe *you* will love to own it as a scion of the parent plant.'

"Some other one will probably go in my stead. I shall always love to think of and pray for those who go, if *I* am not permitted to help 'build the house.' I have felt, in the decision of this question, the peculiar sweetness of trusting the Lord. Oh, it is good to leave all with our Father in heaven, and walk in the path he points out. . . . .

"Accept my thanks for your letter, and for the freedom with which you spoke. It was what I asked. My ardent desires for your usefulness do always attend you; true happiness will follow.

"Affectionately yours,

"FIDELIA."

The considerations which led Miss Fiske's mother, sister, pastor, and other friends to advise, against her going to Persia, related chiefly to the state of her health. Never very strong and robust, she had not fully recovered from the effect of her severe sickness in 1840; and it seemed to them but a reasonable fear that she would not be able to endure the exposure and hardships of a missionary life. Miss Fiske herself shared in this fear; and the thought how she should bear sickness away from all her kindred was a source of no little anxiety to her when leaving home. She afterwards was wont to speak of her generally good health in Persia as given in answer to prayer, and as a special token of her Father's loving kindness.

Another cause of solicitude to her, when revolving the great question of duty, was the liability to frequent changes incident to a missionary life. Her local attachments were strong, and it was trying to think that in Persia she would probably have no permanent abiding-place. She always remembered the time and the spot where she kneeled and gave up all anxiety on this point; and with gratitude she recognized as another special mercy of God the fact that while on missionary ground she never found it necessary to change her home nor even her room for any length of time.

When, constrained by the advice of friends, Miss Fiske decided not to go to Persia, another was selected to go in her place; but she, likewise, on laying the matter before her friends, found them so averse to her going that she yielded to their judgment. When her decision became known at the seminary, the question of duty immediately presented itself to Miss Fiske for reconsideration. That night she could not sleep from thinking over the subject. In the morning expressing to a friend her willingness to go, even at that late hour, if her relatives would give their consent, it was proposed to go and talk the matter over with Miss Lyon. After conversing with her a few minutes, Miss Lyon said, "If such are your feelings, we will go and see your mother and sisters;"

and in about an hour they were on their way. After a thirty-miles' drive in an open sleigh, on that cold, wintry Saturday, through snow-drifts in which they were several times upset, they reached her mother's home on the Shelburne hills about eleven o'clock in the evening.

The family were aroused from their slumbers to receive the unexpected guests, and to hold an unexpected consultation. Prayers and tears mingled with the solemn and tender discussions of that hour. There was little sleep beneath that lowly roof that night, and the consideration of the subject gave a peculiar interest and sacredness to all the duties and services of the following day. Before the Sabbath closed, that mother, whose fond heart at first pleaded so hard against separation from a loved daughter, was enabled cheerfully to say, "Go, my child, go." Other friends could no longer withhold their consent, and the great question, involving such momentous and blessed consequences, was definitely settled.

On Monday morning Miss Lyon returned to South Hadley, Miss Fiske remaining to spend a few last days with loved ones at the home and amid the scenes of her childhood. A stated meeting of the church in Shelburne, occurring on Thursday, it was changed into a kind of farewell meeting. This gave Miss Fiske an opportunity to say "Good-by" to most of her friends in her native town. The next day she looked, as she then supposed, for the last time upon the face of mother, sisters, and kindred, upon the home endeared to her by so many hallowed associations, and upon the snow-clad hills she loved so well. Reaching South Hadley in the afternoon, she found that nearly the whole school had improved every leisure moment during her absence in sewing for her, and that a very good outfit was in readiness. A farewell meeting was held in the seminary hall that afternoon, conducted by the Rev. Mr. Condit, the pastor of the village church, and in the evening she met again for last words the teachers and pupils; and at two o'clock the next morning she was on her way to Boston, whence she was to embark. At the following anniversary of the seminary one of the compositions publicly read, entitled "The Missionary's Farewell," touched a tender chord in the hearts of many present. It alluded thus to the last night Miss Fiske spent there: "Shall we ever forget how affectionately she implored her sisters in Christ to live faithfully for him? How tenderly she entreated the impenitent to listen to mercy's call? Shall we forget the tones of that voice which had so often led us in our devotions, as she once more commended us to her God and our God? But that hallowed hour passed away, and a sadder one came. It was the parting hour, and we gathered around to bid her a last adieu. She wept not herself, but smiled sweetly and said, 'When all life's work is done we shall meet again;' but tears and stifled sobs were our only reply. Sadly and silently we went away, yet turned to gaze once more on the form we might never see again."

Spending a few hours in Boston, on Saturday, she went to Andover, where on the Sabbath the missionaries received their instructions from the Prudential Committee of the Board. On Monday she returned to Boston, having but two days in which to complete her preparations for the voyage. Of her visit to Andover she wrote: "I there met many who had known and loved Uncle Pliny. It would have been very pleasant for you to be there, and see in what sacred remembrance his name is held after he has so long slumbered in the dust. The older members of the Prudential Committee were such when he left. They spoke with tears of those days when they gave to him a farewell in the Lord. Oh, that I might be as faithful in my labors as he was in his!"

Dr. Perkins thus concludes his narrative of those eventful days: —

"The story of Miss Fiske's hasty departure from home and native land, fully told, is one of thrilling interest; her own beautiful and energetic traits of character, and those of her revered teacher, Miss Lyon (the two in many respects alike, yet quite unlike), appearing most admirable in this connection. Miss Fiske carried a full tide of sympathy with her from the seminary. She was one of its first missionary offerings, and many of the estimable young ladies, from among both teachers and pupils, soon followed in her luminous track, — the result in part of her fragrant memory, and of her intensely interesting letters to the school."

How fully her mind rested in her first decision not to go to Persia, and how readily she turned to other methods of Christian usefulness, will appear from the following extracts from a letter written a few days after the decision was made, yet containing no allusion to the subject that had so engrossed her thoughts and stirred her heart.

"SOUTH HADLEY, Jan. 31, 1843.

"MY DEAR COUSIN: — . . . Oh! may you be faithful to them (her children). Perhaps you are rearing for the world those who shall hereafter stand on Zion's walls, and sound the gospel trumpet. And should they prove faithful ambassadors of Christ, in our own or heathen lands, you will feel for all a mother's anxious cares a thousand-fold repaid. I love to look on that child who, like Samuel, has been consecrated to the Lord, and is now training for usefulness. Your station is no unimportant one. You feel it to be so, and I am glad you do. I am thus led to hope you may the better discharge its most important duties. And while you are quietly employed in the care of your interesting charge, it shall be my prayer that your dear children may be early sanctified by grace, and may grow up to be ornaments to the church of Christ, by their abundant labors for the redemption of a fallen world. Give them unreservedly to your God. It is your great privilege. I was recently exceedingly interested in knowing the facts of one pious mother's consecration of her little ones to the Lord in their early years. She had been out to a missionary meeting, where she was led deeply to feel the claims of a dying world. She asked herself, 'What can I do?' Of worldly substance she had little; but, as she entered her dwelling, and saw her three lovely children engaged in their plays, she said, 'These will I give to my God.' She retired to her closet, and there, in a covenant not to be forgotten, she surrendered them to her Father. In due season one by one he called for them. The eldest, a daughter, married one of our most devoted home missionaries, and now labors amid the desolations of the West. The second was called to a foreign land. Her life was short, but it proved a blessing to benighted souls. She was for a time a member of our beloved institution. We have had transmitted to us the account of her brief career and early death. We seemed to see her enter heaven and receive her 'little crown and little harp,' as she expressed it. The third, a son, has just finished his studies, and in a few weeks will leave for Persia, there to spend his life in laboring in the cause of Christ."

It might be added, that another son born subsequently, and in like manner consecrated to the Lord by that devoted mother, has for years been engaged in missionary work in Turkey.

CHAPTER VI.

EMBARKATION, VOYAGE, LAND JOURNEY, ARRIVAL.

Company. — Farewell Note to her Mother. — Life on Shipboard. — Studies. — Care of Judith. — Storm at Sea. — Gibraltar. — Letter to her "Section." — Smyrna. — Children of Missionaries. — Donkey Ride. — Constantinople. — Visits Schools. — Mosque of St. Sophia. — Trebizond. — Erzroom. — Arrival at Oroomiah. — Welcome. — Letters of Dr. Perkins and Miss Lyon.

On Wednesday, March 1st, 1843, Miss Fiske, with others destined to the same general field, embarked on board the bark "Emma Isadora," Capt. Hallet, for Smyrna. Besides Miss Fiske, the missionary company consisted of Rev. Dr. Perkins and wife, and their daughter Judith, who, after a visit to this country, were returning to their Eastern home; Rev. D. T. Stoddard and wife; Rev. E. E. Bliss and wife, who expected to labor among the Mountain Nestorians, but were stationed at Trebizond; Miss C. E. Myers (afterwards Mrs. Wright), and Mar. Yohannan, a Nestorian bishop, who had accompanied Dr. Perkins to this country. Impressive religious services were held on board, when the parting words and looks were interchanged with the numerous friends who had gathered there, and at half-past four o'clock, P. M., the bark left her wharf, spread her sails, and, moving quietly down the harbor, was soon out of sight of those who had, with a tearful interest, watched her departure, and who breathed after her many a fervent prayer.

Amid the hurry of those last busy days in Boston, Miss Fiske found little time for the use of the pen. The following brief note to her mother bears marks of the haste with which it was written.

"BOSTON, March 1, 1843.

"MY DEAR MOTHER:—In about one hour I leave for the vessel. I am happy in the prospects before me; and your own last comforting words have been a source of rich consolation to me. Oh! trust ever in the Lord, and he will support you. Pray much that I may be faithful in the Lord. If I can only be faithful, I shall regret no sacrifice.

"Yours in love,

"FIDELIA."

Of that parting hour she subsequently wrote: "It was to me a day of intense interest, when my feet stood on the deck of the vessel which was to bear me to an Eastern land; my heart overflowed with gratitude. Yes, I was thankful that I might leave all for my Redeemer; that I might go and spend and be spent for those sitting in darkness."

The following extracts from Miss Fiske's letters give us glimpses of her manner of life on shipboard, and show with what spirit she went forth to her missionary work.

"ATLANTIC OCEAN, March 13, 1843.

"It was half-past four, P. M., when the sails of our frail bark were filled to the wind, and we found ourselves receding from the shores of loved America.

I stood on the deck and watched the forms on the shore until they faded away in the distance. I then felt that I had separated from, to meet no more, my dearest earthly friends. I knew not, until then, how well I loved you all; still I could not wish to retrace my steps. I stood where I had longed to stand, nor was the peace that filled my bosom less than I had anticipated. I knew that in all human probability I should meet those I had loved, on earth, no more; but I hoped I was called by my heavenly Father to leave them, and, if so, I could but rejoice in it. Earth, and earthly things, seemed as they had seemed, on what I supposed was a dying-bed, and I felt it sweet to lean on the arm of the Beloved. I felt that it was now for me, in a great measure, to forget the things behind, and seek to prepare myself for my new field of labor. I stood on the deck till I could see my native shores no more, and then returned to the cabin where all our little missionary band were soon assembled. We spent a little season in communing of heavenly things, but soon, one by one, we felt the approach of our dreaded foe, sea-sickness, and were compelled reluctantly to retire to our staterooms. That night and the succeeding days brought very rough weather, which doubtless increased our illness."

"*March* 14. — You will like to know how I pass my time, and I as gladly tell you. I have taken little Judith (a darling child) to be my companion part of the time. She sleeps with me, and I dress and prepare her for breakfast, which, with the care of myself, takes until breakfast-time, which is usually at eight. After this I have some time alone. And this I would record as a signal blessing, for I may be as uninterrupted as ever I was in my 'mountain home.' After this the bishop is ever ready to give Miss Myers and myself a lesson in Syriac. . . . At ten we have Hitchcock's Geology. Mr. Perkins thought it very desirable that we should possess considerable knowledge of this before our land journey. Mr. Perkins and Mr. Stoddard are our teachers. I enjoy the lessons very much. Perhaps I may become better fitted to make selections for your cabinet. We have two hours for religious reading together, in the afternoon and evening. The rest of the time we can spend on deck or in the cabin, studying, writing, or doing what we please. The days seem not long, and time passes very pleasantly.

"My health is good, and I can truly say my cup overflows with blessings. I ask but a holy, thankful heart, which shall prepare me for everything which is before me."

"*March* 15. — St. Michaels, one of the Western Isles, is now fully in view. It is a beautiful island, about thirty miles long and six or seven broad. We can distinctly see its houses and beautiful green wheat-fields. I have been seated an hour on the 'house on deck,' gazing at it. The sun shone out most brightly on us, the nautiluses played abundantly in the water by our side, and once and again we beheld a sail in the distance. Is there not enough in nature everywhere to lead the mind to God, if we will but behold it? Why should we so often deplore the loss of comforts while so much remains? Oftener does my heart weep over what is left than over what has departed. Perhaps you will ask if I did not desire to set foot on this land. Had it been the place of my destination I would gladly have done so. But, as it is, I would rather be on the deep waters hastening to my Persian home. I care not how soon I rest there, or rather labor there.

"May I, my dear sisters, speak to you as when with you? Well, then, let me tell you how precious has been to me the hour of prayer, since I have been on board. Does one trying thought enter the soul, there seems a voice gently whispering, 'The remedy's before thee: pray.' When earthly friends are diminished in number, or absent from us, there is a sweetness I knew not when with them, in leaving all with God. O my dear friends, will you not often pray that I may never trust myself, or lean on any arm of flesh!"

"*March* 17.—We have passed the last of the Azores, and are now bending towards Gibraltar with a favorable wind. Since commencing our lessons in Turkish our time is as completely filled (that is, if we devote as much as we wish to writing our friends) as ever were days at Holyoke. I little expected in one fortnight to find my time so occupied. But I like it so much the better; it seems like my last loved home. Mr. Perkins says to-day, 'You like enough to do, do you not?' And he says, at Oroomiah I shall have all I desire. If it is my Father's will, I hope my life and health may be spared to labor there."

"*March* 21.—This morning we hoped that the day might be pleasant, and might find us bidding adieu to the troubled Atlantic. But vain were our hopes. We are now probably little nearer Gibraltar than in the morning. The rain is pouring down in torrents, and the wind has increased to a gale. One moment we are borne aloft on the wave to the mountain's height; the next, the waves literally encompass us. From the window of the 'house on deck' I look out to trace a Father's hand in this wild commotion, for I cannot go on deck with any safety. The men are all at their posts; the captain, with an anxious countenance, is much at the helm. But oh! there is to me a sweeter thought: '*My Father is at the helm!*'"

"*Thursday*, 23. — Rejoice with me, my dear friend! We have left the rude Atlantic, and are now in the peaceful Mediterranean. The storm of Tuesday was more violent in the evening, or rather in the night, than in the day.

"From early childhood I have been familiar with Gibraltar's reported grandeur; but, when my eyes really beheld it, I stood in mute astonishment. It was half-past four when we passed it, — about noon with my dear Holyoke friends, and their recreation day too. Oh that I could for a moment be with them, and tell them how a kind Providence has watched over us and brought us safely over the Atlantic waves in just twenty-one days, — as short a passage, the captain tells us, as he ever had, and still as rough a one. We passed through the Straits at the rate of eleven miles an hour, and now, that my eye had looked on Europe and Africa, I felt that I was really far, far from home.

"After passing the rock, we went to tea with joyful, and, I hope, thankful hearts. We found our table spread without the usual 'rack' for keeping our utensils in place, and it was so quiet that we needed it not. I cannot tell you how pleasant it seemed to be once more quiet! We shall probably have no more so rough 'seas.' In the evening we returned to our reading with more than ordinary interest. We are now reading in the evening 'D'Aubigne's History of the Reformation.'"

"*March* 23.—I need not tell you I think often and much of you, and I thank the Providence that brought us together this year. Oh, may it be found in the last day that our spiritual interests were promoted by it! How precious to me is the recollection of those last days spent with you, and of that last night, when, for the last time, we bowed together before the throne of grace! Oh, it is Christian intercourse that binds hearts by the strongest ties! Has not such intercourse been ours? May it not still be so on earth, and may we not hope to be forever engaged in this blessed employment in the world to which we now hasten?"

"*Wednesday*, 29.—Another recreation-day with you. Is it your day for a missionary meeting, or was it last week? Have you remembered your unworthy sisters on the far-off seas? It may be that my usefulness will greatly depend on your prayers for me. Sisters, pray for me; it will be the greatest blessing you can confer upon me. O my dear sisters, your own hearts will be warmed, and you will feel that you are rewarded a hundred-fold for all your labor, even in this life."

TO SECTION "NO. 4," NORTH DIVISION, MT. HOLYOKE SEMINARY.

"MEDITERRANEAN SEA, April 1, 1843.

"BELOVED FRIENDS: — I cannot repress my inclination to write one sheet to you on the deep waters. All of Holyoke's sisters were dear to me; but, as you were placed under my especial care, I loved to call you 'my own,' in its truest sense; and since separated from you, not a day has passed without my thinking of you. Precious to me is the memory of the last few days I spent with you. How was my heart warmed to see the interest you manifested in the cause of missions! Oh, may you never lose it, but may it increase and increase, until you shall all be found doing all in this blessed work which your heavenly Father would have you do! Many of you now hope that you are the children of God. In your expressed desires to be whole-hearted Christians I was deeply interested; my prayer to God shall be that you may be such, — that you may have humble, holy hearts, fitting you to labor abundantly for your blessed Redeemer. If you do really desire to live lives of active piety, enough will be given you to do, yea, more, — strength to do it.

"But some of you I left strangers to God; and is such still your estate, beloved ones? I sometimes hope that, before this, you have found the Saviour precious to your souls, and that each of you can say, with a good degree of confidence, 'I love the Lord.' Again I think, perhaps it may be otherwise. Then I ask myself, is there anything more I can do for those I love so much? A still monitor then seems to say, 'Praying breath is never spent in vain;' and, in the solitude of my little state-room, I seek Heaven's blessing for those whom I may no more ask to go with me to the New Jerusalem as I take their hands in mine. It is a solemn thought that I can never again speak personally to you. I feel that I have been unfaithful to you. Will you forgive me? Oh, let no neglect of mine keep you from the way of eternal life! The day hastens on when we shall consider an interest in Christ as of more value than all that the world can give.

"The difference in our time prevents my observing with you the time of the recess prayer-meeting; but I am happy in the thought that my own beloved section will all observe it. Is it not so? No seasons of prayer when I was at Holyoke are now remembered with more interest than those meetings. Fail not to remember when you are together those whom your eyes have never seen, and never will see until the judgment-day. Be faithful in prayer, and you may in that day see some who have been saved in answer to your supplications. . . . .

"Ever remember me, my dear young friends, in your prayers, that I may be faithful in my Master's service. Enclosed is my tenderest love for each and every one of you.

"I am now, as on the day I left you,

"Affectionately yours,

"FIDELIA FISKE."

TO HER MOTHER AND SISTER.

April 4. — "Last evening I stood on the 'house on deck,' and saw the sun go down. It was a delightful scene. The golden clouds were reflected from the gentle water's surface, with no common splendor. Reluctantly I turned away, and retired to the cabin. But I remained not long, for the beauties of an evening at sea, and on Grecian shores, rested upon and around us, and called me forth. The new moon in the west was shining on the placid waters, which only played at this time in gentle ripples. Methought this little orb of night seemed arrayed in a lustre not her own, for never had I looked on her when she seemed so lovely. Her gentle beams, reflected from the water's surface, caused it to seem like a sea of glass; the stars, those sparkling 'gems of night,' did literally 'bestud the sky.' As I looked on that scene I could only exclaim, 'How beautiful, how glorious are thy works, Parent of good!' And there was to me, as I gazed, one sweet thought. It was, that on these same nightly objects my own dear mother and sisters may look. But this was not all, nor the sweetest thought of that hour; for then I remembered that our Father, our Guide and Keeper, was the same. This morning I arose at half-past four, and went out to take a morning view of what lay around and above us. Jupiter, Saturn, and Venus were still visible, and the heavens seemed slowly preparing to welcome the king of day. At length he came, in all his glory. His appearance was sudden, and I would not, for much, have lost sight of it. It was as though a huge ball of fire had suddenly arisen from the water's edge. Not a cloud played about him, nor aught to mar his ascending glory."

TO FRIENDS AT MT. HOLYOKE SEMINARY.

"SMYRNA, April 8.

"We are now in our first desired haven, and here I will pen a few lines to you. Yesterday, at half-past three in the afternoon, we anchored in Smyrna harbor. We were in sight of the town in the morning, but were a long time in beating up, for the winds were contrary. Before three, a boat was seen coming towards us. As it approached, we found that it contained Mr. Van Lennep and brother. It was pleasant to us all to meet him, but particularly so to Mr. Bliss. Our captain went on shore about this time, and returned with the health officer of the custom-house, who, after examining the health bill of the passengers, and scrutinizing our very selves, permitted us to go on shore. But, before we were in readiness to go, our hearts were made still more glad by seeing Mr. Temple, and Mr. King from Greece (the latter was on a visit here) approaching us. It was good to see these missionary fathers coming to bid us welcome in the name of the Lord.

"The meeting with Mr. King was wholly unexpected, but not the less pleasant. He remembered the time when he had laid his hand on my head, saying, 'I wish you were old enough to go with me to Greece.' And now he says, 'I will bid you welcome to this land, if I may not to Greece.'

"Let me tell you of the strange feeling that filled my mind when I first stepped ashore. It was a rainy afternoon, which added not a little to the unpleasantness of the scene. When our little boat first came along the shore, we could behold people of various nations and costumes, and, as our ears soon told us, tongues. It seemed to us all a perfect Babel. Our trunks being landed (nothing else was brought on shore, but put from the ship into the steamboat, which carried us from Smyrna to Constantinople), some dozen of *hamnouls* (porters) contended for the privilege of carrying them to our boarding-place, at Mr. Temple's. For this, they would expect to receive perhaps a piastre (four cents). They, having taken two or three trunks apiece on their backs, proceeded on their way, while we followed through the dirty, narrow streets, too narrow to admit a single carriage, until we reached Mr. Temple's, which was not far.

"There are many interesting associations connected with Smyrna. It is pleasant to remember that here was once a church of the living God, whose works, tribulation, and poverty were known by the blessed Redeemer, although scarce a vestige of it now remains."

Miss Fiske spent a week very pleasantly and profitably at Smyrna. She enjoyed exceedingly her intercourse with the missionary brethren and sisters at that station, and their families. Much as she needed rest after her boisterous voyage, she spent most of the time in visiting the schools connected with the mission, and in gaining an insight into the details of missionary work. She was deeply affected by her first view of the moral condition of those who had never felt the benign influences of a pure Christianity. "My heart," she writes, "bleeds over the wretchedness which meets my eye here. Had I ten [illegible] lives, I would gladly give them all away to help raise these degraded ones. But they are very difficult of access here; much more so than in the field to which we go."

The children of the missionaries excited in her a lively and tender interest. In their behalf she thus appeals to her Mt. Holyoke friends: —

"Will you not love sometimes *particularly* to remember them in your seasons of prayer? I have felt more than ever before, since I have been in missionary families, the need of prayer for these children. We cannot begin to know at home the temptations to which they are exposed. Nor can we know the anxiety of their dear parents in their behalf. Beloved sisters, bear with me while I again entreat you to pray for them. The answer to your prayers may send comfort to a mother's heart when ready to sink under the cares that devolve upon her in this land of darkness."

All that need further be said of her stay in Smyrna is contained in an extract from a letter to her mother: —

"We remained in Smyrna just one week. It was a busy, pleasant, and I hope profitable, week. It was good, after thirty-six days at sea, to find so pleasant a home as Mr. Temple's house afforded." . . .

"Connected with Mr. Temple are Messrs. Adger and Riggs, with their families. They are in Bournabat, — a pleasant village eight miles from Smyrna. The day after we reached Smyrna, Messrs. Adger and Riggs, being at Mr. Temple's, invited Miss Myers and myself to go home with them and spend the Sabbath. We gratefully accepted the invitation, with the understanding that we should thereby enjoy a 'donkey-ride.' And here let me say, that I saw not a carriage in Smyrna, and but few horses. Transportation is chiefly by porters, donkeys, and, perchance now and then, a string of camels. About half-past four the donkeys were brought to the door, and we found ourselves mounted, for the first time, on these little creatures, upon whom we might with little difficulty have seated ourselves by a single step from the ground. I had a saddle, but no bridle; however, I was attended by a Greek muleteer, who carried in his hand a sharp-pointed instrument, with which he continually goaded the animal, so that we pressed forward at no very slow rate. The eight miles were soon passed, and I found myself in Mr. Riggs' very pleasant family." . . . "We remained at Bournabat until Tuesday, when we returned to Smyrna. We left at an early hour, walked three miles over a pleasant portion of the country, gathering the beautiful flowers that abounded there. In this walk we passed several wells, digged in other days by Mohammedans, for the benefit of the weary, thirsty traveller. By these acts of benevolence they were believed to be entitled to high seats in the heavenly kingdom. But we found the wells deep, and nothing to draw with; so we passed on, unbenefited by their cooling waters. Our walk of three miles brought us to the water. Here we took a boat; but the waves were so high as to render rowing impracticable. A sail was therefore raised, and we went dashing forward at 'Atlantic speed.' While on the ocean I often longed for a good dash of salt water, but it never came. But now it came to my heart's content. The waves rolled over us, pouring off from our bonnets in sheets. Mr. Riggs felt very sad that he had brought us into such a 'fix.' But we comforted him by telling him that we enjoyed it right well; and so we did, although, when we reached the shore, we were completely drenched. We had then a mile to walk, and I imagine that we presented no very pleasing appearance as we passed through the streets. But safe and sound we reached Mr. Temple's, and suffered not at all from our adventure." . . . "The afternoon of Thursday we spent in visiting the remains of ancient Smyrna. These are on a hill overlooking the present city, which is very low. Before us, as we here stood, were the ruins of the ancient fort, and the amphitheatre where were celebrated the Grecian games, and also the spot pointed out and believed to be that of Polycarp's martyrdom." . . . "Thursday evening the missionaries assembled at Mr. Temple's for a prayer-meeting. Some others were present, making our whole number about twenty-five. It was to us, 'ready to depart on the morrow,' a most precious season. The departing, and remaining ones were commended to a covenant-keeping God, in whose presence we all hope one day to meet. Nor were our friends at home forgotten; and here let me say that I have not heard a prayer offered, since I have been among missionaries, in which the friends at home have not been remembered. Are missionaries as constantly remembered by those they have left behind? Friday morning, after making necessary preparations for leaving in the afternoon, we called on Mrs. Van Lennep, the widow of one of those brothers with whom Uncle Pliny resided when here. She spoke of him with the deepest interest, saying to me, 'And now our house is just as when he was with us; this was where he dined;' and, pointing to another room, 'there he preached.' Mr. Jacob Van Lennep, the surviving brother, is consul-general in Smyrna. He had twice called to see me when absent, and, when he knew I was at Mrs. Van Lennep's, came again. He wished (to use his own words) 'an affectionate remembrance to all the brothers and sisters of his early and loved friend, Mr. Fiske;' and he added, 'also to your own mother; tell them all that I treasure their names among my choicest ones, and, when I met you, I felt more as if beholding an old friend than a stranger.'"

The missionary band left Smyrna April 14th, in the Austrian steamer *Siri Parvas.* "We reached Constantinople," writes Miss Fiske, "after a pleasant passage of thirty-eight hours. It was as clear a morning as ever lighted an eastern sky, when we entered the harbor, giving us a most delightful view of the city. It being the Sabbath, the captain kindly consented that our effects should all remain undisturbed till Monday. Arrangements having been made for us in the families of Messrs. Dwight and Holmes, we went to our temporary homes, enjoying a pleasant and quiet Sabbath."

Miss Fiske spent nearly three weeks in Constantinople. These she turned to good account in making herself more familiar with missionary operations, treasuring up a store of facts, and suggestions, and counsels, which were exceedingly valuable in reference to her own future work. She took a special interest in the schools connected with this mission, and carefully studied the methods employed to secure the mental and moral improvement of the Armenian youth.

She was fortunate in having an opportunity to visit the Mosque of St. Sophia, of which she thus writes: —

"This, as you probably know, was once a temple of the living God. It was built by the Christian Emperor, Constantine, and the pillars, which graced his temples when an idolater, were brought by him from various places to support this vast fabric. My own eyes have seen the eight pillars of beautiful porphyry, perhaps two and a half or three feet in diameter, which he placed in his great temple. After the time of Constantine, the building went into decay, but was rebuilt by Justinian. When the city was taken by the Turks, it was converted into a Mussulman's mosque. No Franks are now, or ever have been, permitted to visit it, except by a special firman from the Sultan; and this is obtained only by the payment of a considerable sum. But fortunately for us, while in the city, the lady of Mr. Payson, American Consul at Messina, visited Constantinople, and obtained a firman for visiting this and other forbidden spots. We were invited to join her company, and gladly accepted the invitation. At the hour appointed we repaired to the house of Mr. Brown, American Chargé d'Affaires at this place. It was a wet day, but we suffered not at all from it. We first visited the Turkish Armory, where are multitudes of the arms of other days. We visited one small mosque before we went to St. Sophia. We reached the last-named place just before noon, — the time for prayers. There were hundreds assembled to repeat the Mohammedan prayers, and bow towards Mecca.

We were not allowed to go into the body of the house till after prayers; but were permitted to go into the galleries and look down on these poor deluded mortals. Oh, how did my heart weep over them in their lost and ruined state! The galleries are so elevated that persons below looked only like children. It is estimated that they will contain ten thousand persons, and the whole mosque, perhaps thirty thousand. The length of the body of the building is two hundred and sixty-nine feet, and the breadth one hundred and forty-three feet. In the centre is a dome, the interior of which is gilt mosaic work. It has, I think, forty-two windows, and is one hundred and eighty feet from the ground. This dome is one hundred and fifteen feet in diameter, and has an inscription on its inner surface, the letter of which are said to be ten yards long. On either side of the dome are seraphims which are also of mosaic work. In the lower part of the mosque are thousands of small glass lamps, hung in lines, five together, or in splendid chandeliers. From the galleries they look like little diamonds. They are cup-form, and I should think would hold about two gills each. When all lighted they must give to the house a most splendid appearance. Oh that God were worshipped there by humble, sincere hearts! and I have no doubt he will be one day. There is a change coming over these dark regions. A spirit of inquiry is awaking here. May the Lord come, and that speedily! From the mosque we went to the mausoleum of the Sultan. It is a splendid building, beneath which were laid his remains, and those of his family, numbering fifty-four."

The presence of Dr. King, the early friend and associate of her uncle, Pliny Fiske, added greatly to the pleasure of Miss Fiske's visit at Constantinople. Of him, she writes thus to her mother: —

"I enjoyed seeing him *very much*, though the good man said, when he bade me good-by, 'you cannot have enjoyed it as much as I have.' The tears would roll down his cheeks as he spoke of Uncle Pliny, and then looked at me. He and Mr. Goodale both thought that in everything I much resembled him. Mr. and Mrs. Goodale would look at me and say, 'How much you do make us think of your uncle! It does us good to look at you.' You will be surprised that they should think thus, since none of you at home could see any resemblance. Mr. Goodale and Mr. King both wished to be remembered very affectionately to all the family friends, and particularly to you, dear mother. They said, 'Tell her, she has given you to a noble work, and will never regret it. We bid her child welcome to our missionary circle, and feel that those who have been tried in separation from a dear friend will be rewarded for their sacrifice.'"

Miss Fiske, with the company to which she belonged, left Constantinople May 4th, in the Austrian steamer, "Stamboul," Capt. Ford, for Trebizond; grateful for the providential detention which had given her this favorable opportunity of becoming acquainted with so large a circle of excellent and experienced missionaries. She writes, soon after leaving: —

"I wish I could tell you of the delightful seasons of Christian intercourse we have enjoyed with the dear missionary brothers and sisters, as we have passed along. It has been sweet, it has been soul-reviving. I shall carry with me the most pleasant remembrances of them as I go to my field of labor."

From Trebizond she writes: "Our passage of seven hundred miles to this place was a pleasant one of less than three days. Captain Ford is an intelligent Englishman. We felt at his table more as if in the house of a friend than in a steamboat surrounded by hundreds of strangers. We would be grateful for this and thousands of other blessings. And here I would speak of the appearance of the deck of a steamer in these seas. It is covered with hundreds, I might almost say, 'of all nations, kindred, and tongues.' There have been no less than eight or nine different costumes and languages on both of the boats in which we have been. Many of these deck passengers are the most filthy objects I ever saw; others are of considerable respectability among their own people. They bring their own bed and provisions with them, and day and night, men, women, and children, encamp together in the open air.

"Among the passengers of the "Stamboul" was a Persian, who had just left Constantinople with a Georgian female, whom he had bought in the slave market, to be the wife of a friend. He paid for her one thousand dollars. She was accompanied by a colored female, who is to be a kind of second wife, for whom he paid four hundred dollars. The first-named answered to all my ideas of the beauty of Georgian females. She was dressed in a beautiful purple merino loose garment, and her face was nearly covered with a common veil, called 'gashmak.' I should think her about fourteen years of age.

"Mr. Johnston is the only missionary here. He and his worthy companion have long labored here alone, but not without affecting good. They had not seen an American since Mr. and Mrs. Perkins passed this way on their return to America. I need not say they were glad to see us. Two evenings ago we had a prayer-meeting at which Mr. Johnston spoke of their solitude. 'Often,' he said, 'we have sat down at the communion season alone. Last Sabbath was our regular time for observing it, but, knowing of your coming, we deferred it until you should be with us. As he spoke of these things poor Mrs. Johnston was obliged to leave the room, overcome with weeping. She has suffered much from being thus alone."

TO HER MOTHER.

"And now I know you will wish to learn particularly in regard to myself, — if I have been well; if I have not deeply felt the need of a near and dear friend, like a mother or sister, into whose compassionate bosom to pour all the feelings of my heart? A thousand other inquiries I know the love of my dear mother would prompt; and with the same frankness as when in childhood I rested on my mother's bosom, would I answer them. Since the first three days at sea I have not seen an hour of sickness. I have really been unusually well. But I would ever bear in mind that sickness may and probably will come; and that, without a mother's or sister's tender care, I may languish and die. Sometimes such thoughts steal over me for a moment to sadden; but I remember that there is One who loves better than any earthly friend, and can better provide for a sick-bed. Oh, how sweet to trust a divine hand for all we need! A kind Father has provided for us in days of affliction. Oh, how does the remembrance of those days open the hidden fountains of the soul! I weep not alone over the loved ones gone to the silent grave, but over the remembrance of kindness shown to us in those days. . . . In regard to sympathizing friends, I can say I have not felt the want of them. Our company, I think, are all very excellent persons. They have been to me everything I could have asked. Instead of mourning over neglect, my heart has oftener led me to shed tears of gratitude over undeserved favor shown me. The journey thus far has been prosperous, though there has been opportunity for things trying, which have only been avoided by the very great kindness of our guides and protectors. Surely I have great reason to speak of the goodness of God in thus providing for me. To him I would ever commit myself, and trust his loving kindness, and beg you, my dear mother, to feel that I have been happy since I left you. Could I know that the same cheerfulness which I have enjoyed, has been yours, I should feel that my cup overflowed with blessings."

The perils and hardships of the sea were past, but a land journey of seven or eight hundred miles, by no means easy or safe, through unsettled and mountainous regions infested with robbers, and furnishing but poor accommodations for travellers, still lay between our missionary friends and their Persian home. In making preparations for this, the week spent at Trebizond was mostly occupied. They here parted with Mr. and Mrs. Bliss. Under the guidance of Dr. Perkins, who was familiar with the route, they passed safely and pleasantly to Erzroom, and thence to Oroomiah in Persia, their destined home and field of labor. The next day Miss Fiske thus reports their arrival in a letter to her family friends: —

"OROOMIAH, June 15, 1843.

"MY DEAR, DEAR FRIENDS: — From my chosen home I am now privileged to address you. The kind and merciful Providence of other days has continued to watch over me in all my wanderings, and in health and safety I have reached this place. Letters which I forwarded to you by mail from Smyrna, Constantinople, and Trebizond, you have received, or doubtless will receive soon. By these your anxiety for me will be somewhat relieved. Still, you will have had many thoughts in regard to me, as I have journeyed by land over these wild wastes. All these anxious thoughts I would, as soon as possible, have put away by your hearing of our arrival. For, although nothing reaches me, as yet, from you, my pen shall not be silent while health continues. Having made all due preparations, we left Trebizond May 15th, after a pleasant stay of one week in the family of Mr. Johnston. The day was quite rainy in the morning, but, the afternoon proving less so, we thought it desirable to leave. A part of our boxes, the articles of which we might not need for our immediate use, had gone before us. The rest, with ourselves, required twenty horses. Being all mounted, we wished much that our friends at home could look upon us; for we thought could they but see our happiness, they, too, would enjoy much. Mr. and Mrs. Bliss, and Mr. Johnston accompanied us about five miles, when we bade them farewell.

"We found our way over the mountain passes, the vales, and the plains, of Persia and Turkey, not a little toilsome. But we have been blessed with good health and fair weather; and, under the excellent guidance of Mr. Perkins, have probably performed the journey with less fatigue than usual. We reached Erzroom May 23d, having been nine days on the way, yet resting on the Sabbath. Here we found pleasant homes in the families of Messrs. Peabody and Jackson, enjoying their society, and gaining renewed strength for our further journey.

"When we left Erzroom, May 29th, we felt that we had really set out on our journey, for we had no more missionary friends to visit, and we expected that our next resting-place would be our final one on earth. Mr. and Mrs. Peabody, and three Armenian friends accompanied us for a few miles out of the city, and then again to our loving friends we said farewell. The journey before us was now about five hundred miles, and some of it through a very dangerous portion of country, much infested by Koordish robbers. We felt that our path was insecure; but, committing our way to the Lord, we went forward, and he has kindly preserved us. On the 10th instant, we were met by two Nestorians, who had come, knowing us to be on the way. They brought letters from the different members of the mission, which led us to feel ourselves very near them. The next day we came to Khoy, which is only three days from Oroomiah. Here, the bishop, being exceedingly anxious to reach home, with one of the Nestorians, left us for his own village, Gavalan, two days distant. Finding the weather becoming very hot, we rose at one, Monday morning, and rode about eight hours. The next morning's ride brought us to Gavalan at half-past seven o'clock. The news of our approach had gone before us to Oroomiah, and bishops, priests, and deacons were anxious to meet us. Some, leaving Oroomiah just at night, rode until almost morning, to be at Gavalan in season to meet us still further beyond. But in this they were disappointed, for we had started earlier than they expected. Seeing us, however, a little distance from the village, they sprang upon their horses and with lightning speed advanced towards us. First came Joseph, a brother of the bishop, who has been educated by the missionaries. He leaped from his horse, embraced Mr. and Mrs. Perkins, kissed their hands, and with tears of joy bade them welcome, and also the rest of us. Then came good Priest Abraham, with Moses and John, two of the scholars, and gave us the same welcome. In their rather broken English, they said again and again, 'I very glad see you.' Before we arrived, a 'multitude on foot' had come to us, among whom was the bishop's father. As we came in, the hill that overlooks the village was literally covered with men, women, and children. Their tattered garments and great filthiness showed their extremely degraded condition. Yet their willingness to hear inspires us with the hope that something may be done to raise them to the ranks of 'freemen in Christ Jesus.' When we reached the dwelling of the bishop, we found it, like those about it, a miserable hut of mud. But he had made all the preparations for us in his power. We were taken into the best room of the house, which was entered by much stooping. Luncheon was soon brought, consisting of new baked bread, milk, honey, butter, and cheese. The bread, which is in thin cakes, perhaps half a yard long and half that width, was laid on the waiters; then were set two dishes of milk, with wooden spoons, with which to help ourselves; then dishes of honey and butter, which we spread upon our bread with the help of another piece of bread. But it was all very sweet, and we ate with good relish. The room was soon filled with others who had come to welcome us, among whom were Mar. Yusuph, (Joseph), Priest Yohannan, and others mentioned in Mr. Perkins' book.

"When our tents came we repaired to them, as they were more comfortable. There a dinner was brought us, served in the same style as our former meal. The fatted lamb had been killed for us, and all things made ready. After dinner, Mr. Stocking, Dr. Wright, and Mr. Breath arrived. They remained and returned with us the next day. At night some eight or ten more priests and deacons arrived to take us joyfully by the hand. The next morning (Wednesday), we left about two o'clock, accompanied by all those mentioned above, and rode for about five hours, when we encamped for a little time. Here we were met by Mr. and Mrs. Holladay, Mr. Merrick, and Mr. Jones, besides very many natives. Others we met on the way, until our company amounted to nearly fifty. Three hours' ride brought us to the city. According to previous arrangements we all repaired to the house of Mr. Jones. Here we met all the others. After laying off our riding-dresses, and resting for a little, it was proposed that we give thanks and sing. Mr. Merrick read the 107th psalm; we sung 'How blessed are thy servants, Lord,' and then Mr. Merrick led in prayer. This, with the kind welcome given us, was almost overcoming, and I wept tears of joy."

The following testimonial in regard to the favorable impressions which Miss Fiske had already made upon her associates, together with the reply which it called forth, may fitly close this chapter: —

FROM REV. JUSTIN PERKINS, D. D., TO MISS MARY LYON.

"OROOMIAH, July 7, 1843.

"DEAR MADAM: — Having had a very fair opportunity to form an opinion of Miss Fiske, — the very estimable young lady whom you so kindly interested yourself to furnish from your seminary for our mission, — I will redeem the pledge I gave you, to communicate my impressions. This I can do in a few words. We have found her all you promised, and even much more. I have not yet observed a blemish in her character, and her excellences are very prominent, yet so happily blended as to unite in a symmetry that shields them from observation, until she is known by acquaintance. You, doubtless, appreciate her fully, as you must, of course, well understand her worth; and I state my own impressions, not for your information, but to apprise you that we, too, have learned something of her rare merits.

"Miss Fiske has usually enjoyed excellent health since we left Boston, and has also been in fine spirits. She has won the hearts of all our missionary friends on the way, nor less the hearts of our associates here. Mrs. P. and myself feel personally under great obligations to her for her invaluable assistance in taking care of our little girl, both on our voyage and during our journey. She at once secured the affections of the child to such an extent as to relieve Mrs. P. almost wholly of the charge of her, which, in her delicate health, was a greater aid than you can well conceive. Miss Fiske had both the strength and the disposition to do most that the child needed to have done for her, without much inconvenience to herself. And so good a traveller has she proved as to impose little care on me, in addition to that required by the rest of our travelling party.

"She appears entirely contented, happy, and pleased with her situation and circumstances, and bids fair to be incalculably useful in the important sphere she will fill, in promoting the interests of our mission and the salvation of the Nestorians. We feel under very great obligations to you, dear madam, for the deep interest you took, and the prompt and laborious efforts you made, to secure for us such a helper as Miss Fiske. If, under her fostering care, a scion of Mt. Holyoke Seminary shall gradually spring up on the plains of Oroomiah, to enlighten and bless benighted Persia, I know you will feel yourself to be amply rewarded. May the Lord also give you the satisfaction of seeing Miss Fiske's mantle rest on scores of your pupils."

MISS MARY LYON TO REV. JUSTIN PERKINS, D. D.

"SOUTH HADLEY, Feb. 6, 1844.

"DEAR SIR: — Your kind letter, bearing date July 7th, I have received, for which please accept my cordial thanks. Your testimony to Miss Fiske's happiness and usefulness is very gratifying. Her own letters, too, are all suited to make her friends happy in having given her up for such a work. It is my opinion that the leadings of Providence should be decisive to justify our encouraging an unmarried female to go on a foreign mission. My impressions on this subject were strengthened as I saw Misses Fiske and Myers bidding farewell to friends, and home, and kindred, and country. How different was their situation from that of the rest of the company! Every other missionary had *one* intimate friend, and that one the dearest friend on earth. But Miss Fiske has been admirably prepared by the endowments of nature, by the dealings of Providence, and by the influence of grace, for just such a sacrifice. I rejoice that her heavenly Father has called her to this self-denying work, and that she was not disobedient to the heavenly voice. I rejoice, too, that the finger of Providence pointed *her* out to go, rather than any other one about whom we had conversation. I doubt not she will find many ways of doing good besides that of teaching. As you wander along together, a lonely band, through this vale of tears, and as you are laboring and suffering for Christ's sake, I doubt not that Miss Fiske will often be able, in her own quiet way, to come to one heart and another, as an angel of mercy and kindness. Sometimes she may be able to give to some of her companions in toil a cup of consolation, when others, who would fain enjoy the privilege, have not the time nor the strength granted them.

"Miss Fiske has been very faithful in writing letters; and I think this is not among the least of the ways given her to serve the cause."

CHAPTER VII.

STATE OF THE NESTORIAN MISSION IN 1843. — FIRST IMPRESSIONS AND FIRST LABORS.

First Missionaries. — Reinforcements. — Mountain Nestorians and Dr. Grant. — Residence at Seir. — Letters. — Study of the Language. — Good News from Holyoke. — Governor of Oroomiah. — Call on his Wives. — Preparations for the School. — Hymns Translated. — Removes to the City. — Girls come to Read. — Chamber upon the Wall. — Sympathy for her Mother.

MISS FISKE was not a pioneer in the missionary work in Persia. The ground was already broken; others had labored, and she felt it a privilege to enter into their labors. For nine years the mission among the Nestorians had been in successful operation. Mr. Perkins, and Dr. Grant, who, with their wives, were the first to enter the field, — the former in 1834, and the latter in 1835, — had, from time to time, been reinforced by efficient co-laborers: Rev. James L. Merrick, in 1835; Rev. Albert L. Holladay and wife, and Rev. William R. Stocking and wife, in 1837; Rev. Willard Jones and wife, in 1839; Austin F. Wright, M. D., and Edward Breath (printer), in 1840. Mrs. Grant had, in 1839, rested from her labors.

Much had already been accomplished by this excellent band of missionary brethren and sisters. They had met and borne the peculiar privations and hardships incident to the occupancy of a new field. They had secured in a large measure the favor of an intolerant government, and the confidence of a degraded and oppressed people. They had laid broad and solid foundations for the noble structure which was destined, ere long to rise in that far-off and benighted land. True, the number of hopeful converts was, as yet, small. No revival of religion had been enjoyed.

Miss Fiske writes : "Soon after our arrival, one of the older members of our circle remarked that he did not know of five in the whole Nestorian nation whom he could look upon as true Christians."

The gospel had for some time been statedly preached in several of the Nestorian churches. Some forty schools had been established in the villages on the plain of Oroomiah, and a printing press had been put in successful operation.

No one appreciated more fully than did Miss Fiske the great advantage of entering a field already brought so largely under cultivation, and of being connected with so large a band of experienced fellow-laborers.

A part of the Nestorians dwelt in the mountains of Koordistan, which look down from the west on the Province of Oroomiah. These mountains were also the home of fierce, lawless tribes of Koords. The region was nominally under Turkish jurisdiction, although the Persian government also laid claim to it. The people, however, both Nestorians and Koords, were really subject to neither power, and enjoyed a kind of wild independence. From the founding of the mission, Dr. Grant had set his heart upon doing something for these mountain Nestorians, and, by persevering effort, had gained a foothold among them; but in 1842, he was driven away by a terrible war, in which thousands of the Nestorians were cruelly put to death by the Koords, while many, who escaped the sword, found their way down to the plain of Oroomiah, and were there brought under the influence of the missionaries.

Two days after her arrival at Oroomiah Miss Fiske, with other members of the mission, repaired to Seir, where she remained several weeks, resting from the fatigue of the journey, acquiring the language, and making herself familiar with the operations of the mission, and laying plans for entering upon her own specific work as teacher. Her own pen will best acquaint us with the feelings and employments of those first weeks of missionary life.

TO MISS MARY LYON.

"SEIR, July 5, 1843.

"Were I by your side, I know you would wish to ask many questions in reference to the time that has passed since I saw you. And I should love, as in other days, to tell you the joys and sorrows of my heart. You would, doubtless, wish to know my feelings, as far my experience goes, in regard to young ladies going out single.

"Many were ready to say to us, on our leaving, 'Your journey will probably be to you more trying than anything after you reach your field.' The reverse, however, will doubtless prove true in my case. So far from anything trying being my lot on the way, I rather enjoyed each day and hour. Nothing was wanting on the part of Mr. Perkins to render our journeyings and our short stays pleasant. And that 'delicate regard to the comfort and feelings of the young ladies,' so strictly enjoined on the other members of our company by Dr. Anderson, has surely been heeded. . . . .

"Although my journey has been thus pleasant, I can see many ways in which a young lady might be exceedingly tried. I believe, and I am frank to confess it, that my feelings five years ago would have been very different from what they have now been, had I passed through the same.

"O my dear Miss Lyon, I do, I am sure I do, most sincerely thank you for all those kind instructions you have so often given me, and which I have felt more than ever before, during the last months, to be the light of my path. The feelings of missionaries on the way, with whom I conversed on the usefulness of single ladies in the missionary field, are invariably the same. They feel strongly that there are very wide doors of usefulness at present open to them, and more, that their labors are almost indispensable in gaining access to the females in many places. But these same good brethren feel not less strongly in reference to the qualifications of young ladies for such a work. One qualification, in reference to which Dr. Dwight (whose judgment, by the way, I do highly prize) spoke more strongly, perhaps, than of any other, was a willingness to labor year after year, when little good might seem to be effected. He felt that few were to be found who would not soon ask for a change of place or circumstances. And yet, he said, could such be found, none would be more welcome to our field, and none could be more useful. With such views constantly brought before me in regard to the possibility of great usefulness in my present station, you will be assured I feel not less interest in the work than when I left you. As I am permitted to see more and more of the poor degraded females of this nation, if I know my heart, I do feel a deeper interest in them, and a stronger desire to spend and be spent for them." . . . .

TO A COUSIN.

"SEIR, July 17, 1843.

"My home is in the family of Mr. Stocking, and I feel myself highly privileged in having so good a home. I studied Turkish, as a spoken language, on the way, but am now giving all my energies to Syriac. The first fortnight after my arrival I was not able to study, but am now quite well and able to study as closely as when in America. Reading from right to left, with new characters, was at first somewhat puzzling. But its novelty has now all passed away, and I am becoming quite familiar with the style, not to say the matter. We are reading the history of Joseph, as translated from the ancient into the modern Syriac. I can read with tolerable ease, and am beginning to translate a little; also to speak a little. I cannot tell you the thrill of joy that fills my soul at each new acquisition in this language. Oh, I do long to have its shackles thrown off from me, and my tongue loosed! The hope that I shall, ere long, be able to begin to labor for my poor Nestorian sisters makes study a pleasure. I hope to begin to labor in the girls' school when it opens in the autumn, with the assistance of a native teacher. If I can but be instrumental in a small degree in raising them from their present degraded condition, my heart will be glad. Yes, I shall feel it sweeter here than in my native land, to live and labor, and from here go to my eternal home."

TO A TEACHER IN MT. HOLYOKE SEMINARY.

"SEIR, July 19, 1843.

"MY DEAR, DEAR MISS M.: — My pen cannot express, nor, were I by your side, could language express, the feelings of my heart to-day. Do you ask me why? It is not that sorrow fills my heart; but it is that I may rejoice over new-born souls in Holyoke. And have you enjoyed another precious season of refreshing from the presence of the Most High! Oh, how I do long to know the particulars! But not a word from the pen of any of you has reached me as yet. But I do and will believe you have sent forward the glad tidings to cheer a sister's heart in this land of moral darkness, and that soon I may receive them. . . . . Was it when I was on the deep waters that you were thus blessed? Oh, how often was I with you in spirit, in my little state-room in the 'Emma Isadora.' In that, to me, precious place, I used, one by one, to open those letters so kindly prepared for me to read on the voyage. There were many from those not pious. These breathed a spirit peculiarly interesting to me. There were expressions of feeling which I had never been able to elicit in conversation. With one exception, they contained earnest entreaties for remembrance at the throne of grace. There were many expressions like these: 'When your eye glances over these lines, on the broad waters, will you not offer one petition for me, that I may not be lost forever?' 'Pray for me that my present feelings be not lost, that I may come to Jesus *now*.' 'While you labor for Persia's daughters, will you not sometimes offer a petition for your unconverted friend on Christian ground?' With such petitions for remembrance before me, when I came near to my Father's seat, surely I was not wanting in subjects of prayer; and I used to try to pray for them day by day, and could but feel that there was mercy very near to some of them. But I was not prepared to hear, without deep emotion, that in less than two months from the time I left you, all but six of Holyoke's pupils were rejoicing in hope. The messenger came in on Saturday the 15th instant; but brought me no letters from America. The letters of others contained no intelligence in regard to you, at the seminary. Much as I wished to hear from you, I contented myself with the thought that letters were probably on the way. I said 'the trial of not hearing from those I love in America may be one to which I shall often be called on missionary ground, and which, perhaps, more than most others, I need grace to bear.' But while thus soliloquizing and reasoning with myself, I did not think it possible that this very packet brought news to make glad my heart. On the Tuesday following (yesterday), we were all invited to John's wedding. Accordingly we all went down to the city. Mr. Merrick's family reside there, and we went into their house until time to go to the house of ceremonies. While sitting there I took up some New York Observers which the last messenger had brought. I had read but a few minutes when my eye rested on a notice of 'a precious revival' in the seminary, in which it was said, 'Of sixty young ladies unconverted, all but six are rejoicing in hope.' Such intelligence, so unexpected at that time, relating to interests so precious, was to me overcoming. I burst into a flood of grateful tears. My tongue refused utterance; and as kind sister-spirits around me inquired, 'Why do you weep?' I could only in silence point to that on which my own eyes had rested. Oh, that this first intelligence from you might be but an earnest of what I shall receive while I dwell in this strange land! I need not tell you that in imagination I have to-day lived over with you the scenes of the last months in your peaceful home. I have seemed to hear the inquiry for the way of life from those I have loved so well. I have heard their song of joy after having tasted redeeming grace, and have seen them humbly sitting at the feet of Jesus. And who are those that still refuse to sit there? Are they my own dear lambs? those of my own precious section? Such a revival has brought my sister-teachers a time of deep interest and deep anxiety. I would have loved to share it with you, if such had seemed our Father's will. Oh, there is a sweet delight in pointing souls to the Lamb of God!

"SEIR, August 9, 1843.

"MY DEAR BROTHER AND SISTER, — . . . . I have written you in regard to my pleasant situation. I feel that my cup overflows with blessings. . . . Seir is a small village, the people mostly Nestorians. I love to go out to their mud huts, as attempting to speak with them helps me to speak. When they see me coming, they run to bring a mat or something of the kind for me to sit on. I take my seat, as sister A. will remember I used to love to sit in childhood. Really, sister, this once considered sad defect of mine comes now well in use. When I enter a house, in scriptural style, and, in accordance with the usage of this people, I say, '*Shlama lahone*' (Peace be to you), their reply is '*Shlama mashana*' (Be it returned to you a hundred-fold). Then follow many expressions like these: 'I am your servant.' 'My children are your servants,' etc. Then they will cluster about me and seem exceedingly pleased with conversation. You would be amused to see me surrounded by fifteen or twenty Nestorian women and children, dressed in the manner described in Mr. Perkins' book, seeking to improve my conversational powers. I do exceedingly long to have the time come when my tongue shall be loosed, and I shall be able to speak freely with them on religious subjects. It will be pleasant to gather a little band of these poor females together, and unite with them in prayer and praise. I hope you may long think of Fidelia as going from house to house, or in the school-room surrounded by these poor degraded little girls. Yes, if it is my Father's will, I hope long to live and labor for Persia's daughters. And will not you rejoice that this privilege is mine? Oh, could you see these poor females, as they are, you would be thankful that you have a sister to spare to them! None of them read, and few of them have any correct ideas of eternity, or the God to whom they are accountable. Their days are spent in those labors, which, in our country, are performed by the other sex alone. To the fields they carry their little ones, as they engage in their work. I have seen the little child of a few months sitting in the field by its mother, while she was harvesting grain. At night they return to their homes, milk their cows, prepare supper for their husbands, and then eat alone. To eat with their husbands is the height of indelicacy in their view. They marry very young; often at the age of eighteen they are the mothers of two or three children. To be the mother of sons is considered a great blessing, but of daughters a great misfortune. Very many of the children die in infancy and childhood, owing, doubtless, to the climate. It is confidently believed by the missionaries that not one fourth part of those born survive the years of childhood."

"SEIR, August 9, 1843.

"MY OWN PRECIOUS MOTHER: — I will not ask if you wish to hear from Fidelia; for I will not for a moment believe that you have forgotten your daughter. If other friends forget, I know my own dear mother will not. It is to me a trying thought, that I have not for more than five months heard one word from you. When I think of it, my feelings would lead me with the wings of a dove to fly to your side. Yes, my dear mother, I would love to look upon you, and more to talk with you, and know the inmost feelings of your soul. I have tried to commend you to a covenant-keeping God, and I trust that he has kept you in perfect peace. Yes, I hope that you have been peaceful and happy in our separation. It is not mine to be by you, my dear mother, to comfort you, but I will try to do it by my pen. And perhaps I may thus do as much as if with you. You will, I trust, be as happy in thinking of me, as if I were at Holyoke. Yes, I trust you will be ever able to rejoice that you said to me, 'Go, my child, go to distant Persia.' Had a dear father lived to see the day, methinks his blessing would have followed me; and may it not be that now he comes to my lonely spirit with messages of love? I love to feel it may be so.

"I often fancy that I hear you inquire with all a mother's tenderness in regard to my happiness. Be assured that I find everything more pleasant than I expected. I have a pleasant home, kind friends surround me, and, what is to me more blessed than all things beside, I feel that a wide door of usefulness is opened to me. May I be permitted to labor many years for those for whom I gave myself! I suffered slightly from a bilious attack a few weeks after my arrival, but I am now as well as ever I was in America. I mention this, because I promised always to communicate every such thing to you, that you might always be perfectly at rest in regard to anything being kept from you. You shall, my mother, know my sorrows as well as joys. My most earnest request of you is, that you will remember me unceasingly in your prayers, that I may labor untiringly in the cause of my Master, until he shall call me home. May you be long spared to pray for your far-off, but happy daughter. Accept, dearest mother, once more the unchanging love of your own

"FIDELIA."

TO MISS A. F.

"SEIR, Aug. 14, 1843.

. . . "If I know my heart, it is my great desire henceforth to live entirely for God. I am surrounded by an interesting field of labor, such an one as for many years I have desired. And never, from the time I first began to love my blessed Saviour, did I relinquish the hope that such a privilege was in store for me, till my severe sickness. And since my Father has thus raised me from weakness and bodily infirmities to health; and has, in his own good time and way, opened the door for me to come to this land of darkness, ought not my heart to overflow with thankfulness, and my every power be devoted to the cause of Christ? Oh, pray for me, that I may be faithful!" . . .

"You are aware that the 'powers that be' in Persia are all Mohammedan. The poor Nestorians groan under a yoke of bondage. The Governor of Oroomiah, Malek Kassim Meerza, is more lenient than most of the Eastern princes. He is a son of the late King of Persia, who, as the son says, had 'a hundred children.' He is particularly fond of Frank customs, so much so that his father used often to call him his 'little Frangese.' He has shown himself friendly to the missionaries, and has learned our language so as to be able to communicate tolerably well in it. Like others in authority, he has many enemies. Through their influence, he was secretly summoned by the king to appear before him at Teheran. A part of his harem he took with him; others are at different places, while three were left in Oroomiah. I think he has, in all, nine wives. Those remaining in the city, he was exceedingly desirous that we should visit during his absence. We had purposed to do so earlier, but did not find it convenient until yesterday. In anticipation of our visit, we left Seir at an early hour, went to the city, and took breakfast with Mr.

Merrick. After breakfast we sent word to the ladies that, if they pleased, we would call on them. As it pleased them that we should call, about ten o'clock we left for the purpose. As their forms of etiquette forbid that any of the gentlemen should accompany us, we took some of the Nestorian boys, for we might not go alone. They remained at the gate while we were within. As we advanced towards the house, we perceived that our boy John, who was taking the lead, was conducting us into a back, narrow, dirty way. We asked why he did so. He replied, because the prince (referring to the governor pro tem., Malek Monsom Meerza) is sitting in the gate, and it is not good that you should stand before princes. These are their ideas of female propriety. Notwithstanding our darksome way, we were safely led to the beautiful court of the prince's house. The attendants of the mansion ushered us into a pleasant room, where we met the three wives of the prince. They bade us welcome with such a multitude of expressions as in our country would lead one to 'withdraw his foot from his neighbor's door.' The prince is about forty years of age, but these ladies are all young; the youngest, I think, not twenty. Their style of dress, to eyes unaccustomed to it, is not a little amusing. Their under-garment they call a shirt. It is made just like a gentleman's under-garment, except being not more than half the length. These garments are always thin; perhaps of printed muslin oftener than anything else. They were trimmed with coarse cotton edging, such as is two or three cents a yard in America; the only article of the kind found in the country. They wear over this a kind of quilted spencer, which does not come together in front, but leaves the under-garment wholly exposed. The spencers are met by skirts, which, in this case, were silk, — two red, the other a bright yellow. They are made in the form of drawers, each part having seven breadths. On the head they wear a pretty little shawl, pinned under the chin. Can you think how they would look by this description?

"The room in which we were entertained was furnished with sofas and chairs, — things not common in this country. In the walls were two rows of recesses, one near the upper, and one near the lower floor. In the upper recesses were, perhaps, a hundred decanters filled with perfumery, etc. They were beautifully arranged, and presented no unpleasant appearance. After sitting and conversing some little time (some of our number can speak Turkish), one of the numerous attendants brought in a water-pipe and passed it to each of us, inviting us to smoke. Of course we had no disposition for '*quaffing*.' It was accordingly passed to the '*hannums*' themselves; and each in her turn showed herself skilful in this branch of business. The cup was held for them to drink by their waiting-maids. And, as time after time it was passed to them during our stay, we could but mourn over such evidences of Eastern indolence. As is their custom, tea was brought in before we left. One of the maids brought the tea-tray, and set it in the midst, and then poured the tea and passed it to each of us. After taking a cup with them we proposed to leave, as we had other calls in view; but they held us by the skirts of our garments. As a device for detaining us, they invited us to go over their house, which invitation we accepted, nothing loath. You would have been exceedingly amused with the appearance of their best room, the walls of which are covered with some twenty kinds of calico. Not so bad a spectacle, however, after all; for, with its numerous recesses, and the taste displayed in covering them, there was a little air of pleasantness. When they finally allowed us to leave them, they used our English "good-by" with much apparent pleasure. Nazaloo *hannum*, the favorite wife of the prince, as if to show her more perfect appreciation of English customs, bestowed a kiss on either cheek of one of our number. As we see their prejudices giving way, we hope and pray that the door may soon be opened for doing them much good spiritually. Leaving the ladies of the prince, we next called on the wife and daughters of a Kahn. Here we were also detained for a long time. We walked in their garden; gathered grapes from the vine, and received roses from the hands of the attentive daughters. They insisted that we should stay and take fruit, according to their custom; we could not well refuse. There were apples, grapes, muskmelons, and watermelons. We partook, seated on the floor, for they had no chairs in their house. Our long stay made us late to our mountain home; but we reached it in safety, and I trust with increased desires for usefulness. To-day has found me again poring with delight over my Syriac."

TO A TEACHER IN MT. HOLYOKE SEMINARY.

"SEIR, Aug. 15.

"My thoughts dwell on it" (her school) "by night and by day. I inquire, as far as I can, after what has been and what may be done; and I hope I seek heavenly guidance in my plans. But I may be mistaken, and my Father may see fit to disappoint me. Yet I can but hope there is something here for me to do; that I may help to raise these poor females to the place which their Maker designed should be theirs. Already I find that I am becoming attached to these poor children much more strongly than when in America. I often feel like fondly embracing them and loving them as I would children at home. I strive to prevent their extreme filth and degradation from severing them from me. They are bound to the same eternity with myself. At the judgment-bar I shall meet them. I would encircle them in the arms of love, and pray God that he will encircle them in the arms of everlasting love."

TO HER MOTHER.

"SEIR, Aug. 16.

"It is an unspeakable comfort to know that you are happy in my being away from you. Perhaps you can say with another mother, 'My child, if I could, I would not raise a finger to call you home.' O my dear mother, you will be rewarded, I know you will, for every sacrifice you have made for the blessed Saviour! He will not forget it. And should he, in the last great day, lead to you one Nestorian girl, or one Nestorian mother, 'clothed in white,' as the result of your sacrifice, will you not be grateful that it was yours to give one cup of cold water in the name of a disciple?"

TO MISS A. F.

"*Aug.* 22. — To-day dined with Mr. Perkins, that we might employ the hour in conversing about the girls' school, which we hope to open in a few weeks. I proposed to him that we have some hymns translated into Syriac for the 'benăte' (daughters) of this people to sing. The proposition met his approval; and in a few hours a hymn was translated. Mrs. Stoddard sung it most beautifully. The natives who heard it were exceedingly delighted. We hope Mrs. S. will teach singing in the school."

"25. — Another day is gone, and I am alone in my room. Was busily occupied this morning in preparing some work for a native woman, in reference to the girls' school. It was making some beds. Would you like to know the materials? They were a coarse ticking of native cloth, filled with wool, which is here an article of trifling expense. Would you not like to help me make beds, etc., for the Syrian girls? I am sure, were you here, your heart would enter with sweet delight into the duties which are ours to perform. Did life ever look desirable, it has been since my arrival here. Ere I am aware, I find my petitions going up to Heaven that my life may be long spared. But I would not be anxious. I am but a worm of the dust. My Father can carry on a work of grace in benighted Persia just as well without me as with me. But I do feel that it is a blessed privilege to do something for my adorable Redeemer. And it is not long that we can labor for him on earth; soon we shall go to our eternal home. Oh, let us try to be faithful, whether in America or Persia!"

"SEIR, Sept. 12, 1843.

"MY OWN DEAR MISS W.: — Our monthly messenger is just in, but brought me no note or tidings from you. I had fondly hoped to hear from you, and, when I was told that there was nothing for me, I could not refrain from tears. They were almost my first tears beneath a Persian sky. But I soon wiped them away, and said I will not weep for this; it better becometh me to weep for a world lying in wickedness. . . . I often regret that I did no more, while it was in my power, for the cause of Christ at home. The seminary was a precious field of labor. I sometimes think that, were I again there, I would strive to do more for the good of those about me. But I know I could not trust my deceitful heart. It is God alone who gives the heart and strength to labor for him. Had I been more faithful in labor for souls at home, I feel that I should have been better fitted for my present work. The same spirit that leads us to daily effort for the salvation of souls in America is greatly needed on missionary ground." . . .

Miss Fiske left Seir with Mr. Stocking's family September 14th, and took up her abode in the city of Oroomiah. It was not deemed best immediately to open the school, of which she was expected to have the charge. Her imperfect knowledge of the language was still a serious obstacle to direct missionary efforts in behalf of the people. But she was impatient to be at work, and in various ways began to make herself useful to those whose sad condition excited her liveliest sympathies. A few extracts from her correspondence will give us a glimpse of her life during those weeks of waiting: —

"OROOMIAH, Sept. 14.

"Spent this morning in arranging my room. I have a pleasant little place in one end of Mr. S.'s house. There are two small windows, one on the east and the other on the west side. A door on the north side opens into one of Mrs. S.'s rooms, and one on the south opens towards the girls' school-room, and also to the yard; so I can go-out and receive company without disturbing any one."

"17, *Sabbath.* — Spent much of the day in reading with and instructing Isabella, a girl in Mr. S.'s family. Mrs. S. has given her wholly to my care. She is somewhat wayward; and I feel that I need much wisdom from above to guide her aright. In our female prayer-meetings we have taken her as a subject of prayer."

"18. — A little girl, from the girls' school, that I had asked to come and read with me, came and spent an hour or two. She said the other little girls, when they saw her come, cried because they could not come. I told her to say to them, if they would make themselves clean, they also might come."

"20. — Yesterday nine little girls came and read and spelt with me. The funds of the mission are not such that they deem it expedient for our schools to commence at present. In the mean time I shall do what I can for those about me, who can come to my room. This is the beginning of my school in Oroomiah. I feel exceedingly happy in the prospect of being able to do something for the daughters of this land."

"*Oct.* 2.—Yesterday I went out again to a Nestorian service in the church-yard; attendance about as last Sabbath. After the service, several of the girls came to my room, and, with Isabella's help, I read to them some portions of 'Nathan Dickerman' in Syriac. Perhaps you will wonder that I should attempt anything of the kind, when my knowledge of the language is so imperfect. I hesitated in regard to doing it; but, my dear L——, I saw them going down to the dark world of woe, with little instruction fitted to point them to the Lamb of God. My spirit was stirred within me, and I said, cannot I do something? With the help of one who can speak English, I hope to give them some ideas of God, of their souls, and of the world to which they haste. Oh, pray for me, — will you not?—that the Holy Spirit may bless my efforts."

"17.—The schools all began yesterday. Until then I had kept my little class. I can say nothing in regard to the prospects of the schools the present session; but I shall be able to speak of them at the end of the month, when I will write some of you again.

"When I look at the opportunities for usefulness before me, I often feel that one of a holier heart, and of more entire consecration to the Lord, should be here in my place. Oh, that my heart might be full of the Saviour's love!

"The present is a trying time with us. The emissaries of Rome have again made their appearance here, and are seeking to draw after them this weak people. A few have actually gone with them, bribed by gold, which they love more than their souls. We feel that we are called to renewed watchfulness and faithfulness. May the trial through which we are passing do us much good, making us so humble and faithful that it will be consistent for our God to bless our labors."

During these first months of her missionary life, Miss Fiske not only felt most keenly her separation from the home friends, whom she ardently loved, but found her heart constantly going out in tenderest sympathy to that widowed mother, who, in giving her up, had been called to so great a sacrifice. Referring, in after years, to the deep solicitude she then felt for her mother, she says, "I think I can see now that those remembrances of and anxieties for my mother were peculiarly chastening. My heart would not thus have clung to my work had it not been riveted to it by a mother's sacrifice. Those dear Nestorian girls were all the more precious in my eyes, because they had taken me from my mother."

CHAPTER VIII.

OCTOBER, 1843, TO JUNE, 1844.

THE FEMALE SEMINARY. — Condition of Nestorian Women. — Houses and Beds. — Lying, Profanity, Ignorance. — Mrs. Grant's School. — A Boarding-school Desired; Appropriation for one. — School Opened. — First Pupils. — School-room. — Duties of Teacher. — Six black Pins. — First Convert among the Women. — Walks with Pupils. — Sabbath School. — Meeting for Women. — First Bible Lessons. — Visits to Villages. — Sympathy for the Sick.

So closely was the missionary life of Miss Fiske identified with the female seminary at Oroomiah, that it becomes necessary, at this point, to glance at the origin, character, and early history of that institution. But, in order to appreciate the work accomplished by it, the deplorable condition of the Nestorian women, at the time the mission was established, must be considered.

It is a sadly significant fact, that the language of the Nestorians contained no words corresponding to home and wife, the nearest approach to them being house and woman.

"The Nestorian house," writes Miss Fiske, "was formerly a single large room, and there the work of the family was mostly performed. There they ate, and there they slept. Several generations occupied the same, each son as he married bringing his wife to his father's house. Their beds are much like a good comfortable filled with wool, or more frequently with cotton; a heavy quilt and a pillow completed a set of bedding. They took up their beds in the morning, piling them upon a wooden frame, spreading them again at night. It was customary at night to lay aside all the clothing of the day, and to take nothing in its place. The house was lighted by an opening in the roof, and the smoke went out at the same place. It had only a floor of earth, covered in part with mats and pieces of carpeting. There was hardly a possibility of cleanliness. Vermin abounded in most of the houses. The inmates were covered, not only with fleas, but often with lice, which were found not only on the head, but on the entire body."

The women were regarded by the men as drudges and slaves, and were compelled to spend most of the time in out-door labor, among the vineyards and wheat-fields, often going forth to their work carrying not only their heavy implements, but also their infants in the cradle. When, at evening, they returned from the field, however weary, they must milk the cows, prepare their husbands' supper, and wait till they had finished their meal, before partaking themselves.

For husbands to beat their wives often and severely was a well-nigh universal practice; and, of course, wives rendered to their husbands anything but affection and reverence, and were little disposed to meet even their reasonable requirements. "They would come to me," says Miss Fiske, "and tell me their grievances, and would fall down at my feet, begging me to deliver them from their husbands. They would say, with many tears, 'Have mercy on us; if you do not help us, we must kill oursėlves.' I had no fear of their doing that, and would seat them by my side, and tell them of my own dear father; how good he was; but that he was always *obeyed*. They said, 'We could obey a *good* man.' I replied, 'I am very sure you would not have been willing to obey my father.'"

There was, of course, an absence of all those delicate and thoughtful attentions which are so much needed in seasons of sickness and suffering.

"Mr. Perkins," continues Miss Fiske, "tells us of a visit to a family in Kowry, where the principal room was given up to the guests, and in the morning he found that a little son had been added to the family, — born in the stable. He supposed that he and his family had taken the place designed for the mother. But it was not so. Nearly all the Nestorian children begin their life in a stable. The mother almost invariably resorts to that place to meet her hour of sorrow; and there she often meets death."

Lying was almost universal among both men and women. "We all lie," was their frequent, self-justifying plea when reproved for the practice.

Women and children, as well as men, were shockingly profane. Speaking of her early pupils, Miss Fiske says: "My little girls would swear and use the vilest language. It needed but a slight provocation to lead them to call each other 'buffaloes,' or 'donkeys;' and it was no uncommon thing for one of them to call out to a companion, 'You are a Satan.' 'Why, do you think the people will believe me,' said one, when reproved for her profanity, 'if I do not use the name of God very often?'"

The women, in their deep degradation, were naturally coarse, passionate, and quarrelsome. "When you see a whole village of women engaged in a quarrel, their hair all loose and flying in the wind, while they are throwing stones, brickbats, and spoiled eggs at each other, with almost unearthly shrieks, you say, and justly, other women than these were 'last at the cross, and first at the sepulchre.' But *those* may once have been like *these*."

When the missionaries went to Persia, there was but a single Nestorian female who could read. She was Helena, the sister of the Patriarch, whose superior rank secured her this accomplishment. The others were not only ignorant, but entirely content to remain so. When asked if they would not like to learn to read, they would reply, with a significant shrug, "I am a woman," — "I am a girl," — "Do you want to make a priest of me?" The prejudices of the mothers against the education of their daughters were stronger than those of the fathers.

It was among such "fallen sisters" that Miss Fiske went to labor as a missionary teacher. To their elevation, mainly through the instrumentality of a Christian school, she cheerfully consecrated her life. Speaking of their condition, she says: "I felt deeply for my poor sisters before going to them; but there was a deeper feeling, even anguish, when I realized, from mingling with them, how very low they were. I really knew at first very little of the *pit* into which I was descending. I did not wish to leave them, but I did often ask, 'Can the Saviour's image ever be reflected from such hearts?'"

In 1836, the first three missionary schools were

opened for Nestorian children in the villages Ada, Geog Tapa, and Ardishai. The number both of schools and scholars rapidly increased. But very few of the girls could be induced to attend; and it soon became evident that they could be reached only by the establishment of a school exclusively for them. In the way of such a measure were formidable obstacles. These, however, were at length, so far overcome, through the indefatigable zeal of that rare missionary, Mrs. Grant, that, on the 12th of March, 1838, a school was opened by her with four little girls. The number was soon doubled, and then quadrupled. This was, in some sense, the nucleus of the female seminary, which has done so much for the social, intellectual, and spiritual improvement of woman in Persia.

After the death of Mrs. Grant, in January, 1839, the school was continued by the help of native teachers, under the care, first, of Mr. Holladay, and then of Dr. Wright; the ladies of the mission rendering such assistance as they could. "Although," says Dr. Perkins, "the girls learned well, considering their opportunities, they still did not make very rapid progress for five years." During those five years it was simply a day school, the pupils boarding at home, and spending only a few hours daily with their teachers in the school-room. The disadvantages of this arrangement were obvious and manifold. Comparatively little could be done, especially for the moral improvement of the girls who were still, more than half the time, breathing the tainted atmosphere in which they had been nurtured. Miss Fiske, from the first, was exceedingly desirous of changing the character of the school, making it a boarding, or family school, in which the pupils might remain several years, and be under the continuous and exclusive care and training of the teachers. The very idea of such a school was so repugnant to all the hereditary views of social propriety among the Nestorians, as to seem almost chimerical. And when it was proposed to make an effort to secure six pupils, with whom to start a school upon this basis, even those of the mission most interested in the project doubted its success. Says Miss Fiske, writing ten years afterwards, "While every member of the mission approved of an attempt to do something for females in this way, several were so frank as to say that they did not believe that six girls could be obtained for a single year, and that not one would remain with us for two or three years. They were almost certain of this, because they were familiar with the true state of society here. At that time scarcely a girl could be found more than twelve years of age who was not betrothed; and several years previous to that age were usually spent in making a rude kind of embroidery, a certain amount of which must be ready for the wedding-day. While the male seminary numbered its hundreds, priests, deacons, fathers and sons, not one could be found among them willing to give up his little girl to be taught by us for a few years. They feared that, by so doing, their daughters would lose some favorable opportunity for marriage; and, more than all, as girls could be neither priests nor deacons, they could see no reason why they should spend many months in study. These parents were also apprehensive that if their daughters remained long with us they would not be able to carry so heavy burdens in the fields, nor to wield the spade so successfully as their companions who had never learned to read. Even Priest Abraham, who was then, perhaps, our most intelligent helper, and who has for years done more for female improvement than almost any other native, said to us, with strong feeling, "I cannot bear the reproach of having my daughter with you as a boarder."

But, notwithstanding these misgivings on the part of some members of the mission, to the great joy of Miss Fiske, the measure was approved, and an appropriation was made for the support of six boarding pupils, if they could be obtained.

To secure these six girls was now an object of deep solicitude with her. She writes: "The first Syriac word I learned was 'daughter,' and as I can now use the verb 'to give,' I often ask parents *to give* me their *daughters*. Some think that I cannot secure boarding scholars, but Mrs. Grant secured day scholars; and when I hear men, women, and children say, 'How she loved us!' I want to love them too. I mean to devote at least five years to the work of trying to gather girls into a boarding school, as Mrs. Grant desired to do. She has gone to her rest. I wonder that I am allowed to take her place." She was cordially seconded in her efforts by others, especially by Mar. Yohanan, who said to her, "You get ready, and I find girls." But when the day fixed for opening the school (Oct. 16th) came, it was not known that a single boarding pupil had been secured. About fifteen day scholars appeared, and Miss Fiske was beginning to fear that she would be disappointed in regard to the plan on which she had set her heart, when from her window she saw Mar. Yohanan in the court approaching, leading two little girls; one, his own niece, Selby, of Gavalan, seven years old, and the other, Khanee, of Geog Tapa, ten years old. Miss Fiske hastened to meet them at the door, and, describing the scene, she says: "I wept tears of joy over those first two brought to me. Their little hands were placed in mine as the bishop said to me, 'They are your daughters; no man shall take them from your hand.' I shall be glad to give them to the Lord Jesus; and love to think of them as the beginning of my dear school. Mar. Yohanan said, 'Now you begin Mount Holy Oke in Persia.'"

A beginning was thus made, and, though humble, was deemed the pledge of success. Could the number be increased? "Many of our future attempts to secure pupils," says Miss Fiske, "proved fruitless. Several who came to us, after remaining a few days, either ran away or were carried away by their friends. There were many poor, destitute girls, wanting only bread, who applied for admission, but were refused, as not being desirable pupils.

"Notwithstanding all the difficulties we had to encounter, before spring we had secured the desired number of boarders. Yet so strong were the feelings of the friends in regard to them, that they would allow them to remain with us only on condition that they should lodge in the room with or near their teacher, and never go out except in her company. These requests were complied with, and those six little girls were as much the companions of their teacher as ever the child is of the mother."

Of her school-rooms, Miss Fiske thus writes: "We have two rooms for the school and the boarders. The one occupied by the school is rather small, but answers very well for the accommodation of its thirty and three occupants. Its mud floor is covered with straw mats, which render it comfortable. There is one window, of oiled paper, which admits far more light than I supposed a paper window could. A stove, built of brick, and a few rude benches, are the only furniture in the room; but, enlivened as it is by bright and smiling faces, it becomes to me a pleasant place indeed. The other room is much larger than this, and is separated from it by a small entry. This is the kitchen, dormitory, and parlor of my little ones. There are two windows, of native glass, which admit the light, but give no view of the yard. The floor is covered like the other room, with the addition of a thick woollen mat upon which to spread the girls' bed."

Instruction was by no means the only nor chief duty imposed upon the teacher. Attention must first be given to the personal cleanliness of her pupils. "It is no pleasant work," she says, "to do for these children when they first come to us. You can have little idea of the filth and degradation from which we take them. We must first try to make them outwardly clean; and we are glad to do this, asking Jesus to give them a new heart."

To correct the prevalent habit of lying and stealing among her pupils was no easy task. Nothing was safe except under lock and key. "Miss Fiske could not keep a pin in her pin-cushion; little fingers took them as often as she turned away, and lest she should tempt them to lie she avoided questioning them, unless her own eye had seen the theft. No wonder she wrote, 'I feel very weak, and were it not that Christ has loved these souls, I should be discouraged; but he has loved them, and he loves them still.' If the pins were found with the pupils, the answer was ready, 'We found them,' or, 'You gave them to us,' and nothing could be proved. But one summer evening, just before the pupils were to pass through her room to their beds on the flat roof, knowing that none of that color could be obtained elsewhere, the teacher put six black pins in her cushion, and stepped out till they had passed. As soon as they were gone she found that the pins, too, were gone, and at once called the girls back. She told them of her loss; but none knew anything about it. She showed them that no one else had been there, and therefore they must know. Six pairs of little hands were lifted up as they said, 'God knows that we have not got them;' but this only called forth the reply, 'I think that God knows you have got them;' and she searched each one carefully, without finding them. She then proposed to kneel down where they stood, and ask God to show where they were, adding, 'He may not see it best to show me now, but he will do it some time.' She laid the matter before the Lord, and, just as they rose from their knees, remembered that she had not examined their cloth caps. She now proposed to examine them, and one pair of hands went right up to her cap. Of course she was searched first, and there were the six pins, so nicely concealed in its folds that nothing was visible but their heads. This incident did much good. The pupils looked on the discovery as an answer to prayer, and so did their teacher. They began to be afraid to steal, when God so exposed their thefts, and she was thankful for an answer so immediate. The offender is now a pious and useful woman.* "

Miss Fiske was obliged to provide their food and beds. "I am, to all intents and purposes, a house-keeper as well as teacher. I purchase all their food; keep the bill of their expenses; attend to their washing, and, in short, all that pertains to their living. They spread their beds on the floor, as is the custom of their people, and we have not thought it best that they should change in this respect, for our object is not to have them conform to our customs entirely, but to give to them those habits of neatness and industry which will fit them for usefulness among their own people. They eat with their hands, as knives and forks cannot be obtained in this country, and we have no reason to suppose they will ever have them after leaving us.

"Their clothing also must be provided, for they are all ragged as well as filthy. Our children come to us with only what they have on. Our first business is to make them clothes, that they may be comfortable. These we make wholly in the native style. The care of this made me very busy the first few days of school. They must be cared for not less when out of school than when in. When I go out and when I come in I take these children with me, for I dare not leave them to themselves. Oh, they are a precious charge! I do desire to be faithful to them as well as to my whole school. I am assisted by a native teacher,

* "Woman and her Saviour in Persia," pp. 22, 23.

who is perhaps as faithful to his trust as any Nestorian." This native teacher heard the children read; and to acquire greater facility in the use of the language, Miss Fiske used to take her place in the classes and read in turn with them. A portion of her time was devoted to the preparation of scriptural questions in Syriac. The Bible, not only from choice, but from necessity, was made the principal-text book in the school. Notwithstanding all that was peculiarly trying in the charge of such pupils, she felt an affectionate interest in them, which deepened daily. "I find my heart going forth to them," she writes, "the same as towards children at home. Yes, I can and do love them as well as ever I loved children; and if I can lead them in the way to heaven I shall feel that my joy is full."

In addition to her school duties and the care of her little family, she found time to go out almost daily, and call upon the Nestorian women in the city, and try to cause some ray of heavenly light to penetrate their darkened minds. She was thus very busy, and very happy in her work, except as her heart was burdened with anxiety for the salvation of those by whom she was surrounded. She felt most deeply the need of the special influences of the Holy Spirit to give success to her own labors and those of her associates; and her mind was ever watchful for the first indications of his presence. She writes, "I think I have seen an increasing spirit of supplication among the members of the mission since our arrival; and knowing that fervent prayer is all powerful with God, I can but hope that spiritual blessings will descend in rich abundance; and I seem to feel that even now the Spirit's gentle influences are in the midst of us. But, oh, the work of laboring for souls is emphatically a work of faith and prayer! I used to think that I felt this in America; but I was never so overwhelmed with the feeling as since I have been here. A door of usefulness is opened to me here; but I often feel that I can only pray."

A few days later, Dec. 7, she thus wrote: "On Sabbath afternoon, as the children were in my room, Moressa said, 'May we not have a little prayer-meeting?' I said to her, 'Yes, all of you who wish to pray, can.' We knelt, and Isabella, Yonan, and Moressa, all led in prayer. While we were gone to the monthly concert, Monday evening, we found that the children observed a season of prayer together. They seem to be feeling more tenderly than at any time since I have been here. I feel that the gentle Spirit is coming very near us, showing his willingness to bless. Oh, for more of the spirit of prayer and of devotion to the Lord's work! I have often thought, of late, that, if God should come to bless us, we should hardly believe our own eyes when we should see him passing before us."

The close of the year was at hand. Miss Fiske became extremely anxious that the new year — her first new year on missionary ground — might open with some tokens of the Spirit's special presence. She recalled, with lively interest, those "most precious seasons" of prayer, which she had enjoyed at her "dear Holyoke," on the first Monday of the year. She remembered how, on the last of those seasons, Miss Lyon had said, "Perhaps next new-year's day will find some of you on a foreign shore. If so, we pledge you a remembrance within these consecrated walls." It was sweet to think that she with her charge, and the mission, would be particularly remembered in prayer by many dear friends in her native land. She felt it reasonable to expect blessings in answer to their prayers; and thus writes, Dec. 30th, to an associate at Seir: —

"There are seasons when it becomes us to watch most diligently for the tokens of a Saviour's presence. And is not the first Monday of the year, and the days following it, a time when we should expect a blessing? Will not our God hear the prayers that shall ascend from a multitude of Christian souls in our beloved land? If he does not, must we not feel that we are hindering the mercy-drops all ready to fall? Oh, what a solemn thought! — *hindering* those very souls from going to heaven, for whom we profess to have left the precious privileges of our loved native land! O my sister, may we be enabled to lay aside everything wrong, and seek unto God with *all* our heart, that to-morrow and Monday may be to us a season of great good!"

Not all the "mercy-drops" were hindered from falling, as the following extracts will show: —

"*January* 31. — Went out, just at night, so see a woman whose attention at meeting had attracted my notice for two Sabbaths. Found her in a somewhat interesting state of mind. It was most affecting to me to find an inquiring sister. Such an one has never been found here before."

"*February* 2. — Saw the inquiring woman, of whom I spoke under the last date. She spoke of her sinfulness in strong terms. Another woman standing by became exceedingly angry, and beat upon her breast, saying, 'Why do you thus speak? Do you think I am a heathen, going to hell, with the Mussulmen? I am a Christian.' I said to her, 'Do you not believe the words of Jesus Christ?' 'Certainly,' she replied. I then repeated to her some texts of Scripture, showing her that not all bearing the Christian name are Christians indeed. She seemed quieted, and listened with attention. What a treasure are the words of our God! I often deplored my ignorance of them in America, but much more here. When I proposed to go to another house, these women, with others, accompanied me, for they said, 'We wish to hear more.' On entering the house we found an infant crying; said one of the women to the mother, 'Get it quiet, and we will hear the words of God.' They listened attentively to all I could say; but, oh, 'these bonds,' arising from an imperfect knowledge of the language; and still greater bonds of remaining sin in the heart, and want of entire consecration to God! O my sister, may you be freed from them! May your heart be greatly enlarged in prayer for dying souls! Will you unite with me at half-past seven this evening in prayer for that inquiring sister in this village? Do you not think God will hear our prayers? Let us cast ourselves and our petitions into the arms of our heavenly Father, as in early childhood we used to recline upon our earthly father's arm."

"15. — Our congregation of women was full today and very attentive. Mr. Stocking preached to them. Many were affected to tears, and after the services closed, lingered to speak of their souls.

It is deeply interesting to see those poor oppressed people asking for the bread and water of life.

"Our poor sister, for whom you have united with me in prayer, seems to be sitting at the feet of the blessed Immanuel. And is it true that one of our Nestorian sisters is a true Christian? When I was first led to believe it, I almost felt like old Simeon: 'Now lettest thou thy servant depart in peace.' But I would not ask to go home. No, I would rejoice to spend many years in this dark land, if here I may but serve my God. The first intimation I had of a change in this woman's feelings was yesterday afternoon, as we were coming out from the Syriac service. The few women present, as usual, gathered about me to speak a few words. As we walked along she drew a little nearer, and whispered in my ear, 'I have hope in Jesus Christ.' I said to her, 'But you told me two days ago that there was no hope for you in Jesus Christ.' She replied, 'I told you so, but now I have hope and peace in Jesus Christ; it came to me yesterday.' As she spoke, a peaceful smile lighted up her countenance, like that you have seen in those beginning to love the Saviour. That load of guilt, which for days had seemed to be bowing her to the dust, she now hoped had been borne by the Lamb of God."

This first instance of conversion among the Nestorian women filled the missionary's heart with liveliest joy and gratitude. A few days later, speaking of this woman, she says: "She continues to appear well. It would do you good to see her. I have passed some of the most interesting hours of my life with her. Oh for the privilege of leading one such soul in the way to heaven, who would not leave father, mother, brother, sister, and all that this world calls dear?"

It was an interesting circumstance that the Holy Spirit apparently began his work in the heart of this woman, through the efforts of an unconverted daughter, who was a member of the school. Miss Fiske writes: —

"She was led to serious consideration, and taught to pray by her little daughter, who is in school, but who, I suppose, has not a particle of grace in her heart. The fact has greatly encouraged me in my labors for my little girls, hoping that they will themselves sit down at the foot of the cross, and lead their mothers to the same blessed spot."

The hopes which the missionaries cherished of witnessing an extensive revival of religion among the Nestorians, were not, at this time, realized. While the Spirit wrought upon many minds, awakening them to unusual seriousness, and attentiveness to the truth, the number of conversions was limited.

In May one more was added to the number of her boarding scholars. She thus mentions the fact: "I added another little girl to my family, day before yesterday. You certainly never saw such a pitiable object as she was when she came to me. I should hardly suppose she had been washed for five years; and she is all covered with sores. Oh, may I do her good!"

Among her early efforts for the religious instruction of the young, was the establishment of a Sabbath school. At first, a few girls came to her room, with whom she spent an hour each Sabbath. In a short time the number increased to fifty; and thus the first seeds of divine truth were sown in many youthful minds, which were destined to spring up and bear precious fruit.

Nor were Miss Fiske's labors confined to the young. As we have already seen, she became deeply interested in the mothers as well as in the daughters, and was unwearied in her endeavors to do them good. She first sought to secure their attendance at some public service on the Sabbath. But the feeling was strong and universal that it was improper for women to join in a public assembly with men, — especially with priests and deacons, — or to listen to preaching. They could not be persuaded, therefore, to attend the ordinary services conducted by the missionaries on the Sabbath.

But Miss Fiske found that a few were willing to come to her room at the same hour with the public service. She prayed with these, and read to them the Scriptures, with such explanations as her imperfect knowledge of the language permitted. As the number increased, she persuaded them to allow one of the missionary brethren to come in and conduct the meeting. In this way their prejudices were overcome, and they were in time prepared to unite in the regular service, and separate meetings for them were discontinued.

Her first efforts to interest the women in the Bible were sometimes amusing. "She would seat herself among them on the earthen floor, and read a verse, then ask questions, to see if they understood it. For example: after reading the history of the creation (for she began at the beginning), she asked, 'Who was the first man?' Answer: 'What do we know? we are women.' This was about equivalent in English to 'We are donkeys.' Then she told them Adam was the first man, and made them repeat the name 'Adam' over and over till they remembered it. The next question was, 'What does it mean?' Here, too, they could give no answer; not because they did not know, for the word was in common use among them; but they had no idea that they could answer, and so they did not, but were perfectly delighted to find that the first man was called *red earth*, because he was made of it. This was enough for one lesson. It set them to thinking; it woke up faculties previously dormant. . . . Another lesson would take up Eve (Syriac *Hawa*, meaning *Life*). Miss Fiske would begin by saying, 'Is not that a pretty name? Would you not like to know that you had a great-great-grandmother called *Life*? Now, that was the name of our first mother, — both yours and mine.' It was interesting to notice how faces, previously stolid, would light up with animation after that, if the preacher happened to repeat the names of our first parents, and how one would touch another, whispering, with childish joy, 'Didn't you hear? He said Adam.'" *

Miss Fiske was not content with reaching the few women who thus came at her invitation to attend religious meetings, and receive religious instruction at the seminary. She visited them at their homes, going from house to house, where filth and vermin

* "Woman and Her Saviour in Persia," pp. 83, 84.

would have repelled any woman of refinement, whose heart did not glow with love to Christ, and love to perishing souls for whom he died.

She frequently extended her visits to the neighboring villages. Under date of April 8th, she writes: "I have, this afternoon, been to walk with my children; of course, with a guard, for without one I never go out. We went to Dizza, a village just outside the city wall, but about a mile from our premises. Word had gone before that I was coming, and seemingly the whole village came out to meet me. Entering a house, and seating myself on a mat, they gathered about me until the house was so completely filled that they literally trod one upon another. After speaking with them a few minutes, one of the older women said, 'Now, we are all here together, will you preach to us a little?' By preaching, they mean religious conversation. I talked to them some time, while they gave breathless attention. When I left them, they wished to know if I would not come every Sabbath and speak to them. Could I go about here as safely as I used to do at home, I am sure I should do it. Oh, that I may be better fitted for my work!"

May 7th, she writes: "Went to Howsee and Nazee to-day. The first is about ten and the other about eleven miles from the city. Our company consisted of Mr. Stocking, Priest Yohannan, — a man in Mr. S.'s employ, and little Jerusha. We took Jerusha to relieve her mother, who has not yet fully recovered her strength. At both these villages are schools. We first went to Nazee, and visited the school. I then went into a house, and a large number of women came to see me. I found that I could succeed much better in speaking with them than ever before with strangers. It encouraged me very much in my hopes of being able soon to communicate freely with all. After I had talked with them a while, Mr. S. came in, and they all immediately arose, ready to run away. It was with difficulty we could persuade them to stop. You have no idea what a hindrance to their improvement are the false notions of these people in regard to intercourse with the other sex. From Nazee we came to Howzee. Priest Yohannan had provided dinner for us; and a good dinner it was, too, consisting of little fishes (which are plenty in the river near Howzee), eggs, rice, new cheese, bread, etc., etc. I wish you could see us seated at a native table. I have learned to eat with my fingers very well. After dinner, Mr. S. went to the school; but I thought it best to remain behind, and thus have an opportunity to see the women. They filled the room in which I was sitting, and I had a pleasant interview with them; but as soon as Mr. S. returned they all fled. It being now late, we set our faces homeward. In America, I should have thought a ride of ten miles on horseback a formidable thing; but here it is only pleasure. My little pony carried me safely over the ground; and, although dark clouds gathered around, we outrode the rain, and safely reached home before night. I am now a little tired, but hope for more such excursions soon."

The sick of either sex among the Nestorians soon learned that in Miss Fiske they had a most kind and sympathizing friend. "A report of sickness," says Dr. Perkins, "was always a sufficient summons to carry her to the sufferer's bedside." In her letters at this period occur passages like the following: —

"*April* 12. — I have to-day been to see a brother of Mar. Shimon, who is sick, and perhaps near his end. Poor man! we have no reason to suppose that he is prepared for death. I have been trying to prepare some little things for his comfort this evening. Your heart would ache, my dear mother, to see this poor people in sickness."

"19. — Have been out this afternoon to visit the sick near us. I found the brother of the Patriarch no better. Was glad to find that he thought himself unprepared for death. Oh, may his proud heart bow to Jesus! To go among the sick here, is, I feel, one of our duties."

In the mission families her services as nurse were invaluable, and were often put in requisition. The care of infants by day and night was no slight addition to her other numerous duties, but was cheerfully assumed; and no one but herself saw any reason for saying, "You will pity both mother and child with such nursing." "I should not have thought at home," she adds, "that I was fit for such a thing. But the little one has seemed to do very well, and I am beginning to feel that I must not think there is anything I cannot do. Every kind of knowledge turns to account on missionary ground."

About the middle of June her school was dismissed for the summer, except her boarding pupils, now numbering twelve, whom it was thought best to take with her to the health retreat at Seir.

An extract from a letter to one of the teachers at

Mt. Holyoke Seminary will close our review of this period: —

"After having been so little while on missionary ground, I feel that I am unfit to speak in regard to missionary qualifications with confidence. But to you, dear sister (not to the world), I may speak with all freedom. I feel more and more that the missionary must have fully counted the cost of his work to be useful. If he has failed to do this, as far as he was able to, in his own land, disappointment in the people to whom he is sent, their extreme filthiness, wretchedness, and ignorance, and still more their wickedness of heart, will induce a despondency which it will be exceedingly difficult to rise above. It is not usually the trials of a temporal nature that so much affect the missionary; it is want of spiritual success. It is the same unwavering confidence in God; the same cheerful, active, persevering piety, which is so valuable at home, that is needed on missionary ground. Are you surrounded by youthful hearts longing to point heathen souls to the Lamb of God? O my sister, enforce upon them the importance of being wholly devoted to the work of God at home! If they are faithful at Holyoke, laboring faithfully for their own and others' souls, they doubtless would be faithful in Persia, China, or India. The same love which prompts to faithfulness there, would be carried to a foreign land. Oh, could I whisper one word in the ears of those dear young sisters I left behind, it would be this: 'Be faithful in all things in your present situation, and, if your Father has a work for you on missionary ground, he will thus fit you for it.'"

CHAPTER IX.

JUNE, 1844, TO JUNE, 1845.

Visit to Ardishai. — Miss Fiske "Preaches." — Pupils taken to Seir in Vacation. — Persecution. — Schools Disbanded by the Patriarch. — Payment of Money to Day Scholars Discontinued. — Mothers of the Pupils Convened. — Miss Fiske's Narrow Escape. — Entertainment for Friends at Close of School.

At the close of her school, Mr. Stocking invited Miss Fiske to join him and his family in a visit to Ardishai, a village some twelve miles from Oroomiah. Her account of the visit, written years afterwards, will disclose the nature of her work among the women, and her tact in prosecuting it: "On reaching Ardishai Saturday morning we were surrounded by people, few of whom ever before had seen foreign ladies. Our tent was soon spread on the roof of a house. We went up to it by a ladder, and there made ourselves comfortable. It was my first day in a large village, and I became so tired *with*, not *of*, the crowds, that I cannot now think of that June Saturday with other than a most tired feeling. We were very near the lake, and all night long had swarms of mosquitoes in our tent. There was no sleep for some of us, and the morning brought the crowds again, not as inquirers, but merely to see some new and strange thing. About nine o'clock we went to church, where Mr. Stocking preached. There were a goodly number of men present, and a few women.

The latter sat most lovingly near me, and during the sermon were occupied in making comments on my dress, etc. Mr. Stocking was always able to preach, even when the women did talk, by raising his voice above theirs. At the close of the morning service, Priest Abraham, who was with us, rose and said, 'There will be two meetings this afternoon, one in the other church for the men, and one here for the women. I want to have all the women attend, for Miss Fiske, who has come from the New World, will preach.' I was taken greatly by surprise at the announcement, for Priest Abraham had said nothing to me; but it was not the time or place for me to say anything. I told Priest Abraham that he had done wrong to tell them so. He said, 'I knew they would come if they heard that you were to preach, and you *can* preach very well; the girls told me so.' I asked Mr. Stocking to help me out of the trouble; and the priest was greatly disappointed when he found that his notice had left him alone to preach to the men. We went to the church, where were at least five hundred women with half as many children. I looked over them with a sad feeling, for I was sure there was not one there asking to know the truth. They were a rude, noisy company. Mr. Stocking was able to preach and gain a little attention; but it seemed to me that there was not a moment when not half a dozen voices were heard beside the preacher's. When he closed, as many as a score of voices called out, 'Now let Miss Fiske preach.' So the good brother withdrew, and left me to the mercy of the crowd. My preaching was soon done. I told them that when I knew their language better I would come to talk to them in a meeting, only I could not talk when they were talking, for God had given me very little voice; and I had some words for them that would no more mix with their words than oil would mix with water. They said, 'Oil and water *never* mix: we will be silent if you will come and preach.'"

Of a subsequent visit to the same place Miss Fiske says: "The women remembered my promise, and hundreds came together; but they did not remember to be silent. As soon as I began to talk, they began to talk also. I knew I was not heard, and when I asked them to be quiet, each began to exhort her neighbor to be still, but entirely forgot herself. After trying for some time to no purpose, I said, I cannot say anything more unless you will all put your fingers upon your lips, and not say one word. All their fingers went up, and I said, I have a very good story to tell you, but I cannot tell it if one takes her fingers from her lips. Then, with half-suppressed voices, they began to say, 'Be still, be still, so that we can hear the story.' Some minutes passed before the four hundred women were so quieted that I could tell my story. But at last there was silence; and I am afraid you will think I gave them a strange Sabbath-day talk. But I did as well as I knew how, and it did not seem as strange on the spot as it does in telling it; and it did good. It was a kind of preparatory work. I said, 'Once there was an old woman. I did not know her, and my father did not know her, and I think my grandfather did not know her, but he told me the story.' Here they began to inquire after my grandfather, and I was obliged again to get all the fingers on the lips, and tell them that

10

they would not hear any more about the woman if they talked about my grandfather. 'Now, this old woman went to meeting, and always talked in meeting. I should think she might have been one of your relatives. At last they told her she must not go to meeting any more. She pleaded very hard to go, and promised not to say one word. They let her go, but, poor woman, she could not be still. As soon as the minister began to preach, she began to talk, when, hearing her own voice, she said, "Oh, I have spoken in meeting! There, I have spoken again! What shall I do? And again! Why, I keep on talking; I cannot stop!" Now, you are very much like that woman. I do not think you can stop talking, so I must stop.' Their fingers were now all closely pressed to their lips. They did not answer me at all. I took the Testament and read to them of Mary, and told them I was sure that she never talked in meeting, and that if she had, Jesus would not have loved her so much. I talked to them about fifteen minutes more, and prayed with them, and they went out very still."

Writing from Seir, June 22d, Miss Fiske thus speaks of a church which she visited in the village of Mar Sergis: —

"Here is a large stone church, which is much resorted to by sick persons and others. Here they present offerings, consisting of pocket-handkerchiefs, pieces of calico, silk, etc., all of which are hung upon the walls of the church, and for which they expect to have their requests granted. The walls of this great church are almost entirely covered with these things; and many a Nestorian, and also Mussulman, is ready to testify that the lame have been made to walk, the sick been made well; and, above all, that many a child has been given in return for these votive offerings. The church bears the name of a former bishop of Oroomiah, and often have I heard him invoked in words like these: 'O Mar Sergis, give me a son!' It is very painful to see superstition thus maintaining its sway here."

For about two weeks Miss Fiske was pleasantly occupied, at Seir, in instructing her boarding pupils, whom she had taken with her, hoping that she should be able to do much for their improvement, while they were thus removed from the temptations of the city; but her labors and plans were suddenly interrupted by a storm of persecution which burst upon the mission.

When, after the sacking of the mountains by the Koords, Mar. Shimon, the patriarch, fled to Mosul, his brothers found their way to Oroomiah, and were received by the missionaries, for a while, as their guests. They soon, however, manifested such a haughty and overbearing spirit, that the mission felt obliged to decline longer giving them a support. At this they were greatly enraged, and vowed vengeance. Their first hostile movements were directed against the missionary operations at Seir. For several years Mr. Stocking had been in the habit of assembling, by invitation, the teachers of the school for a short time, in order to give them special religious instruction. The interest in these meetings having increased this year, the invitation included others besides teachers, and about seventy in all were gathered at Seir, whom the brethren of the mission were greatly interested in instructing. On Friday, the fifth of July, an order came from the brothers of Mar. Shimon that the teachers should be disbanded, and should appear before them at the city.

"It came," says Miss Fiske, "like a thunderbolt to many, and they knew not how to interpret it. It was deemed best to dismiss the school (of teachers), and allow all to go according to orders. An investigation of the case on Monday led the mission to feel it best to discontinue their operations, except so far as there was a decided wish on the part of individuals to receive instruction. Threats of excommunication from the Nestorian Church were sent to these few on Tuesday; but they heeded them not. Said one good native brother, in reply, 'I fear not the curses of men; they are, I trust, my Father's blessings.' On Wednesday the threats were again repeated, in something like this form: 'Know ye, all ye readers at Seir, if you do not come to us to-morrow, we will excommunicate you from our holy church; your finger-nails shall be torn out; we will hunt you from village to village, and kill you if we can.' These denunciations, much as they might and did affect some, moved not these. Their language was, 'We fear not what man can do to us.'

"The expression, 'all ye readers,' as you will perceive, included my little girls. That it was the design of the Patriarch's brothers to remove these children, we were not certain. Indeed, we hardly supposed it was; but it was thought best, after consideration, that the girls should be sent away, lest they should finally take them away, or prefer some false charge against us for detaining them. I called them together, and Mr. Stocking briefly told them the reasons why they were to be sent away. I wept like a child, and they all burst into audible weeping. I have wept before when called to part with those for whom I had been permitted to labor; but, oh, I knew not then the bitterness I now felt! I was about to send back these children to a darkness almost like heathenism. Oh, what a thought! Had I not remembered that the Lord taketh care of his own, and believed that he would bring light out of darkness, my feelings would have been insupportable. It was near night when the message for their departure reached us, and we could only send away those whose homes were nearest us, on that night. When ready to go, each one fell upon my neck and wept a long time. Jesus took such little ones in his arms and blessed them; but those professing to be his followers were forbidding us to do it. The children who were to remain till morning requested that they might go a little distance with their companions. I gave them permission to do so; but no sooner were they out of the gate than they all began again to weep most bitterly, exclaiming, 'Oh, we shall hear the words of God no more!' The sight of the grief of these little ones affected stout hearts to tears. Said a German Jew (who is with us, and who has been in different countries), in broken English, 'I seen much bad to missionaries in other countries, but nothing bad like this, to take little children from words of Jesus Christ!' This was on Wednesday evening, 10th inst. The other children left on Thursday morning, with the exception of Priest Abraham's daughter. He takes decided ground against these wicked men, and insists on his daughter's remaining. I have felt exceedingly lonely since that day. It seems as if death had been in the midst of us, and I would be admonished by this to be faithful while the day lasts."

The hostility of the patriarchal family increased in bitterness, through papal influences, until all the schools scattered over the plain, about fifty in number, were broken up, and the thousand children instructed in them scattered. The very existence of the mission was threatened, and at one time it seemed probable that our missionaries would all be driven from the country. But, through the kind offices of the Russian ambassador at Teheran, the plans of their enemies were thwarted, and they were permitted to remain and to go on with their work, though not without great opposition.

When the missionaries had most reason to fear expulsion from the country, Miss Fiske thus wrote: "The thought of turning our back on those whom we had hoped to be instrumental in raising to life and immortality is truly painful. The possibility of its being so has cost me many a struggle; but I hope I am now willing to go anywhere that my Father sees best to send me. Yes, if he sees best that I should return to my native land, I trust that I shall go cheerfully and happily, and there do his holy will. Yet, I do pray that, if it be his will, I may live and labor here. I knew not before that my affections had become so closely entwined around this poor people, nor how severely I should feel a removal from them."

In November, Miss Fiske had the pleasure of welcoming back to her school-room in the city all her scattered pupils, who brought others with them, the school opening with twenty, — all boarders.

From the beginning, her strong desire had been to make it a boarding school. The day scholars had, up to this time, been more numerous than those who remained under her constant care. Twenty-five cents a week had been paid to them, instead of their board. The discontinuance of this, it was thought, would induce more to become boarders. Accordingly, when she closed her school in the spring, Miss Fiske told her scholars that no more money would be paid them. Of this step she afterwards said, "I do not now see how I ventured to do it, and I remember that it was said in the mission, at the time, that it would probably be resumed; but it never was, and was dropped in the boys' school soon after."

The success of the measure fully justified its adoption. The number of pupils gradually increased, and Miss Fiske thus writes, December 16th: "I have now twenty-five little girls, all under thirteen years. They are a great charge, often wayward, and causing my inmost soul to weep; and yet I have so much to encourage me that I am far from sinking. I have as an assistant a Nestorian deacon, who magnifies his deaconship by his faithfulness, and is, I hope, a true Christian."

Under date of March 1st, she thus writes: "Most of my girls leave me to-day for a week's vacation. I find that I am needing rest. You may wonder that I should be worn with no larger school, and with native help. But you must know that I must be mother, and house-keeper, as well as teacher. The girls come to me needing a great deal of care at first.

Each one must be separately cared for as she comes in; otherwise the filth, etc., that she has brought from her home, will spread through our partially purified family. . . . I must look to all their food and all their clothes. I must see that they are in readiness for every duty, and also that they perform it. I must see that they are all quiet at the hour of sleep, and that they are awake at the hour of waking; in short, there is no hour in which I can sit down and feel perfectly at ease in regard to my little ones, if I am absent from them; and yet, I doubt not that I have found more help than many who undertake such a charge in foreign lands. It is no small work to prepare lessons, even in the imperfect way I give them. I have enjoyed much in reading the Bible with these children. We spend hours each day thus employed. God may yet sanctify them through his truth; though now they seem far from it. When tried with the filth and degradation of these girls and of their mothers, I am comforted by the thought that Jesus has been in just such homes and blessed their little ones. How much more he felt these things than I *can* feel them! I love to rest in this thought, when a new child is brought to me; and when I am wandering in the lanes of our city."

Two years had now elapsed since Miss Fiske left her native land. Alluding to this fact she says, writing to her mother: "Surely goodness and mercy have followed my every step. It is good to trust in the Lord. You, my dear mother, know the preciousness of such trust. You have felt it, I know, since I have been separated from you. May you be enabled firmly to confide in the Lord all the days of your life. I feel that distrust is one of the Christian's greatest sins; and I feel that I, of all, am the most guilty. When I look back on my past life, and remember how distrustful I have been of my Father's leadings, I wonder that he has borne with me, and is giving me the privilege of living and laboring for him. Oh, pray for me, my dear mother, that I may always exercise a humble trust in the Lord, and be ever found doing his holy will."

In her engrossing labors for her pupils, Miss Fiske did not forget their mothers, but in various ways sought to reach and benefit them also. March 8th, she writes: "Not long since I invited the mothers of all my children to spend an afternoon with their daughters. Almost all came; some walking five or six miles in the snow and mud. It was an interesting hour when we could thus bring mothers and daughters together, and enforce upon them their relative duties. I hope the afternoon was not spent in vain, and that I shall enjoy many such precious privileges with the mothers and daughters of this fallen Israel."

She encouraged among her pupils habits of industry, as well as of study, and often evinced great tact in turning little incidents into incentives to effort. Some friend in America had sent to her a few copies of the "Youth's Companion." The girls were exceedingly interested in them, and wished they could receive the paper regularly. "Wishing to test the strength of their desire," she says, "I asked them how they would pay for it. They immediately inquired if they could not knit stockings and send to the editor. They thought of this expedient, having just learned to knit, and, highly valuing the acquisition, supposed they could accomplish anything by it. Seeing their earnestness, I told them it would not be well to try to send stockings to America; but that I would give them six cents a pair for socks until they had knit enough to pay for the paper one year. They were soon busy at their work, and it is now more than half accomplished, and soon I hope these little 'friends of youth' will be winging their way to far-off Persia, followed by the prayers of Christians."

It was no longer difficult to obtain the desired number of pupils as boarders. Parents who, the year before, thought it would be a disgrace to place their daughters in Miss Fiske's school, were now greatly disappointed and grieved to find that they could not be received. There were so many applicants that, when no more could be taken as boarders, Miss Fiske consented to admit a few day scholars; these, with the least advanced of the boarders, constituting a distinct department in the school.

This day school was taught by Selby, a girl fourteen years of age, who had been one of the most promising pupils in the seminary, but had left the year before, and was married to a little boy, a year younger than herself. Her father-in-law consenting, she returned to take the place of teacher, and soon after became an earnest Christian.

Her conversion was followed by the awakening of several of the pupils. Miss Fiske writes: "I think I now see far more of the Spirit's workings than at any time since I have been here. Some of the girls in school manifest religious interest. My soul is full when I think of them, and it is only when I can cast them upon Jesus that I can feel happy. If they are ever converted, it must be the Lord's work; I feel this more and more."

Miss Fiske greatly enjoyed the release from the confinement and labors of the school-room, which an occasional ride to Seir afforded. During one of these rides, May 13th, an accident befell her, which came near being fatal. The account is best given in her own words: "Feeling the warm weather very much in the city, Mr. Stoddard proposed that we ride to Seir and breathe the mountain air. Accordingly after dinner Mr. and Mrs. Stoddard and I left, accompanied by little Jerusha, Willie, and Hattie, in the baskets, a man riding on the horse that carried the baskets. About half a mile from the city is a river which we were obliged to ford in going to Seir. At this season of the year it is much swollen by the melting of the snow on the mountains. The day we rode, it was higher than usual. Mr. Stoddard first went into the river, and Mrs. Stoddard and I followed. Mrs. Stoddard's horse went directly through, but mine, when he came to the middle of the stream where the water was some three or four feet deep, stopped. I immediately struck him, and he as quickly lay down in the water, and I was thrown over his back. After being thus plunged into the water, I saw my horse coming over me, while I was between his fore and hind legs. But he passed over without touching me. Before I could regain an upright position, I had floated some distance down stream, my head being under water a part of the time. Recollecting that I must not breathe under water, I did not strangle, and soon recovered myself and reached the shore. Mr.

Stoddard, on seeing me going down stream, sprang from his horse to help me; upon which his horse immediately commenced quarrelling with Mrs. Stoddard's. She sprang from her horse, but her riding-dress caught on the saddle, and for a moment she was in a most perilous condition. But her riding-skirt, being of thin material, gave way, and she was thus saved. The horses, being loose, ran about us in anger, as if determined to do us harm. But we were mercifully preserved from them. Mr. Stoddard came up just as I got out of the water, and, seeing it would be in vain to try to secure the horses, we set out for home in our drenched state. We were pitiable objects, I can assure you, as we entered the city. I had not a dry thread in my clothing, and my head felt as if it had had a most thorough *inside* as well as *outside* washing. But I find that I suffered no harm from it, except something of a bruising from the stones in the river. Surely the Lord was my keeper, and not mine alone, but of all our company."

As the term was drawing to a close, Miss Fiske thus speaks of her efforts and her success in making her school what she desired it to become: "I have been able this year to reduce my school to a much more orderly state than last year, although it is yet far from what I would have it. The want of conscience in many of the girls has led me to forbear bringing them to a strict account. But from month to month I can see an advance in conscientiousness, and have little by little brought them to give some account of themselves daily. The questions I ask are these, 'Have you combed your heads to-day?' 'Have you been in the boys' yard?' 'Have you been to the boys' room?' 'Were you present at prayers?' 'Were you late at prayers?' 'Have you all of your knitting-needles?' 'Have you spit on the floor?' 'Have you chewed gum?' (They have a bad practice of always having their mouths filled with gum.) It is seldom, now, that I have a failure on any of these points. I shall soon add to these, 'making communications in school.' I have hardly dared to do so yet, lest they should be tempted to depart from the truth."

The second year of the seminary closed June 5th. On that day a simple entertainment, prepared in the native style, was given to the parents and friends of the pupils in both the male and female seminaries. Several hundred were present. Of the occasion, Miss Fiske thus writes the next day: "The gentlemen of the mission ate in one room with the men and boys, and the ladies in another with the women and girls. It was gratifying to us all to see the apparent confidence reposed in us, and the kind feeling manifested by those present. Most of the children left us last night, evidently pleased to go to their homes for a short time, but with no wish to remain away permanently. We deem it important that they be happy both with their parents and with us. I feel more and more the desirableness of frequently allowing our pupils to spend a few days with their friends. They thus have an opportunity of showing what education is doing for them, and of gaining for us the confidence of their parents. Most of the girls carried home with them a copy of the gospels in modern Syriac, which they had paid for with their needles during the leisure hours of the last few weeks. We also presented each of them with a copy of the 'Dairyman's Daughter,' which has recently been printed in Syriac. I never so much realized the intrinsic value of this little work as since I have seen its effects on the Nestorian mind. Many mothers brought their infant daughters to me yesterday, saying, 'These are yours. We give them to you that you may teach them.' Oh, may I live and have the privilege of teaching them the way to heaven! Were I at Holyoke I should say, 'I am very busy *shutting up house.*'"

CHAPTER X.

JUNE, 1845, TO JUNE, 1846.

A Sabbath at Geog Tapa. — School-rooms Enlarged. — Visit to Ada and Gavalan. — First Revival. — Prayerfulness of the Converts. — Interest in the Monthly Concert. — The Woman who could not Pray. — Interest in Geog Tapa. — Influence of the Revival on the Minds and Manners of the Girls. — Sketches of Sarah, Hannah, and Dea. Gewergis.

Early in her summer vacation of 1845, Miss Fiske spent a Sabbath at Geog Tapa, and found many of the women who, on former visits, cared to talk only about dress, now eager to hear the word of God and to converse about their souls. The day, though filled with exhausting labors, greatly cheered and refreshed her spirits, and inspired her with a more confident hope that a brighter day was already dawning on the degraded women of Persia.

About the 20th of June she removed to Seir, taking with her five of her pupils, whom she hoped to retain during the vacation; but the state of her health soon compelled her to dismiss them all.

The constantly increasing number of pupils in the seminary rendering enlarged accommodations desirable, the mission placed at Miss Fiske's disposal the house of Mr. Merrick. To adapt it to its new use, it was necessary to make extensive alterations, which she superintended, surprising and amusing her associates by the architectural skill and good practical judgment which she evinced, and the tact with which she managed the native masons and carpenters employed on the work. Of this change she thus speaks: —

"I have had but one room (except a small room for cooking) for my school exercises and for the girls' eating and sleeping. This has kept my own room filled with classes or visitors, so that it has been difficult for me to find any opportunity for ventilation, or for rest and retirement, from before light till late at night. I have never kept a bed made up in it, but have at night prepared one on a kind of sofa frame, used for a seat. Now, I have a large room for the prayers of the school, and for the reception of company; also a small sleeping-room for myself, and three small rooms for my school. I trust that every convenience will add to my usefulness. I look forward to the coming winter with an overwhelming feeling of responsibility. Oh, shall my dear pupils this year become Christians! I can never forget how much interest Bro. Stoddard felt in the new arrangement, nor how he came into the best room, and, firmly planting his foot, said: 'May this room be *wholly consecrated* to the Lord!' We prayed that it might be, before it was furnished, and it was the room where, during the following January, there was such a marked descent of the Holy Spirit."

Writing to a friend, October 23d, she says: —

"You will be glad to hear that my school is reassembled for the year. I do not think the fond mother more anxiously longs for the return of a loved absent child than I do for the return of my dear ones. It would have done you good to see the pleasure depicted on their countenances as they again entered our dwelling. As we are crowded, and obliged to refuse many applicants, we insist that none but those perfectly happy with us and willing to abide by our every rule shall remain with us. Selby is not with us this year. We hoped to have her here, and her heart was strongly set on coming, but her avaricious father-in-law demanded such pay for her services that we could not think of employing her. I feel deeply for this lamb of Jesus (for such I believe she is) in her seclusion from Christian society. But the Lord knows his own, and will keep them to the end. In her place I have a young deacon of good abilities, but who gives no evidence of piety. Pray for him that he may become the Lord's. Perhaps the Lord has designs of mercy towards him, and for this reason has brought him to us.

"It is exceedingly gratifying to see that our pupils have not lost their religious interest during their absence. The last sound that falls from their lips at evening is the voice of prayer. They retire to their rooms for the night about eight o'clock; after a few moments we ring a bell for their lights to be extinguished, and for them to cease speaking one to another. After this, often five or six are known to engage in audible prayer. There is something affecting to me, as I pass by their door, in hearing their supplications and in remembering that Jesus hears the infant's prayer, if offered aright.

"I often feel obliged to seek my pillow before nine o'clock, having no time to rest during the day. I never looked upon my school with a deeper feeling of responsibility than I now do. Oh, may it be, not only what its patrons in America, but also what the Lord, would have it be!"

A few days after the opening of her school, Miss Fiske, still eager to do good in every possible way to the women in the villages, made an excursion with Dr. and Mrs. Perkins to Ada and Gavalan. In the latter they spent the Sabbath, and she thus speaks of the day: —

"Mr. Perkins preached to a congregation including almost every person in the village. After the meeting some twenty-five girls gathered about me in the open field for instruction. Oh, how did my heart bleed for the poor ignorant creatures! I inquired of them why the Sabbath was given them. They replied, 'To sit still.' 'But,' I asked, 'was it given for no other purpose?' 'What else can we do?' they replied; 'we cannot read, and there is no one to read to us.' I felt it to be an unspeakable privilege, for once, to tell these poor ones of their sins, and of the Saviour who died for them. We left Gavalan early Monday morning, and, after a long and tiresome ride, reached home at evening. I feel that I derived much benefit from the excursion, getting renewed strength for my school."

The year 1846 was a memorable year in the history of the Nestorian mission. It witnessed the first of that series of extensive and remarkable revivals of religion with which that mission has been so signally blessed. Years of toil and prayer were rewarded with an abundant harvest. Up to this time the number of conversions had been small. Much had been done for the general education and the religious instruction of the people; but all this fell short of that higher spiritual work to which all truly missionary effort is ultimately directed. As the husbandman waiteth for the precious fruit of the earth, so that band of devoted missionaries in Persia waited in earnest desire and strong hope for the time of the ingathering of souls.

During the autumn of 1845 there were some slight indications of increasing religious interest among the pupils of both seminaries; but not until the following January did the work of the Holy Spirit become deep and general. The account of this revival will be given, as far as possible, in Miss Fiske's own words. The first Monday of the new year was observed by the mission as a day of fasting and prayer. "We had spoken," says Miss F., "of passing that day in 'wrestling for souls.' But we had only begun to *seek*, not to *wrestle*, when we learned that souls were pleading for themselves. I went into my school as usual, at nine o'clock, and, after telling the pupils that many prayers would, that day, be offered for them by friends far away, I prayed with them, and then asked them to retire to another room, where they would study with a native teacher. All but two passed out. As these two lingered, I said: 'Did you understand me?' They came nearer, and I saw that they were in tears. 'Have you heard bad news?' I inquired. They gave no answer; but, coming still nearer, whispered, 'May we have to-day to care for our souls?' One of them (Sarah) adding, 'Perhaps, next year, I shall not be here.' I had no private room or closet to give them, but the dear children would find a place. They went to the wood-cellar, and, taking sticks of wood, made their own closets;

and there they spent that cold day, seeking the forgiveness of sin. Nor did they seek in vain; they were soon trusting in Christ, and we were led to hope for yet greater blessings."

"Monday, the 19th, there were such marked indications of interest in my school, that I asked those who felt that they must now care for their souls to come to my room at five o'clock. I had been out of my school but a few minutes, when I found that a number of the girls had sought places of prayer. While asking for wisdom to guide the dear children, Mr. Stoddard came to the door, and said, 'I cannot stop, but I want you to know that four or five of my boys are much distressed on account of their sins. How our hearts went up to Heaven in thanksgiving at that hour; and how were they filled with trembling and anxiety! I turned away from Mr. S., to meet five of my girls, who seemed to feel deeply their sinfulness. I cannot well describe the scenes of that week. One after another bowed under a sense of sin. Every place was occupied for prayer. We could hardly command our own rooms long enough to bend the knee therein; while we were glad to write, on all around us, 'Immanuel, Immanuel!' The two schools hardly knew anything of each other's condition till Friday, when they met in the usual weekly prayer-meeting, in the room which Mr. Stoddard had asked might be 'wholly consecrated to the Lord forever.' We felt that evening that the room was no longer ours, but the Lord's, and we all wanted it to be his forever. The boys sat on one side, and the girls on the other; and I never saw a company that seemed more fully impressed with eternal realities. The careless ones had stayed away, and those present were earnest seekers. It seemed to me that Mr. Stocking and Mr. Stoddard were Heaven-inspired that night, as they spoke of sin, and of Him who saves from sin. Souls were born there; and we do not wonder that many of our native friends think the place a Bethel.

"For three weeks after the revival commenced we had but little company. The time seemed to be given us to labor expressly for our pupils, and it was to us like one continued Sabbath. Every place in our house was consecrated by prayer, and all our work was for souls.

"At the end of three weeks, Nestorians from without began to flock around us, and now our dear pupils were true helpers. I often had as many as ten or fifteen women to pass the night with us. Then I used to gather together all the spare pillows, cushions, and quilts in the house, and make our sitting-room one great dormitory. I often stayed with them till midnight, and then, from my room, heard them pray all night. I love to remember those nights of watching with the Lord Jesus for those precious souls. Oh, how easy it is to watch when he is with us!

"Two months after the first cases of interest occurred, we gave our pupils a vacation. Mr. Stoddard calls our last meetings with them 'Thanksgivings.' As they left us, they said, 'Pray for us! pray for us!' I remember that one little girl said, 'Did you ever see a new-born lamb cast into the snow and live?' Thank God, most of them did live, and we trust are to live forever."

Extracts from other letters, written at the time, will give further details of this interesting work of grace and its results. To two of the teachers at Mt. Holyoke Seminary, she thus writes: —

"OROOMIAH, Feb. 28, 1846.

"MY VERY DEAR SISTER: — The week on which my last letter to you was closed, was one of most striking demonstrations of God's Spirit in the conviction of sinners. On Saturday and the Sabbath almost the whole school seemed affected. The close contiguity into which they were thrown led me to feel that while there was no doubt of the Spirit's presence, there was also much of animal excitement among the younger ones. To avoid this, we separated them as much as possible one from another, recommended them not to speak at all to one another, and gave them much time to be alone with their God. Those deeply affected were soon manifest, and in our conversation and prayers with and for them, we sought to show them the wickedness of their hearts, their utter alienation from God, and their need of a change of heart, and thus lead them to the sinner's only Friend. From that time to the present, the interest has increased; and now there are only two in the school over ten years of age (including more than half the school), who have not been deeply affected. Many of these appear to be true Christians. Time alone can show the genuineness of their conversion. But I do believe that God is gathering to himself a precious band here. Several under ten years of age have appeared to be deeply convicted of sin, and seem now to love

Him who delights to take little children in his arms and bless them.

"Dear children! I watch over them with the greatest anxiety, feeling that at every step I hear my Saviour's voice saying, 'Feed my lambs.' Their confidence in us, and their natural frankness, lead them to be exceedingly free in expressing their feelings. I am often awaked in the morning by a dear child standing at my bedside with some inquiry in regard to the way of life. Their freedom renders it a delightful, and, at the same time, a responsible task to guide them. Oh, do pray for me, that I may be guided aright! I never felt so weak, and, at the same time, such tremendous responsibilities resting upon me.

"Prayerfulness has thus far been strikingly exhibited in those hopefully converted. They love their closets, and it is one of their greatest trials that they cannot have a closet as they wish. I have many little meetings for prayer with them. It is delightful at such hours to hear those who have but just begun to love the Lord, pleading for entire consecration to him, and also, with the deepest apparent feeling, wrestling for their impenitent friends. Can it be, I often think at such times, that these are indeed sisters in Christ, redeemed by his blood, and heirs of heaven! If so, what an inroad has been made on Satan's kingdom! God has brought to pass in a day what years of man's labor could never effect. To his name we will give the glory.

"I spent yesterday in Geog Tapa, in a most interesting manner. You may wonder that I should leave my school for a day. Could other ladies have gone out to look after our lost sisters, I should have felt sure that it was my duty to remain at home; but, as they could not, I felt equally sure that it was my duty to go; so I went forth, committing my flock to Israel's Shepherd; and, with such a Keeper, and under such circumstances, you will not be surprised to know that they had an interesting day. I found them all quiet and prayerful when I returned. Sixteen women from different villages had been in for the purpose of religious inquiry during my absence. The older girls, feeling that they must take my place, took each of those by the hand, and conversed and prayed with them. Our intercourse with the women is becoming very extended through the medium of our school. One's whole time might be profitably devoted to such labors without doing anything for the school."

"OROOMIAH, PERSIA, March 31.

"MY DEARLY BELOVED SISTER: — Our school is so changed that we can hardly realize it is our school. We often pause to ask ourselves, is it possible that those, whose voices we now hear in prayer and praise from morn till night, are the same individuals over whom we mourned three months since as 'dead in trespasses and sin'? What has the Lord wrought! Oh! I want to love him more and serve him better.

"Our pupils promptly returned at the close of our vacation, and apparently feeling more deeply than when they left us. I know you delight in quiet returns after vacations. I wish you could have seen my school return last Friday. You would not have supposed an individual was in the house. Many burst into tears as they again met their companions; but all was perfectly quiet. The closets were all immediately filled with these praying souls, and remained so until the hour for retiring.

"In nine villages besides Geog Tapa there are from one to four or five individuals for whom we hope. Most of these persons have been first awakened by visiting our schools, and seeing the tears, and hearing the penitential confessions of our pupils in prayer before God, and several have here hoped that they found the sinner's friend. I think that an individual now seldom comes into our yard without being urged to repentance, and prayed with by several individuals. These dear young Christians seem to have no disposition to go to heaven alone, and while we can see them humble and prayerful, we feel no desire to check them in their labors of love. I trust that they inherit the same faith and will abound in the same self-denying labors which led their fathers to plant the standard of the cross among the snows of Tartary, amidst the burning sands of India, on China's inhospitable shore, and among the Eastern isles.

"You will rejoice to hear that there is much interest among the middle-aged females here. Three of the girls' mothers we hope love the Saviour; others are interested. I find my labors almost as much out of school as in. I long for one of Holyoke's daughters to help me in this very interesting work. My own health is very good, and I am happy in my labors. Oh, why was it given to me to labor here, and others, so much better, denied the privilege?"

The prayerfulness of the converts has already been alluded to. With reference to this, Miss Fiske further writes: "Twice or even thrice a day does not suffice for communion with their heavenly Father. They want to be much at the mercy-seat, and many of them spend hours every day there. I often see three or four sitting by a closet, with tearful eyes, that they may be the first to enter when the place is vacated. How do I then sigh for those closets in America where a prayer was never offered!

"If they do not pray several times a day, they feel that they are becoming very cold-hearted. To-day, as they were going out to walk, one of them, who, perhaps, had not prayed for three hours, felt that she could not go until she could have a few moments alone. I have the whole school divided into little circles of five or six each, and have a prayer-meeting with one circle every day. These are precious seasons to me, and I trust to them also.

"One night the girls of the school, while walking with their teacher, came to a grove, when one of them said, 'See, here is a grove; what doth hinder us to be praying?' So they scattered in different parts of the grove and all prayed."

Under date of April 13th, she writes: "Last monthly concert-day was a most interesting day to our pious natives. We have, heretofore, had so few praying souls about us that our service has generally been for imparting instruction rather than for prayer. But now we could but feel it a privilege to unite with dear native friends in supplications for a dying world. Never did I hear more feeling prayers, than I heard on this day, for the coming of Christ's kingdom. My girls, not satisfied with the public services, wished for another concert among themselves. Oh, what supplications did I hear from their lips until the sun went down! I felt that I was near to heaven, or at least that the kingdom of heaven had come near to us. They could only be persuaded to leave their meeting by a promise of a similar meeting there the next day. With this promise they left for their closets, there to supplicate Israel's God; and the next day found them in their meeting, praying for the salvation of souls; so that the sun, having run its course, and witnessed the concerts of prayer on all sides of the globe, found a continued one here."

Miss Fiske often went to Geog Tapa for a day, to labor among the women, and to rejoice in seeing the same fruits of the Spirit there, which had so gladdened her heart in the city. She thus writes, May 19th: "The general aspect of the village is much changed. Almost all who have come to years of discretion give good outward attention to the preached gospel, and not a small number, we hope, are truly and anxiously inquiring for the way of life. It is difficult to speak definitely of probable results among such a people. But we hope that as many as fifty have become Christians, some from all classes. Quite a number of ecclesiastics, formerly intemperate and profane, appear now to be humbly sitting at Jesus' feet. Poor, degraded women have been made free in Christ Jesus. Many laboring men, who, a few weeks since, seemed almost as ignorant as the beasts they followed at the plough, are now intelligent Christians. With their spades in their hands they now preach Christ and him crucified, from morning until night; and the fields and vineyards are made vocal with their prayers and praises. I often spend a day there, with Christian sisters; and I need hardly tell you that this work has bound me more closely than ever to my Persian home. I feel it a great privilege to labor here; and here, I hope, if it be my Father's will, to make my grave; and from here, with many dear ones in Christ Jesus, to go up to meet the Lord, when the final trump shall sound."

The labor connected with such a revival, however delightful, is very exhausting. Miss Fiske found herself, in June, too much worn to continue her school duties. The school was accordingly dismissed for the summer. "We feared," she writes, during the vacation, "the effects of their long absence from us; but as far as we have been able to learn, those hopefully pious are walking as becometh Christians. Many of them are very diligent in their Master's service, being missionaries indeed, doing, as we believe, more than we could ourselves do for their poor people."

The permanent effect of this revival on the general deportment of the scholars was marked and gratifying. They became more gentle, affectionate, and tractable. Faults which their teacher had long labored in vain to correct almost entirely disappeared. "God made me feel my utter helplessness, and then he did the work," writes Miss Fiske. Stealing and lying, to which they had been addicted, were afterwards of rare occurrence. Great tenderness of conscience was manifested; sins of which they had not been suspected were confessed, stolen articles were restored. "Khanee, one of my girls," says Miss Fiske, "came to me greatly troubled, saying, 'Do you remember the day, when, two years ago, Sawdee's new shoes were taken from the door?' I said

'Yes.' 'You thought a Moslem woman took them;' and then, bursting into tears, added, 'but I took them. I was angry with Sawdee, and I threw them into a well, where no one could get them. What shall I do? I know Jesus will not receive me till I have confessed it to Sawdee. Can I go and tell her to-night and pray with her, and then go and work to get money to pay her for the shoes?' She paid for the shoes, and became a bright and shining light in her dark home. There were many cases just like this."

The intellects of the girls seemed greatly quickened by grace in the heart. They had better lessons, wrote better compositions, and were in all respects better scholars, strikingly illustrating the power of the gospel, when received by faith, to elevate and improve the whole character and life.

Brief sketches of two or three of the converts will further illustrate the character of this revival, and will serve as a fitting close to this chapter.

SARAH, — DAUGHTER OF PRIEST ESHOO.

Of the two pupils, who, as already mentioned, requested of their teacher, on the first Monday in January, 1846, permission to spend the day "in caring for their souls," one was Sarah; or, as the Nestorians pronounce it, Sarra. Miss Fiske's own pen has furnished the following account of this lovely child: —

"Sarah was a tall, dark-eyed girl of twelve or thirteen years, when she first came to my school. We had few books except the Bible, and so our pupils studied that most of the time. Sarah learned her

Bible well, and could repeat large portions of it, and tell all its stories. I could scarcely ask her to find a text, to which she would not turn at once. I called her my concordance. But she did not learn that she was a sinner till January, 1846. She was the first at that time to ask the way to heaven, the first to find the way, and the first to enter heaven. She lived just five months after she said to me, on that first Monday in January, 'Perhaps next year I shall not be here.' Only a few days after her conversion, her father said, 'Sarah knows the way to heaven better than I do.' He never felt that his 'daily bread' had been given him, unless he had knelt with the dear child in prayer, and been carried to heaven by her petitions as well as his own. Mr. Stocking used to enjoy conversing with her very much. He often said, 'If I want to write a good sermon, I like to sit down first and talk with Sarah, and then be sure that she is praying for me.' You can easily imagine that it was a most delightful privilege to watch over the dear girl as she was nearing heaven. We would sit for an hour at a time, and talk of the home of the blest, while she, seeming to see its glories, would sing, 'It will be good to be there;' then her thoughts would turn to perishing souls around her, and she would say, 'But I would labor a little longer for them, if it be my Father's will.' I never knew a young person more anxious to save souls. She was very feeble at the time of her conversion, but she would work for Christ. The girls, and women too, always loved to have Sarah tell them 'the way.' They would say, 'We can see it when she tells us.' I do not wonder that they saw it, for she seemed to see it all the time. I depended upon her so much, that I doubt not I let her do more than she was able to do. As early as March we felt that she must die, and she realized it herself. But she clung to her school and did not leave it till May, although she passed her nights at her home, which was close by. She would be in our meetings, even when it was necessary for some one to aid her in reaching the chapel. Her emaciated form, and hollow cough, and eye bright with a lustre not its own, all told that she was about to go from us; and I have sometimes heard those young disciples say, as she took her seat in the house of God, 'Have we not an Elizabeth Wallbridge among us?' Never, perhaps, was a young Christian going to the grave watched with more interest than was Sarah. 'Will her hope sustain her at the last?' 'Will Jesus stay by her?' 'Will he come for her?' they asked, ready to test the Lord's faithfulness by the manner in which he should support this young sister in her trial. Their expectation was not disappointed; and, since Sarah died, the Nestorians have looked upon death as never before. Heaven's gates are wider opened to them; and it is to them more a blessed reality that Christ comes himself for his own.

"I said that Sarah left us in May, but she did not leave till we saw that she must do so, or take a room in our house. When I told her, she said, 'I think it better for me to go to my father's, and stay there, but I want a little while here before I go, never to come back again.' With weary steps she bent her way to her closet, or rather the closet where she gave her heart to Christ. On reaching it she found it occupied. She then sought another, where she passed an hour in earnest pleading, and then came to me, and sweetly said, 'I am ready to go now.' Two of her companions accompanied her, and I cannot easily forget how she stopped in the court to look back upon the home where she had found her Saviour. It was her last look. I watched her as she stooped to gather some of the roses by her pathway, and realized that my work for her was almost done. She lingered till June, and I saw her almost every day, and often found her with her open Bible, and several women by her side, whom she was seeking to lead to Christ. She always wanted me to pray with her, and she would be supported and would pray with me. Her praying companions often had meetings by her bedside. Each visit made me feel that she was getting nearer home; yet she was very happy. One Saturday it was proposed to her father to go to Tergawar and preach. He said, 'I will see what Sarah says.' The question whether he should go was asked as he bent over her lowly couch, and her answer was, 'Go, father, and I will pray for you.' The father left on his errand of love, and the child prayed. The beautiful Sabbath sun rose, and I was by Sarah's side. I saw that she was almost home, and I told her so. It was good to commit the happy soul once more to Him who was ever near. I was obliged to return to my school; but said to her mother, 'Send for me when the Master calls for the dear child, for, if I may not go over Jordan with her to-day, I wish to go with her to the swelling stream.' In the afternoon, realizing that she must soon go, and forgetting for a moment, she said, 'Call my father.' When reminded that he had gone to preach, she at once said, 'Oh, yes, I remember; don't call him, let him preach. I can die alone.' She then said, 'Call Miss Fiske.' Her sister left her side to go for me, but the dying child remembered that it was the hour of our prayer-meeting. So she beckoned to her sister to come again to her, and said, 'It is the hour when she prays with my companions; don't call her. I can die alone.' So I was not with her when she died. Had I been by her side, perhaps she would not so clearly have seen the Lord Jesus. Soon after calling for me, she said, 'Mother, raise me, that I may commit my spirit.' She was raised, supported as she had been hundreds of times by her mother's strong arms, and on the bended knee, with upraised eye, she said, 'Lord Jesus, receive —' Here her voice ceased. Prayer was ended, and praise began. In my own room (the Bethel) I heard footsteps on the stairs; the door opened, and one stood by my side with the message, 'Sarah is asleep.' I was so thankful to be told in this way, for I knew she was not dead, but sleeping till Jesus should say, 'Arise.' Sarah was buried that same evening, according to the custom of the country. I followed her to the grave with the whole school, and we laid her very near dear Mrs. Grant. Will you wonder if I tell you that I trod the way to that grave in sadness? The great loss I had sustained seemed to crush me. I realized that Sarah would help me no more, and when I reached the place I could only look into the grave. But, just as the coffin was lowered I looked up, and there was the bright star of evening; and I seemed to hear a voice saying, 'Thus your dear child has risen, a bright star in heaven.' Then I was glad she was there; I was glad that the first to love the Saviour was the first to go home. I love to think of her as there, waiting for us who prayed with her on earth. Her Christian life was a short one, but she did much, for she taught many how to die."

HANNAH, OF GEOG TAPA.

Miss Fiske furnishes no connected sketch of this beloved pupil; but the following account is gathered from several of her letters written at the time. Hannah became a member of the seminary in the autumn of 1845, and was then about ten years of age. She was one of the first to become interested during the revival of the following spring. After her conversion she often expressed a strong desire to die, and be with Jesus, whom she so loved. One morning she went to her teacher's bedside, and awoke her by asking, "Is it wrong to wish to die?" "But why do you want to die?" her teacher inquired. "That I may go and stay with Jesus and never sin again," was her reply. "She once came to me," says Miss Fiske, "with a tearful eye, and said, 'It seems to me I cannot wait. I do so want to go to my Saviour.' Again she said, 'I fear I have sinned in not being willing to wait till Jesus calls for me.' " This desire for an early removal to heaven never left her. When the girls were arranging their things in the school-room to leave for a vacation, in the spring of 1847, one of them very seriously said to her companions, "Who of us, do you think, will never use these things again?" Hannah, being present, replied, "We cannot know, but I think that I never shall." And when her own bundle of books was tied up and laid away, she said to one of the girls, "Perhaps you will open this; I do not think I shall. When you come together again in the autumn, I trust that I shall be in the Saviour's school above." These words proved to be prophetic. The Saviour was longing to fold this lamb to his bosom. During the following season the cholera made fearful ravages in the cities and villages of Persia. In September it reached Geog Tapa, where Hannah was spending her vacation, and she was one of its earliest victims there. The day on which she was taken sick she was tending a vineyard (a common employment for little girls of her age) with another little girl. Not feeling quite well, about noon, she said to Guly, her companion, "I feel sick, and perhaps I shall die soon." "Are you willing to die?" asked her little friend. "Oh, yes," she replied; "I do not fear to die and go to Jesus." The disease progressed rapidly, and she soon said to Guly, "I feel very sick; I know that I shall die soon. Shall we not pray together once more?" Immediately they knelt together in prayer, as they perhaps had done hundreds of times before. The sick one was commended by her young sister to Him who walks through the dark valley with us. Having finished her prayer, she said, "Now, Hannah, will you pray?" But Hannah's prayers were ended. She was too sick to pray, except to say in broken and half audible speech, "Bless my dear sister, and take me through the dark river." Hannah was soon removed from the vineyard to the house. A fond mother bent over an only daughter; three loving brothers over an only sister. Everything possible was done, but the fatal disease worked on unchecked. As her schoolmates and friends gathered tearfully about her, she many times assured them that Jesus was her all; and that she longed to go to him. Once she called for her Testament, and opened it, but soon closed it again, saying, "I can read these words no more, but do you read them more prayerfully, and love the Saviour more than I have." She lingered in great distress, but with bright visions of the glorious realities just before her, till the early dawn, when she fell asleep. We cannot doubt that Hannah's long-cherished desire was then realized; that Jesus came and took her to himself. Her school companions were deeply affected by her death, and loved to go often to her grave to pray, not for the dead, but for the living; and there to sing: —

"How blest is our sister bereft."

DEACON GEWERGIS.

To persons at all acquainted with the history of the Nestorian Mission, the name of this man is familiar. Of his conversion and subsequent devotion to Christ, Miss Fiske thus writes: —

"In the autumn of 1845, Deacon Gewergis of Tergawar, brought his eldest daughter, then perhaps twelve or thirteen years of age, and begged that I would take her into my school. I knew him as one of the vilest of the Nestorians, and I shrunk from taking his daughter into my family. I should not have received her, had not a good missionary brother reminded me that I was *specially* sent to the lost, and that to none did this more emphatically apply then to Deacon Gewergis. I took the child, but perhaps not quite willingly. The father, during his short stay, showed so much of avarice and supreme selfishness, I could but rejoice, when he left me, that his home was twenty-five miles from us, in the mountains, and that winter snows would soon cut him off in a great measure from us.

"When he went away he wanted to take his daughter's clothes with him. Mr. Stoddard and Mr. Stocking were so indignant that they advised me not to keep the girl. I replied, 'I should like to shame that man.' 'Well,' they said, 'you *may* if you can; we should like to have you.' Perhaps it was all my *will*, but I thought I could not, and would not, do as he desired. I went to the room where he was. He said to me, 'I want to leave my girl here, and I want you should teach her.' 'Oh, yes, I will; she may stay.' 'I want you should teach her just as well as you can; make her a good teacher, so that she can earn money.' 'Yes, I will do as well as I can by her; is that all you want?' 'I should like to take the clothes she has on.' 'Why, Deacon Gewergis, are you her father? Is she your child? I never heard of such a thing. Take her clothes! Yes, you may if you wish to, but I haven't any clothes for her.' He was ashamed, and, holding up his tunic with both hands before his face, said, 'I think I'll go.'

"How little I thought then, that his next visit would bring him over those deep snows, to have his heart melt at the foot of the cross. I did not see him again till February. Then he appeared in his Koordish dress, with his belt of ammunition, his dagger at his side, and his gun thrown over his shoulder. He came in, on a Saturday, among my dear children, many of whom were weeping over sin. I felt that the wolf had truly come into my fold. I tried to guard the dear children, and God took care of the deacon in his own time and way. He ridiculed the girls in their anxiety for their souls. But they felt too much that they were lost, to be much affected by what he said. The daughter, with deep feeling, at length asked him to go alone with her to pray. He laughed at her, but said, 'Do you not think I, too, can pray?' They went by themselves. The father repeated his form in ancient Syriac; the child bowed down, pleaded for her own soul, and then for her perishing father. As he heard her say, 'Save my father, going down to destruction,' he raised his hand to strike her, and he used to say afterwards, 'God alone kept me from it.' They left the place of prayer, and he was not led to it again that day, even by his pleading daughter. Deacon Mured Khan, who was a teacher in the school, and was just beginning to love the Saviour, took Gewergis to his own room, and there reasoned with him till late Saturday night. The Sabbath found him not only despising, but doing all he could to prevent others from coming to Christ. Sabbath noon Deacon Mured Khan came to me and pleaded with me to go and talk with Deacon Gewergis. I wanted Mr. Stocking to go, but he said, 'You had better go now; I will see him afterward.' So I went to the room where he was. He was sitting in the only chair in the room. He did not rise when I went in, or even offer me a seat; so I stood by his side, and told him I had come to talk with him about his soul. He laughed at me and said, 'I am safe,' and laughed yet again. I tried various ways to reach him, but all in vain. He opposed every doctrine of the gospel for more than an hour. I was about turning from him, when I seemed to have a new view of the worth of his soul. I turned to him, took his hand, and said, 'Deacon Gewergis, I see you do not wish me to speak with you of your soul. I promise you that I will never do so again, if you do not wish me to; but I want you to make me one promise: when we stand at the bar of God, and you are found on the *left hand*, as you certainly will be, if you go on in your present course, promise me that you will tell the assembled universe, that on this twenty-second day of February, 1846, you were told your danger. I leave you, to pray for you.' I could say no more; my heart was too full. I turned and was about leaving him, when he burst into tears, and said, 'My sister, I need this salvation. I will go and pray for myself.'

"The hand was withdrawn, and Deacon Gewergis passed into the nearest room. I could hear a low voice, but I could not believe that it was prayer. The bell rang for chapel service. I sent my dear children alone, and I stayed to watch the praying man. I thought he would probably remain for a time, and then steal whatever he could lay his hands on, and depart. I had no faith; so there I stayed and watched, till I seemed to hear a voice saying, 'What doest thou here, Elijah?' I was ashamed of myself, and went and found my place in the solemn assembly, where brother Stoddard was preaching. I had been there but a few minutes when the door opened very gently. Deacon Gewergis entered; his gun and dagger were gone, his turban had fallen over his face, his hands were raised to his eyes, and I could see the big tear-drops falling. He stumbled into the nearest seat, and laid his head upon the desk. At the close of the service I asked Mr. Stocking if he could see Deacon Gewergis, for, I said, 'I cannot see him again now.' This good brother was all ready for his work. He took him to his study, and then and there the deacon cried out in bitterness of soul, 'My sins, my sins, they are higher than Jelu mountains!' Mr. Stocking said to him, 'Yes, but if the fires of hell could be put out, you would not be troubled, would you?' Then the strong mountaineer was bowed to the floor, and exclaimed, 'Sir, I could not carry this load of sin if there were *no* hell.' This brother pointed him to Christ, and he was left alone till the morning. Then brother Stoddard came to see him at my request. I shall never forget how this dear brother came to me, after a short interview, saying, 'Deacon Gewergis's soul is so full of the love of Christ, "My great sins, and my great Saviour!" is all he can say.' I said to Mr. Stoddard, 'You will not be deceived by this man.' He looked mildly upon me, saying, 'My sister, be not faithless, but believing.' I asked Mr. Stoddard if he was willing to take the deacon home with him and take care of him. He replied, 'I shall be but too glad to do it.' But, before noon, the man had left for his mountain home, for he said, 'I must tell my friends and neighbors of sin and of Christ.' We heard nothing of him for two weeks, when one of our helpers was sent to find him. He found him in his own house, surrounded by his friends, telling them 'of sin and of Christ.' The helper spent the Sabbath with him, and Monday they came to Oroomiah. The deacon soon found his way to my room. As he opened the door, I was on the opposite side of the room, and saw him at once. With tears in his eyes, and hand extended, he approached, saying, 'I know you did not believe me, but you will love me, — will you not?' Yes, I loved him, and wondered at my own want of faith. The deacon always remembered the school as the birthplace of his soul, and ever delighted to pray for us. Once when he had been praying in Mr. Stoddard's school, at evening devotions, as he rose from his knees, he exclaimed, 'O God, forgive me, I forgot to pray for Miss Fiske's school!' So he knelt again and prayed for us, and Mr. Stoddard said he did not believe there was a smile on a single countenance.

"The June after his hopeful conversion, I went with Mr. Stocking's family to his home in Tergawar. This was the first time ladies had been into the mountains. The good deacon was greatly delighted with this visit; and we then commenced labors for females there, which we have loved to continue to the present time. One day we went upon the top of a high mountain; the road was rough and difficult of ascent, but the deacon, as much at home on those steeps as the wild goat, could not only take care of himself, but of others. As he offered to help us, we said, 'We get on very well.' As he heard this, I saw his eyes filled with tears, and he said, 'You helped me in a worse way, — may I not help you?' We were made willing to be helped.

"The deacon gave himself, from the time of his conversion, to labor for souls. He loved especially to labor in the mountains. There was always a tear and a smile on his countenance, and he was ever ready, as at first, to speak 'of sin and of Christ.' He went through the mountain districts many times, with his Testament and hymn-book in the knapsack thrown over his shoulders. As he entered the passes among the rocks, he was sure to be found singing, 'Rock of ages, cleft for me;' and when he sat down by the fountain's side, he was ever ready to burst forth in saying, 'There is a fountain filled with blood.' He warned all whom he met, and pointed them to Christ. After years of labor, he was called to his rest, dying of brain fever, March 12, 1856. As his mind wandered in that last sickness, he seemed to dwell much on those days that he spent with us in 1846, when he first understood the way to Christ. He would say, 'Oh, Miss Fiske was right when she pointed out that way,' and then he would shout, 'Free grace! free grace!' till he would sink away unconscious; then, when roused, he would say, 'That blessed Mr. Stocking! Oh, it was free grace, free grace!' Those were almost his last words. The dear child who prayed with him, when his soul was first awakened to its lost state, was by his dying-bed, to catch from his lips those blessed words, 'Free grace! free grace!' and her voice in prayer was the last earthly sound that fell upon his ear."

The walking-stick of this good deacon, which had so often supported him as he journeyed over the wild mountains, preaching the gospel, was brought to this country by Dr. Perkins, and deposited at the Missionary House in Boston.

CHAPTER XI.

JUNE, 1846, TO JUNE, 1847.

Visit to Tergawar. — Cholera. — A Revival. — Copies of the New Testament in Syriac, given to the Pupils. — Presents Inexpedient.

In August, 1846, Miss Fiske visited the district of Tergawar, of which she gives the following account: —

"Since I last wrote you I have spent several days in Tergawar, a mountainous region on our borders. The place is elevated, and delightfully cool, and abounds in most charming scenery. It is just such a spot as one loves to flee to, after being long confined amidst the noise and dust of such a city as ours. I was so worn out with my school duties that, for several days previous to going, I was able to do but little, or, perhaps I might say, nothing. A change of air and place I found most invigorating and delightful. We had long wished to visit this district, on account of some religious interest, which had for months existed there. We were gratified to find some apparently heaven-born souls amid these wild mountains. In one village, as we were resting in our tent at night, we could often hear the voice of prayer on every side of us. How did we magnify the Lord that he had himself thus worked there! No member of the mission had visited the place for nearly three years. I found one or two sisters anxiously inquiring for the way to heaven. During our stay in Tergawar we passed over into Koordistan, and ascended some of the snow-capped mountains. The views of different districts in Koordistan are very fine."

She writes, September 16th: "I visited Geog Tapa little more than a week since, and spent three days there. I was deeply interested in the appearance of the village. It is believed that there are now but few persons in Geog Tapa who do not pray in secret. We do not consider 'Behold, he prayeth,' a certain sign of conversion, but we are rejoiced to know that public prayers in a dead language are giving place to prayers in the closet. In the threshing-floors many little closets are made by sheaves of grain, one sheaf answering for the door. Will not God avenge his own elect here? I do believe he will."

Miss Fiske was very grateful, on resuming her school duties, September 28th, to find that her vacation excursions had quite restored her to her usual health and vigor. In reply to anxieties expressed by a sister, in regard to her health, she writes, October 13th: "I keep nothing back. I solemnly promised our dear mother, just before leaving, that I would ever be frank; and so I will be. Judging from my own feelings, I shall thus save you from a great trial. There is nothing I so much dread as to feel that I do not know the worst. In regard to my lungs being seriously affected, I do not think they are. Some of the time this summer I was entirely free from any difficulty in this respect, and I now very seldom experience any inconvenience. You know that from a child

I suffered often, and seriously, from colds. That I still should thus suffer is not strange. Yet I believe that I suffer less than I should if teaching in America; that is, I think I am able to do more here than I should be able to do there. This is a great comfort to me when I feel the outer man decaying."

The school had been in session only about five weeks when it was interrupted, and the pupils scattered by the appearance of the cholera in Oroomiah. For months this scourge had been advancing in that direction; but it was hoped that, owing to the lateness of the season, its progress would be arrested before reaching the city. At length, however, about the first of November its presence was unmistakably announced. The missionaries, with their families, immediately removed to Seir, and were all mercifully spared. For five weeks the ravages of this terrible disease continued, and in that time it was ascertained that more than two thousand three hundred died in the city of Oroomiah, or nearly one-tenth of the entire population. Early in December the missionaries deemed it prudent to return to the city; but Miss Fiske's school was not reassembled till near the close of the month. In the mean time she was much occupied in ministering to the poor Nestorians of the mountains, who had been driven from their homes by the bloody Koords, and had fled, almost starved and naked, to the city.

The pupils, as well as teachers, having escaped the pestilence which had so suddenly swept thousands around them into the grave, came together with hearts overflowing with gratitude, and were soon visited again by the same gracious Spirit, whose converting power was so wonderfully displayed among them the previous year. The school now numbered forty-one, of whom twenty were hopefully pious, and this number was soon to be increased. January 13th, Miss Fiske wrote: "You will be rejoiced to know that the Lord is again visiting my tender charge in mercy. There had been one case of seriousness in the school previous to the new year; but it was not one of such deep feeling as we desired to see. We hoped and prayed, and yet our Father's face was hidden from us. Such a cloud of darkness sometimes rested on me that I felt I could not be the Lord's, and I feared also that all my girls who were hoping were deceiving themselves. But, rejoice with me, 'He that was lost is found.' Yes, I trust I can now say, 'Jesus is mine, and I am his.' He has also visited the Christians in school, and brought them very near to himself. Nor is this all. The cry of the impenitent for mercy is again heard in the midst of us. The Spirit of God is here convincing of sin, of righteousness, and of judgment. The Tuesday following the first Monday in the year (which was a most interesting day), the girl, mentioned above, became more deeply serious. She attended to her regular duties during the day, and was in at evening prayers. I saw that she was much affected, and after prayers I had a little conversation with her. Finding her much exhausted, I pointed her to the sinner's Friend, and advised her to retire for the night. I had been gone from her but a few moments when she became insensible. We used the most powerful restoratives, but she lay thirteen hours before showing any signs of arousing. When she came to herself she had no peace. The same angry God, she felt, was frowning upon her. She continued thus about a week before she was willing to come to Christ. I watched over her with deepest anxiety, fearing lest she might go back to the world. Her contest was long and severe with sin and the devil. Her physical powers seemed to sink under it. But she has at length, as we hope, fled to Christ. There were no other cases of deep interest in the school till a little more than a week since, when the Spirit came in a wonderful manner to some souls. I have never seen persons so bowed and humbled. Four, I hope, have submitted to the Saviour, and five others seem not far from the kingdom of God. I should like to write you more fully; but the careless soul, the awakened sinner, and the trembling Christian call for all my strength to-day."

A few weeks later she writes: "A precious addition has been made to the number of our praying ones. There is now but one in school, except quite small girls, for whom we have not hope. Several of our scholars are married, or soon will be; of such, those whom we have considered Christians are bright gems where they are set. Their sweet submission in the family circle, and their faithful performance of every duty, excite the interest and admiration of their neighbors and friends. It is as difficult here, as it is with you at Mt. Holyoke, to keep those qualified for teachers any length of time. Some of the older girls are beginning to help me a good deal, but busy ones are already marking out domestic circles for them. It has been trying to me to think that I could not raise up teachers here; and I do not wholly despair of doing so yet; but I am convinced that it will be some time before any one will be allowed to remain unmarried till twenty years of age. I am, however, comforted in the thought that those who would make good teachers will also make good wives and mothers."

April 7th, she wrote to her mother: "Four years ago this afternoon I first set foot on Eastern shores, and, as the anniversary of that day returns, my thoughts are much on the land which I felt, then, more than during the voyage, that I had left forever behind. Yes! sweet home of my birth, of my early privileges, of my fathers' sepulchres, and a thousand tender associations, I have probably taken my leave of thee forever! but not in sadness, I can truly say, if I may only be useful in this dark land. I remember, mother, that you once asked me, just before I left you, if I should feel it my duty to go if I knew that I should not live more than six years. My reply was, 'I do not expect to live more than six years in a foreign land, and perhaps, not half that time, but I still feel that I *must go.*' I often wonder, when I look back on the past, how it was that I felt no more doubt in regard to my duty. Was it a heavenly voice that said to me, 'This is the way, walk ye in it'? Oh that I could feel assured that it was; and more, that I could be *entirely devoted* to my Master's work! To be Christ's is all that is worth living for; and, if we be indeed his, how brief will be our separation from our dear Christian friends! Perhaps our kind Father will allow us to awake, at the same time, in light. Perhaps I may never hear of your death nor you of mine, because in death not divided."

Seventeen years afterwards the mother *saw* the

daughter die, and a few months later, the daughter welcomed the mother into the "light."

While the revival in Miss Fiske's school was in progress, she heard of a revival in the Mt. Holyoke Seminary. The cheering intelligence deeply affected her pupils. "I have not seen," she writes, "so many tender feelings called forth for a long time. It was just before their weekly prayer-meeting on Sabbath evening, at which I am not present, it being also the hour of the mission prayer-meeting. When our meeting closed I went down, supposing that they had dispersed; but, no! they were still praying and praising God with an affecting earnestness. I felt it not best to interfere, but allowed them to continue more than two hours from the time they began, and then they were unwilling to leave the sacred spot. They often speak of their own conversion as being in answer to prayer in your seminary. Born as they were in a revival, they feel peculiar interest in such seasons."

After a continuous term of eighteen weeks, the school was dismissed, May 4th, for a brief vacation. The closing scene was invested with touching interest, by the presentation of copies of the New Testament to several of the girls. The occasion is thus described by Miss Fiske: "We have been able this spring, for the first time, to give the Nestorians copies of the New Testament entire in their spoken language. But it was not thought best to distribute them gratuitously at first, but to lead as many as possible to pay for them. Teachers, and others have paid a dollar for the book, which is somewhat less than its cost. But as our pupils could not for a long time command so large a sum, it was thought best to resort to some other expedient for placing the Holy Book in their hands, and still not give it to them entirely free. A catechism had been recently prepared by Dr. Wright, in which the answers were given in texts of Scripture. These texts, some ten or twelve hundred in number, were from all parts of both the Old and the New Testament. The pupils were told that all who would learn and correctly recite this catechism should receive a New Testament, provided they did it entirely in recreation hours. It was delightful to see the interest with which both boys and girls set about the work. Some completed it in about three weeks; and all the elder girls, with two or three exceptions, before vacation. These two or three were not willing to go to their friends till they had finished the task. About twenty girls in all received the book, and went to their homes saying, 'Precious treasure, thou art mine.' Parents, overjoyed with the gift, as well as with the diligence of their children, threw their arms around their necks, and gave vent to tears. The girls have had interesting times with their friends, reading to them, and communicating religious instruction."

The presentation of books, like that just mentioned, was the only kind of presents, or rewards, which Miss Fiske deemed it wise to make. Articles sent her by friends for this purpose were otherwise used. She says, "Very few presents are used by us for the women; I use *none*. I heartily disapprove of the practice in the present state of the mission. Of course you will not understand me as speaking of other missions, nor of other days here. I only mean to say that I do not think they are now called for here."

CHAPTER XII.

JUNE, 1847, TO SEPTEMBER, 1848.

Cholera. — Visit to Marsheboo. — "Settling it." — Arrival of Miss Rice. — Journey to Erzroom. — Departure of Mr. and Mrs. Stoddard. — Death of Mrs. Stoddard. — Persecutions of Mar. Shimon. — Death of the King.

THE early part of the summer vacation of 1847 was spent by Miss Fiske in frequent excursions to the neighboring villages. She visited many of her pupils at their homes, and was delighted to witness their Christian activity. July 12th, she writes: —

"Yesterday, which was the Sabbath, I spent at Geog Tapa. After the afternoon service I attended a farewell prayer-meeting in the church. This meeting has been established by the girls since vacation commenced, and is now attended by some sixty or seventy. I rejoice in the disposition of the girls to engage in such kind of labors; but, when I remember that they who are to sustain such a meeting are girls only thirteen or fourteen years of age, I tremble lest in some things they should be indiscreet. Oh, may the Lord's honor be perfected in their weakness!"

The cholera reappeared this season in Oroomiah. Of its ravages Miss Fiske thus writes: —

"It is impossible to give you any correct idea of the heart-rending scenes which have been witnessed in our ill-fated city. When we saw the storm approaching we fled to the mountains, so that our eyes have not seen, only our ears have heard, what the Lord has done.' We cannot, at present, correctly estimate the number who have been cut down; but we suppose that one-fourth of the inhabitants of the city may have fallen. Some days since, we heard from the sellers of cloths in the market, that during two weeks they sold four thousand shrouds! The whole population of the city is about twenty-five thousand. During those days almost all business was suspended in the bazaars except shroud-selling. The cry of the mourning women, and of the mourning men also, has gone up continuously all over the city. One night the whole population were out crying for mercy. The work of desolation in the villages, although dreadful, has been less in proportion.

The cholera having disappeared, Miss Fiske reassembled her school about the first of October. Early in November, Mr. Stocking invited her to accompany him to Marsheboo, a place about fifty miles distant in the mountains beyond Tergawar, and in Turkey. Her first thought was that she could not leave her school.

"Your school is not your all," said the good brother. "There are souls perishing in those mountains, for whom you have only prayed, and I want you to go and labor for them."

Three of her eldest girls, readily consenting to take care of the school in her absence, and promising to pray for her, in less than two hours she had mounted her horse, and was on her way.

"No lady," she says, "had ever been there before, and, on account of the difficulties of the roads it had been thought that no one ever could go. But one of my pupils (a daughter of Mar. Shimon's brother) having married and settled there, I felt a strong inclination to try to surmount the difficulties, and to go and tell my sisters there the story of redeeming love. We started Friday, P. M., and by hard riding reached Tergawar just after sunset, where, in the village of Mawana, we spent the night. Our host found it convenient to bring into his one room, with his family (consisting of fifteen or twenty souls), hens, sheep, calves, etc., etc. I can hardly tell you what was, and what was not, in that room: cellar, store-room, pantry, chambers, and stable were all combined in one. You would have been amused to see the motley gathering there that evening. But it had an interest to us, for we could there preach Christ to never-dying souls.

"About ten o'clock, the mother of the family rose, saying, 'Now we will settle it.' I listened to hear the settlement of some family quarrel; but to my surprise her meaning was, 'we will settle where to lie down for the night,' and, as I looked over the room, I thought, surely, some little skill in 'settling' is needed, if we are all to sleep here. But soon she took out three of the children to an empty manger, where she put new hay and quickly 'settled' them; they were covered with an old rug, and at once fell fast asleep. She then returned, saying, 'Now there is room for our guests,' and brought a piece of cotton cloth, which she said was *all* for me. In a short time, one and another were fast asleep. They lay on mats with neither bed nor pillow; and the divers breathing and snoring of men, and calves, and lambs, were soon heard, all mingled together.

"I tried to sleep in vain; my eyelids would not stay closed. The morning came at length, and I was glad to be in my saddle again, for it was infinitely softer than my bed of earth. It is impossible for me to describe the ride of Saturday. The road was more difficult than any I had seen; and it is said that the lady who can reach Marsheboo can go on into the heart of Koordistan. We reached M. after noon, and not only had a kind reception, but were comfortably provided for by my old pupil. I had an interesting season there, and free intercourse with the women, and was permitted to tell some of them for the first time of Jesus' love. I was more than repaid for all my toils in reaching there. We remained till Monday morning, when we left for the city, where we arrived a little before sunset. Can you not believe that I am very well, to be able to ride fifty miles in a day over such a road?"

November 20th, Miss Fiske's heart was gladdened by the arrival of Miss Mary Susan Rice, who was to be henceforth associated with her in the care and instruction of the school, and in her general missionary work among the Nestorians. Writing to her mother, four days after the arrival of Miss Rice, she says:—

"I am much pleased with my new companion. I love her more and more every hour. I feel that she is just the one to come here. The girls are delighted with their new teacher, and well they may be. I do believe she is one of Heaven's choicest spirits. When she told me about her visit to you I could not control my feelings. I laid my head on her shoulder and wept aloud. Oh, it is such a comfort to me to think that she has seen you! I have not forgotten to love you. My heart is as warm as ever, and nothing has brought you more freshly to my mind than seeing this dear sister. I am very thankful that she was able to see you."

Miss Fiske's first impressions of Miss Rice were abundantly confirmed by the experience of eleven years of harmonious and delightful missionary labor. She ever found in her a congenial companion, and a judicious and efficient fellow-worker; and, when compelled by impaired health to leave Persia, it was a great comfort to be able to entrust her school to one so competent to take charge of it, and so devoted to its interests.

One of the teachers, Dea. Mured Kahn, was now transferred to a girls' school established at Geog Tapa, three of Miss Fiske's older pupils supplying his place in the seminary by teaching half the time.

Miss Fiske's heart often turned fondly to her native hills, and to the loved ones there. December 17th, she writes: "I suppose you still live in the brick house among the hills. Has all remained unchanged since I left? I feel as much interest in changes as Uncle Pliny did, when he said, 'Tell me if the old black hen lives.' I suppose your neighbors are nearly the same as when I left; that the hills are as steep as ever, and that 'Ball Mountain' and 'Sluice Brook' have known no change. Oh, how pleasant it would be to look on them again!"

While laying in her winter stores, she writes:—

"You will, perhaps, smile when I tell you that I put up seventy-five bushels of grapes this year for my school. They are hung up in clusters, and dry, or wilt, a little, when they keep very well till spring.

They are much cheaper than apples in New England, and I am sure I like them quite as well."

Five years had now elapsed since she left her native land. Devoutly thankful for the past, she was more than ever hopeful in regard to the future. To her mother she thus writes: —

"OROOMIAH, March 21, 1848.

"MY DEAR MOTHER: — You have, doubtless, thought of me often during the last few days, and remembered that five years have passed since I bade you farewell. How much occasion have we both for gratitude to our heavenly Father for all his goodness to us during this period! When I left you, I know that all a mother's feelings filled your soul. You pictured to yourself many a scene of sorrow and of suffering for your departing child. But grace enabled you to commit me to the Lord, and oh, how has he fulfilled your fondest desire! How gently has he led me! How have mercies unnumbered strewed my path!

"I should love to tell you with what sweet delight I look back on all the Lord's dealings with me in past years. *It was all right.* Yes, I am sure that I feel so; and I would not change one thing that my Father has done. He knew and did what was best. I only ask, now, that I may never distrust him, but go cheerfully, yea, joyfully, forward, where his unseen hand leads. If we do but trust the Lord he will provide, and will strengthen us in every hour; as one has beautifully said, 'If he leads us in a thorny path, he will give us shoes of iron and of brass.'"

Miss Fiske's health having become somewhat impaired by the continuous labors of the winter and spring, it was thought best for her to accompany Mr. Stocking and family to Erzroom, for the purpose of escorting Mr. and Mrs. Cochran to Oroomiah. The unusually cold and wet weather rendered this horseback ride, of four hundred miles each way over the mountains, more fatiguing and unpleasant than was anticipated. Miss Fiske, however, enjoyed much in connection with it, especially the Christian intercourse with the missionaries at Erzroom; and it gave her great pleasure to welcome new laborers to the missionary field in Persia.

The next day after her return, Mr. and Mrs. Stoddard left Oroomiah for Erzroom, fearing that the state of his health might oblige them to go to Constantinople, and possibly to America. The touching record of that journey, and of the sudden death of Mrs. Stoddard at Trebizond, is found in the excellent memoir of Mr. Stoddard. It was a severe trial to Miss Fiske to part with this beloved brother and sister. They had been her companions in the 'Emma Isadora;' they had for five years been intimately connected with her in labors for the Christian education of Nestorian youth; they were moreover congenial spirits, and had in many ways greatly endeared themselves to her. Perhaps no one, save the stricken husband, felt the death of Mrs. Stoddard more keenly than she. "Precious sister! She died far away from us, where we could not give one sympathizing look or deed. Why must it be so? Why might I not stand by that dearest sister's dying-bed? My Father knows why, and I would fain bow in sweet submission to his will, though my heart bleed at every pore. . . My heart's desire and prayer is that this trying providence may lead me to be more faithful while life last. It comes very near to me, and to us all. From my first acquaintance with Mrs. Stoddard she has been all to me that mortal could be. Her heart was tenderly alive to the spiritual interests of those for whom she left her home and friends, and to them she gave all her energies. Few, very few, have been able, in so short a life, to accomplish so much as she accomplished. Her family, our missionary circle, the seminary, and all about us, shared in her untiring labors, and it may be said of her, as truly as of Mrs. Grant, 'She hath done what she could.' If my work were as well done as hers, and if I were as well prepared for my rest, how should I, too, love to go home!"

While the mission was thus deeply afflicted in the loss of two of its members, the hand of persecution was laid heavily upon it.

The patriarch, Mar. Shimon, after his return from Mosul, for a time professed to be friendly; but at length threw off the mask, and manifested the most bitter hostility against the missionaries and all who adhered to them. He even took an oath that he would exterminate the mission, root and branch, or lose his life in the attempt. He made common cause with the Jesuits, and secured the co-operation of the Mussulman officials; while many of the more wicked Nestorians, retaining much of their superstitious reverence for the patriarch, were ready to execute his malicious orders. He threatened with excommunication all who should continue to act as preachers or teachers, or to be in any way associated with the missionaries in their work. He broke up the schools in several of the villages, and caused some of the teachers to be severely beaten; sent men to the churches to interrupt the services, and anathematized Mar. Yohannan, Dea. Gewergis, and Dea. Tamo. "Our little school," says Miss Fiske, "does not escape the patriarch's curses, nor does your humble sister, 'who,' he says, 'is doing a great deal to lead the young from the good old ways.' 'Has Miss Fiske taught you this?' is his frequent inquiry, and then follows the command, 'Give no heed to her.'" He resorted to various artifices to allure her pupils from her. One day, in August, he sent a man for one of the girls, on the pretence that her brother was sick and at the point of death, charging him to be sure and keep his intentions from "that devil, Miss Fiske;" and, in case of failure in his first attempt, to seize her, and forcibly carry her away. The plan was providentially defeated, to the great joy of both teacher and pupil.

"*August* 28. — This has been such a day as we never saw before in Persia. Sometime before noon, the teacher of the school in Charbash came fleeing to us, wounded, having barely escaped with his life, from Mar. Shimon's servants. His crime is simply teaching a few children in his village the gospel. He had but just come in, when he was followed by his almost breathless brother, who said that he, too, had barely escaped with his life, and that they were attempting to tear down their house.

"The affair was committed to the Mussulman owner of the village, who took one or two of the men pris oners, when Mar. Shimon and his company fled to the city. They arrived here a little before noon, and we were just seated at our dinner when we were startled by the cry, 'A man is killed!' and by a rush from all parts of the yard. Mr. Stocking immediately went out and found a large company before our gate, and several forcing themselves in to seize those in our employ. Mar. Yohannan had received a heavy blow on his head, and all was confusion. Mr. Stocking, in attempting to put the rabble out, and to have the outer gate closed, was grossly insulted. It was some time before those of us within could ascertain the cause of the disturbance. I sat with my little flock around me, reminding them that we must not count our lives dear for Christ's sake. The turmoil was soon in a measure quelled; but we felt it of little use to apply to the Mussulman authorities here for help. Their sympathies are evidently with Mar. Shimon. They would gladly see us all out of the country, or falling beneath the bloody knife. Just at this moment a messenger has arrived from Tabreez, bringing an order from the prince, procured by Mr. Stevens, for the protection of those in the employ of the mission. It is timely, and we trust may do something for us. Still we do not feel that we are out of danger. We try to be prepared for life or death, as our Father sees best."

"*September* 6.—The enemies of the cross still triumph, and the followers of the lowly Jesus are insulted at every step. They can hardly pass along a street without being reviled, spit upon, or beaten. We have no arm of flesh to lean upon, and our Father doubtless sees that we could n t bear help from such a source, and so he is leading us into the deep waters, yes, *very deep*, before giving relief. We cannot believe that our God will suffer this vine of his own right-hand's planting to be uprooted. We believe that it will again flourish after it has been pruned as much as he sees to be necessary."

"9. — Letters were received a few days since by Mar. Shimon, from Tabreez, Yahya Kahn (the governor of this province who is now in Tabreez on business), telling him to go on in his course, and he would help him in everything. He further added that an order from the prince had been received for his arrest, but that he should make it all in vain. He also sent another letter to the Kahn left in charge of his affairs here, telling him to help Mar. Shimon till his return. To-day our opposers, strengthened by these letters, go about as roaring lions.

"This Yahya Kahn is a brother of the favorite wife of the King of Persia. He has great influence at the Persian court, and we probably have more evil to expect from him than from any other human being. He will return here soon, and will doubtless do much to annoy us.

"The pious natives around us seem to be driven more and more to the throne of grace, and to feel that the Lord alone is to be their helper."

"11. — Yesterday two sheriffs arrived from Tabreez with an order from the prince there, for the arrest of Mar. Shimon, requiring him either to repair immediately to Turkey (he is a Turkish subject), and to promise not to return, or to appear in Tabreez and answer for his conduct. The same order required the Nestorians who had assisted in his wickedness to appear in the prince's presence. This order was procured by Mr. Stevens.

"14. — As the authorities here felt that they could not resist the orders of the prince at Tabreez, those who had been summoned thither were preparing to leave with the sheriffs this morning, when news came of the death of the King of Persia. He had fallen in an hour; and now, until another is on the throne, all will be confusion. There can be no government without a king in this land. The prince, acting as governor at Tabreez, is heir to the throne, and will probably be placed upon it. . . The death of the king is the fall of Yahya Kahn, the man we so much dreaded. He will probably never return to Oroomiah. Last night we prayed our Father to help us meet that dreaded foe; and this morning we hear that his course is run. How easy for the Lord to cast down, as well as to raise up! To-day we have been praying that religious liberty may be the result of these changes."

"16. — The Lord has kept us another night, while wild disorder has reigned without. Wicked men have felt themselves let loose in their wickedness, and all kinds of crime have been committed. Five men were killed during the night near our premises. We heard the firing of guns all night. We hope that we may be kept in these days of tumult; but we are quite willing that our Father should do with us as he pleases. In his own way let him glorify himself by us."

The Koords, taking advantage of this state of anarchy, came down from the mountains, and plundered and burned many villages; the people, mostly Mahomedans, fleeing for their lives to Oroomiah, naked and starving, to receive sympathy and aid from the missionaries.

"But, thanks to our heavenly Father," wrote Miss Fiske, a month later, "those exciting days are past, and we hope that some degree of order may soon be restored to poor Persia. The young king has been crowned, and all is quiet at the capital.

"After the death of the king, Mar. Shimon retired into Turkey; but was soon driven back for a season by fear of the Koords. He did not, however, dare any longer openly to oppose the mission, or the native Christians."

CHAPTER XIII.

SEPTEMBER, 1848, TO JUNE, 1849.

Saturday Duties. — Monthly Concert. — First Collection. — John "studying Backsliding." — Revival. — Interest in Degala. — "Praying Sarah." — Conversion of the Malek of Geog Tapa. — The Tiary Girls. — Death of Miss Lyon.

It was in the midst of the exciting scenes which have just been described, that Miss Fiske reassembled her pupils to enter upon the labors of her sixth school year. At their own request, a few of the best scholars were allowed to study the English language, in order that they might have access to those treasures of religious and scientific knowledge which they could not find in their own tongue. The improvement of the girls in their studies was more satisfactory than ever before.

A few extracts from letters will sufficiently indicate the character of Miss Fiske's labors at this time: —

"*November* 4, *Saturday.* — Our girls always sew in the forenoon of this day, and the afternoon is given to preparations for the Sabbath. To-day has been a busy day, and my poor aching head asks rest. We have had meetings with the scholars this evening. I met with those who hope that they are Christians, and Miss Rice with those who have no hope. Several, who had hoped themselves to be the Lord's, were constrained to-night to take their places with the impenitent. They said that if they were Christians they needed a new repentance. May it be given to them."

"8.—I have had an interesting meeting with the impenitent, and the doubting ones, in school. There were falling tears among them. Oh, may they prove to have been tears of penitence!"

"23.—I tried yesterday to fill up every moment with some work of the hand or head. All my spare time I spent in writing. The effect of such constant employment has been a rather severe touch of neuralgia to-day. I find it impossible to work all the time. I wish I could, especially as I do not like to have the girls ever see me unemployed. But I sometimes feel so exhausted that I cannot bear even to take my knitting; and, as I have no strong inclination to sleep, I often take a little rest sitting quite still. This soon restores my weary nature to its usual vigor."

"*December* 2.—To-day we had a pleasant monthly concert. Our Syriac service was attended, at three P. M., in the school-room. Near the close of the meeting, and while we were singing the 'missionary hymn,' a contribution was taken; the first one we have had in the city. Our pupils and others have been very busy of late earning money for the Lord's treasury. The result of the collection was quite a little box full, mostly coppers,—more than seven dollars in all."

"19.—I have never been so well satisfied as at present, with the improvement of the girls in their studies, but we lack the one great thing,—the influences of the Holy Spirit."

"20.—John came into my room, this morning before light, filled with anxiety for immortal souls. He said he could not sleep when he thought of our state without the Holy Spirit; and added, 'When I am praying, I feel as if God would come among us.'"

And God did soon come among them in great power. The following weeks witnessed one of the most interesting and extensive revivals of religion which have occurred in connection with the Nestorian Mission.

March 27th, 1849, Miss Fiske wrote to the teachers at Mount Holyoke: "I never before witnessed such thrilling scenes as those through which we have passed the last winter. They have sometimes been almost too much for our mortal frames, and we have been ready to ask to be clothed upon with immortality, while the Lord passed before us. The first tokens of this visitation were seen in December, in John's feelings. For days his head was bowed down as a bulrush, and he was mourning over his backsliding. He dwelt on his wanderings so much, that, on being asked one day by one of the brethren, what he was doing, he replied, in his imperfect English. 'I am studying backsliding, and O sir, I love it very much!' His meaning was not that he loved backsliding, but that he loved to get back to his God. His own quickening was followed by earnest desires for the salvation of others; and all within his reach were earnestly besought to be up and preparing the way of the Lord.

"The first of January was a day of deep interest, both at the city and at Seir, though several days passed before the impenitent began to awake from their sinful slumbers. The hopefully pious seemed to be first called to a season of deep trial, in regard to themselves. Never can we forget the affecting scenes through which we have passed with those whom we had considered as humble Christians. An awful sense of the violation of their covenant obligations fell heavily on *all* of them. For many days some of them would do nothing but weep and pray. 'How unfaithful have I been to my Redeemer, and to immortal souls!' was their universal language. Those whom we had loved, as dear members of Christ's body, sat down with the newly awakened, to mourn over sin, and to give themselves anew to the bleeding Lamb.

"The surviving one of the two girls who were awakened on the first of January, three years ago, spent the day this year in an agony which beggars description. Having occasion to go to her room, I found her in her closet, pleading, with groans, for a Saviour's forgiveness and presence, while her Bible, which lay open at the fifty-first Psalm, was literally bedewed with tears. I could put my finger on no part of those large pages (for it was a large Bible) which had not been bathed in penitential tears. I left the dear child pleading in her closet, assured that, sooner or later, the Sun of Righteousness would dry her tears, and make her a vessel of mercy to many others. Nor has that expectation been disappointed. Having first 'wept bitterly' herself, she has been eminently fitted to lead other weeping souls to the only fountain of consolation. She continues laboring with unabated zeal, both in and out of the school.

"We watch these praying lambs with tender interest. I hope to see many of them bright seraphs above. Our house is now one where they literally 'pray without ceasing.' Our seasons of social prayer with these dear girls are intensely interesting. We often feel that it is sweeter to pray in a *strange* than in our own tongue.

"I should love to give you many *particulars* of the interest in our school, but my time is so limited that I must not dwell too long upon this part of the work."

In an official account of this revival, Dr. Wright says: "The night of January 29th is marked as an era in the history of the revival in the female seminary. Up to this time two or three only of the impenitent had shown any signs of alarm. Most of them had listened to the most pungent exhortations, and the most rousing warnings unmoved. Indeed, they seemed so light and trifling, and to care so little for their immortal souls, that their teachers were almost heart-broken in view of their state. The evening meeting of the above date passed without any incident worthy of note. The bell was rung for the girls to retire for the night, at the usual time; but the signal was not heeded. One of the pious girls came to Miss Fiske, and said that many souls were distressed on account of sin, and that it was the time to pray, and not to sleep. The Holy Spirit had come like a mighty, rushing wind. Most of the school had assembled in one room; and there the pious girls were pouring out their souls in importunate prayer, and the impenitent, with scarcely an exception, were borne down under a sense of their sins, and were crying for mercy. Those of us who witnessed the scene can never forget it. It reminded us of a wreck tossed upon the wide ocean where the unhappy crew were pleading for their lives. One prayer commenced, 'O Lord, throw us a rope, for we are on a single plank, upon the open sea, and wave after wave is dashing over us.' Eternal realities rose up before our minds with awful vividness. Jesus and his salvation were the absorbing theme. Prayer was continued till past midnight, when the girls were advised to seek rest."

The interest extended to many outside of the two seminaries. Miss Fiske thus continues her narrative: "You already know that Miss Rice and I are far from feeling that our work is *confined* to our school. While we hope never to neglect this interesting department, we desire to labor for our sisters of every age, grade, and place, so far as our Father shall call us to it. The encouragement to labor for females *generally*, has been far greater this winter than ever before. We have not been obliged to go out after them, but they have thronged our houses, asking for the bread of life. There have been but few days since the middle of January, in which we have not been visited by many sincerely inquiring souls. Our room has been consecrated by the prayers and tears of those very sisters for whom you have so often prayed. Yes, dear sisters, your prayers have been answered, and you would have wept tears of grateful joy, could your eyes have seen what we have this winter seen,—scores of poor women leaving their daily duties, and coming and sitting down day after day in tearful silence, to learn the way to heaven. They have always eaten and slept in our large room (for we had no other place for them), and thus have been almost constantly where one of us could see them. From our little bedroom near by, we have often listened almost the entire night to their prayers. I need not tell you that it has been very pleasant to part with sleep, even night after night, while poor degraded women were lifting their voices to the Eternal throne.

"The first interest among females outside of our school commenced with the wives of our two teachers, Seiad and Yonan. They, in common with all the brethren who have received *a second baptism* of the Spirit this winter, from their first renewed interest, felt an untold anxiety for their families who reside in Geog Tapa. By their first visits home, after the revival commenced, their wives were brought into a state of thoughtfulness; and they soon found their way to our school and begged that they might stay a few days, for their souls' benefit. I need hardly tell you, that with joy we gave them a place in our room, our labors, and our prayers. Seiad has been in our school for many years, and his wife has, consequently, been a very frequent visitor on our premises. She had always been an opposer of religion in its purity, and I almost dreaded to see her face among our little flock. But oh, how different was it now! Day by day her interest increased, till her view of her sins almost overpowered her fearful soul. Tears were her meat and drink, and prayer her constant employment, for several days. But at length, to use her own expression, 'the Saviour found her,' and then she had peace. When her feelings became quite strong, she asked to see her husband, whose counsels she had ever slighted, and begged him to pray with her. He did so; nor was she backward to mingle her petitions with his. This father and mother have been blessed in their children, so that all three of them, together with a son-in-law, are now numbered with the *praying ones.* It was deeply affecting to us to find this little family in one of our rooms a few days since, each in his or her turn pleading for Heaven's mercies. Happy family! may their God ever be the Lord!

"Yonan, our younger teacher, was married two years since, entirely contrary to his own choice, by his wicked father. His trial was great in this, but grace triumphed, and his great desire has seemed to be, to see her who was thus forced upon him a true Christian. Often at the hour of midnight have we heard him with strong cryings pleading for her at the mercy-seat. That praying breath has not been spent in vain. She apparently submitted to the lowly Jesus in the early part of the revival. Never shall I forget those melting accents which fell upon my ear, when she, for the first time, prayed with her husband. I was in an adjoining room (unknown to them), and could but turn away myself to weep, as their weeping voices in unison sent their requests to Heaven. This dear sister is now most humbly active for others in her village. Because her father-in-law would give her no place in his house for social prayer, she has for some time met several young women, at the hour of sunset, behind the church, for this purpose. The bleak winds of February and March have not chilled their burning hearts.

"John's old mother, over whom threescore and ten years have passed, has entered into the work with an interest, which might cause many a mother in our American Zion to blush. Her business has seemed to be to try to lead aged females to the cross; and to do this, she has taken them one by one, and, in her consecrated closet, besought them *now* to make Christ theirs.

"There has been a very interesting movement among the women of Degala, a village not far from the city, and which has ever been noted for its wickedness. Joseph, who is from this place, has very properly called it 'the Sodom of the Nestorians.' But we hope, even here, there are already righteous enough to save it from Sodom's doom. The first person from the village interested this year was a young man in our employ. He passed through a season of severe conflict before his proud soul could bow. But when it did bow he seemed particularly desirous to give his every power to Him who died for his ransom. About a month after his own attention was first arrested he came to us one day with great apparent emotion, and said, 'I have a petition to make,—WILL you receive it?' We supposed that some worldly difficulty might be besetting him, but said to him kindly, 'Tell us what it is.' He immediately burst into a flood of tears, hid his face in the skirts of his coat, and said, 'My village is lost, my family are going to destruction, and their blood is on my neck. Oh, *will* you let me go to-night and tell them their state, and ask their forgiveness for my soul-destroying example?' We had no heart to deny this young brother his request, and he left us sobbing aloud.

"Dea. Tamo soon visited the village, and was surprised to find several persons serious, and one woman agonizing for her soul's salvation. Her case was exciting the attention of all the village, for she had long been considered the worst person in the place, and so vile as hardly to find companions. Dea. Tamo, in telling us about her, said, 'Oh, I have never seen anybody like this woman, — in such distress and with such a view of sin.' The next day she came to our weekly meeting, and no sooner did I begin to converse with her than she threw herself into my lap, saying, 'Do tell me what I shall do, and where I shall go to get rid of my sins.' I pointed her to the Lamb of God; and for a moment she would seem to seize the dying sacrifice, and then again a view of her sins would bury her in a flood of grief. I asked her to pray with me; and oh! such a prayer I hardly ever heard from mortal lips. I wondered where she had thus learned to pray, for I believed that she had never heard ten prayers in all her life. But when I remembered that the Spirit, and not man, teaches to pray, I was satisfied. This poor woman, borne down with a sense of her sins, and derided by her friends on every side, had learned to pray where the Redeemer first found a resting-place on earth, even in the *lowly manger*. She could find no other place than where the 'horned oxen fed,' to pour out her soul in humble supplications. I found, on inquiring into her case, that she was awakened to a deep anxiety for herself almost as soon as she entered our house on a previous visit, when she was met at the door by one of our warm-hearted girls, who, though a stranger to her, gave her an almost convulsive grasp, saying, 'My sister, my sister, what are you doing? Oh, we are all lost and going right down to destruction. We *must* awake to-day.' These few words, prompted by a tender love for her soul, could not be forgotten. From that hour this sister has gone on seeking, and we believe has truly found, the Saviour. She suffers persecution on every side, but receives it with a meekness which is winning souls to Christ. She is not left alone; several other women are deeply interested, who hold daily meetings for prayer. Their desire for religious instruction is truly affecting. They all love to sit with Mary's spirit at the feet of Jesus' disciples, and drink in gospel truth. One of them, speaking with us, the other day, of her lost state, was asked if she was willing to forsake *all* her sins. She wept most intensely and said, 'Oh, what shall I do? I have one sin that it is very difficult for me to leave; I am afraid that I cannot do it.' She was asked what that sin was. Again she wept most bitterly and replied, "I *cannot live* without these words of God; my husband is not willing that I should go to hear them, and sometimes a little anger rises in my breast. Do tell me what I shall do with this sin.' How little those in Christian lands know of such trials! Many of these women from Degala, and several from other villages about us, often spend the Sabbath and Friday with us. They attend the morning preaching, and then all repair to our room, to be taught and prayed with till the time of the afternoon service. They bring their babes with them; but the little creatures are so quiet that I sometimes think that He, who suffered little ones to be laid in his arms in the days of his flesh, quiets them, that their mothers may learn what it is to be Christian mothers. Their bread, or rather their dinner, is laid upon a cloth upon the floor, and, that no time may be lost while they eat, one of the girls stands and addresses them on their eternal interests.

The scenes of these hours are often tenderly touching. The young disciple, whose lot it is to speak to them, does it with streaming eyes, and with the tenderness of one, before whose vision eternal realities are vividly set forth. The listeners, with sighs and sobs, attempt to eat, but frequently stop, feeling that they have no need of anything but the *bread of life*. After dinner, those of them whom the sisters of the mission cannot see, are committed to the girls, and each one conversed and prayed with alone. If there is time after this, we have a season of prayer together before going to the afternoon preaching. These days are very precious ones to us as well as to our pious girls, and, though we doubt not much of the seed sown falls by the wayside, still we have delightful evidence that some of it is bringing forth fruit to eternal life."

"*April* 3. — The last few days have been days of peculiar interest in our school. The prospect of a vacation, instead of diverting the attention, seemed to lead every praying soul to besiege the throne of grace with renewed earnestness. The voice of prayer 'without ceasing' has fallen upon our ears, except during the most silent watch of the night. Some, after leaving our evening meeting, have spent two uninterrupted hours in their closets, agonizing for themselves and their departing companions. Many of the older girls felt that they could not leave till they had prayed with each of the school alone. They have done this; and, if never permitted to return to this consecrated place, their remembrance of these last days must be pleasant to them through a long eternity. The little band separated this morning with many tears and most fervent parting prayers. The quiet of the scene led our thoughts forward to the sweet rest of heaven, in which we hope to participate with many of our loved charge. Not a loud voice, nor heavy footstep, nor harshly shutting door was heard in all our house. All was so sacredly quiet that we could but feel that we were having a parting blessing. Some of our pupils are too far from their homes to return, and others feel that in their weakness they cannot encounter the rude assaults of a wicked world; and so about one-third of our number remain. When those who left were ready to go, we all knelt together in prayer, and pledged a continual remembrance of each other at the throne of grace. We send forth these lambs with feelings of peculiar anxiety. Some of them go into families where every soul would gladly 'break the bruised reed and quench the smoking flax.' Others go to villages where there is not a praying soul. My heart is full as I think of them to-night. Oh, may Israel's God make a Bethel for them in the wilderness of sin into which they have gone forth! It is now ten o'clock, and still we hear the voice of prayer for the absent ones. I have juts come from a closet, which I intended to enter and to try to persuade the suppliant to leave for needed rest; but, as I listened to her fervent supplications, mingled with weeping, for each of her companions by name, I withdrew, though not without anxiety for the dear one, who is a great bodily sufferer, and who, we sometimes fear, has almost finished her earthly course. She spends so much time in prayer that it is but seldom that I can get an opportunity to pray with her. I do not think she has spent less than four hours in her closet any day for a long time. 'Prayer is the

Christian's vital breath;' and ought we not to allow her to enjoy it till she breathes the purer air of heaven?"

"8.—The last few days have been days of tender, anxious watching over the praying child mentioned above. The next day her disease assumed a very serious form, and, until to-day, we have considered her as standing on the borders of the grave. But her sick-room has seemed to us all the gate of heaven. The Saviour has put underneath her his everlasting arms, and the dark valley has been all light. She has longed to embrace the messenger who should carry her quite over the cold stream. Her sufferings have been intense, but have all been borne with sweetest patience, and resignation to the Saviour's will. Several times we thought she had drawn her last breath; but her Father saw fit to bring her back to pray for his Zion a little longer. She is so much more comfortable to-day that we think she may partially recover. She seems a little disappointed at the prospect of praying instead of praising, but sweetly says, 'Thy will be done.' As I have seen this child supported in the hour of trial, I have felt more than ever how blest is the praying soul when God calls for it. Our house was thronged yesterday (the Sabbath) with inquiring women. I was able to do but little for them, being confined to the sick child, but the girls who are here labored for, and prayed with, them."

"10.—Moressa has just returned from Degala, where she has been laboring for the last few days. Her report of the steadfastness of the praying women there is truly encouraging. They are beaten and turned out of their houses by their wicked, drunken husbands; but still they cling to Christ. Moressa had no rest while there, and has come home completely exhausted."

During this revival an incident occurred which illustrates the active, earnest, and practical character of the piety of the girls in the seminary. The malek, or mayor, of Geog Tapa, — a man of great influence among the people, — had a daughter in the school, whom he called to see just when the religious interest was at its height. Of this interview Miss Fiske wrote: "Awakened, but not converted, she tried to pray with him; then called in half a dozen of her praying companions. They began to pray, with the proud man sitting in his chair. He sat till his feelings so overcame him that he sank down on the floor. Now they felt that their prayers were being answered, and so they prayed the more earnestly. They had permission to occupy my room, and there I left them with the malek for nearly an hour. When I went in, I found him bowed down and the girls surrounding him, praying. He was weeping like a heart-broken child; and he was weeping over sin. Nor was it long before he felt that the blood of Jesus 'cleanses from all sin.'"

This man became a warm friend of the mission, an earnest worker in the Lord's vineyard, and, in 1863, went home to praise him for that prayer-meeting.

The effects of this revival were marked and widespread, changing the whole aspect of that deeply interesting missionary field. At the close of it, all the girls in the female seminary over twelve years of age were hopefully converted; and many of them were from that time bright and shining lights in that dark land.

In the midst of the revival, Miss Fiske was called to the trial of parting with three of her pupils, whom she would gladly have retained longer. They were from the mountain district of Tiary. Their parents were among the fugitives who escaped to the plain after the terrible massacre of 1843. They called at the seminary door one day to ask for charity. Instead of silver and gold, Miss Fiske offered them a home for their daughters. They, disappointed, at first declined the offer; but the girls were attracted by the kind words and manner of Miss Fiske, and were finally permitted to remain. Sarah, Nazee, and Helenah were taken in, washed and clothed. They made rapid improvement in manners and knowledge; and became a connecting link between the seminary and the evangelization of Koordistan. They all became Christians, and helped to kindle the light of the gospel in their distant mountain home. One of them was the "praying Sarah," as she was generally called, mentioned by Miss Fiske on page 221. The pages of her New Testament were often found wet with her tears; and, after she left, her teacher found upon the whitewashed wall of her closet, traces of tears which she had shed in her seasons of earnest prayer.

The parting scene was one of touching interest. Miss Fiske will best describe it.

"It was very trying to the girls to leave. Here were their home, their dear Christian friends, their loved closets, and all the means of grace. How could they leave them all? They had but three days with us, after it was decided that they must go, — days of sadness, tears, and prayers. Many times we asked the Lord to allow them to dwell with us; but he gave us no indication that such was his will.

"It would be difficult to give you a full impression of the parting scene. The whole school came to my room for a last prayer, and for a last look of their loved sisters. All was silence for a moment, when the dear girls came to me, and, in a weeping voice, said, 'Can we not go for a few minutes, and give a farewell to our closets?' Precious children! who can tell us how they prayed in their Bethels? Only our God knows, and he will never forget those last prayers. They returned, overcome with their feelings. A few words were said, and we bowed in prayer. We rose at the close of the prayer, but it was to kneel again, for it was proposed by one of the girls, that 'all who wished to pledge themselves to remember the Tiary sisters in every prayer, should join hands, commit the dear ones again to the Lord, and give to him their pledge.' About twenty soon formed a circle, joined hands, and, enclosing the departing ones within the circle, whispered the promise in the eternal ear, and committed the girls to Christ. There were several prayers, and then they left us. They could not speak as they passed out, except to say, 'The promise! the promise!' We do remember them in every prayer; and will not the Good Shepherd care for these lambs?"

And the Good Shepherd did keep them, although they lived in the midst of wolves. Years afterwards they were found by the native preachers, with the love of Christ still burning in their hearts, ready to welcome and assist them in their missionary labors.

A month later Miss Fiske received intelligence of the death of her revered teacher and friend, Miss Mary Lyon. To the letter which conveyed to her the sad tidings, she thus replies: —

"OROOMIAH, May 29, 1849.

"MY OWN DEAR R.: — Your kind but sad letter of March 5th reached me nearly two weeks since. Oh, how did it cause our hearts to bleed and our tears to flow! And is dear Miss Lyon really gone to join the holy throng about the throne? Blessed one! what a rich reward is she now enjoying in the presence of her adorable Redeemer! We know the change is her gain, still our Saviour will not forbid us to weep, when we remember what we, and thousands of others, have lost in this death. How kind it was in you to write me while her last sands were running! I shall always love you with a fresh love for this kindness. While you were standing around that dying-bed, I was in Geog Tapa, surrounded by scores of inquiring souls. How little I knew through what scenes you were passing! I remember distinctly, that, as the first rays of the sun, on Sunday the 4th, fell upon me, kneeling by a hay-stack, the dear seminary was brought very vividly to mind, and I earnestly sought that the Spirit's presence might be with you; but I do not remember that I asked that you might be supported in trials. You were highly privileged to be permitted to whisper one word of consolation, in that trying hour, to her who has comforted so many while crossing the dark stream. I have found it more difficult to be reconciled to my not being permitted to stand by that death-bed, than to any event that has occurred since I left America. When I parted with dear Miss Lyon six years ago, I did not expect ever to behold her again, till I should see her a glorified spirit; and such has been my feeling ever since. Still I find nature asking that one brief hour might have been mine with her, when she could only whisper 'Sweet Jesus,' and eternity was opening to her view. Her delirium must have been a severe trial to you all. But it was all right. We needed not her dying testimony; her rare life puts her inheritance among the saints beyond all doubt. If her wishes in regard to the seminary are not sealed with her dying words, they are with her living prayers. Will not God bless that dear institution, in answer to her prayers, if not in answer to ours who remain? I long to hear what provision is made for it. Were it not that the Lord Almighty is its Father and Protector, our weak faith might sink in this hour.

"I received a very affectionate and sympathizing note from dear Miss Lyon the last of March. She had Mrs. Stoddard's death particularly in mind in writing me. I replied to it in a few days, and enclosed with it a long account of the revival. I thought, as I sent it away, 'How Miss Lyon's loving, benevolent heart will rejoice in what God has been doing here!' She was not, however, to rejoice on earth with human weakness, but in the eternal city with heavenly capacities. I love to think that she may have been permitted to bear at least one message of love to her children in Persia. Mysterious as her death seems to us, we may be sure that she was not called away till needed on high; and that the great work of redemption will go on more rapidly with her in heaven, than it would with her on the earth."

Again she writes: "My poor pen cannot express my obligations to her; nor would I attempt to write my views of her worth; but most gladly would I sit down, and, with you, shed those tears which now almost blind my eyes as I think that she has passed forever away. . . . Oh, may the bright example of our now sainted Miss Lyon be ever before us, stimulating us to follow more closely that Saviour who is able to make his strength perfect in our weakness!"

CHAPTER XIV.

JUNE, 1849, TO JUNE, 1850.

Women of Degala. — Changes in the School Building. — Moressa praying at her Betrothal. — Arrival of new Missionaries. — Revival. — First public Examination of the School.

THE summer vacation of 1849 was mostly spent by Miss Fiske in the city, superintending certain necessary changes in the school building.

"We have been building," she writes, "a large and convenient school-room, a recitation-room, also a dining-room, besides rearranging the girls' rooms. This work has so completely occupied my time and thoughts that I have seemed to have time for little else. But it is now finished, thanks to our heavenly Father, and our only desire is that our house may be a Bethel in every part."

The work thus referred to prolonged the vacation beyond the usual period. While impatiently waiting for the reassembling of her pupils, Miss Fiske was cheered by such evidences of the silent growth of religious principles in their hearts as the following extracts record: —

"*Nov.* 3. — We to-day received a letter from Sarah, the daughter of Priest Abraham, one of our older pupils. Her father has recently removed to Ardishai, to labor there as an evangelist. This village is an exceedingly wicked place; and it was a great trial to Sarah's mother to leave her pleasant home in Geog Tapa, and be exposed to the trials of a missionary life. But the daughter rejoiced to take up her cross and go. With tears she pleaded with her mother to forsake all for Jesus' sake. The point was gained; and now she writes of her father's deeply interesting labors there, and says she is permitted, Sabbath after Sabbath, to gather a large number of women about her and tell them of the Lamb slain on Calvary. We rejoice that she can do what we cannot."

"5. — Moressa, one of our older pupils, was to-day betrothed. When the time came for placing the ring, which is the seal of the engagement, upon her finger, she was not to be found. The house was searched, and in its remotest closet her plaintive voice was heard pleading for the blessing of the Holy One on what she was about to do. The company who had assembled were long detained, but were deeply interested in thinking that a child of prayer was to be added to their family. It was a day, not of customary mirth, but of deep and holy feeling. May we not hope that she, and the youth of her choice, will indeed be blessed? Only those who have seen the rioting and folly common on such occasions can realize what were our feelings in view of such an engagement begun and ended with fervent prayer."

Miss Fiske and her associate were glad to welcome their pupils to their new quarters about the middle of November. A new year opened upon them without any unusual tokens of the Spirit's presence. But few days, however, had passed, when, on the very anniversary of the commencement of the revival of the previous year, in both seminaries there appeared simultaneously tokens of another gracious visitation. The work which thus began "without observation" was one of great power, and extended to many parts of the mission field. The following account of it was written by Miss Fiske during a short vacation in March: —

"As 1850 dawned upon us, we felt that our prospects for labor during the winter were favorable, yet we mourned the absence of the *special* influences of the Spirit. The first Monday of the year was observed by ourselves, and those connected with us, as a season of fasting and prayer. It was a day of interest, and of more than usual prayer; yet we saw not that agonizing wrestling which preceded the revival of last year. During the week which followed there was more than usual tenderness in the boys' seminary; and the same was also true among our girls. Two of the older ones, in particular, seemed to find no rest anywhere but in their closets. Only the deep tones of the bell would call them from their retirement to attend to their school duties. There was a solemn quiet pervading the whole school, which seemed like that which precedes the breaking up of the deepest fountains. Nothing, however, very special occurred till Sabbath evening, Jan. 13th.

"I was not able to attend the prayer-meeting of that evening, and was left quite alone while all the school were absent. I was apprised of their return by the gentle opening of my door; and immediately saw a little group, with silent and almost breathless haste, pass through my room to apartments beyond. I arose at once to follow the little company, but had scarcely reached the door when I heard some half-dozen voices going up to heaven in earnest supplication. I turned to the stairway which leads to the lower apartments, and there a sound as of many waters fell on my ear. I found that every closet had its occupant, while the poor little ones, left unwarmed and unlighted, were wandering about to light their lamps, or stirring the dying embers within their stoves. I stood silently for a few moments, asking, not what meant the sound of many voices in prayer, but what meant such a simultaneous rushing to the throne of grace. I soon learned that there had been nothing particularly exciting in the meeting, and I sat down with the sweet belief that we were about to be visited by the Heavenly Dove, and that, too, before we had asked. It was a late hour before these young disciples were ready to leave their pleading, and then they retired in perfect silence. The morning found our pupils at the same employment; and what was our joy, in hearing from Seir, to learn that at the same hour in which such a spirit of prayer seemed to pervade our little circle the preceding night, the Holy Spirit came in a far more powerful manner among the pupils there, and the hopefully pious spent the whole night in strong cryings and tears!

"In the girls' school, the week succeeding Jan. 13th was one of deep solemnity. Our older girls, most of whom had given more or less evidence of piety previously, spent every leisure hour, yes, and moment too, in prayer. Their domestic duties were performed most perfectly, and then they fled to their closets. Several of them spent no less than five hours of every twenty-four, of that week, in those secret retreats. When we sometimes besought them to leave praying for necessary sleep, they would reply, 'We *have been* asleep for weeks; doing nothing for God; ruining souls; and how can we sleep till we are forgiven?'

"Saturday afternoon the feelings of several were such that they begged, with tears, to be excused from school duties, that they might give themselves entirely to prayer for a blessing on the coming day. Never did we more gladly bid adieu to worldly cares, and welcome the approach of holy time, than when we saw that evening's sun decline. You will not be surprised to know that we had a blessed Sabbath after such a week of prayer. During the morning service, almost all the school were bathed in tears. Many a seat was vacant at the dinner-table, while prayer, mingled with sighs and groans, ascended from every place of retirement. We heard not a voice, on that day, from morning till night, in all our school apartments, except 'the voice to heaven sent.' When the supper-bell rang, all came, but with countenances which seemed to say, 'Our meat and drink are not here.' A number asked to be excused; but, in compliance with our request, all were finally seated. Never, no, never, can we forget the scene which followed! All those who had previously been interested, with several others, were pouring forth floods of tears in silent sorrow. The blessing was asked, and the steward began to serve, his own big teardrops fast mingling with the contents of the dish from which he served. Each plate was filled, but each remained untouched. Those who felt no interest themselves were awed by such a sight, and gazed in silent wonder, instead of eating. They were urged to partake of their meal. Sighs and sobs sent back an answer from many, while one, rising, seized my hand, and in an agonizing tone said, 'You would not ask *me* to eat if you knew my heart.' They were finally recommended to eat, that they might have strength to pray. Here a tender chord was touched, and each hand, guided as well as dimmed eyes could guide it, was employed on the errand. Would that I could describe to you their appearance as they withdrew from the table to expend their acquired strength in praying! Each watch of that night found these wrestlers in their chosen place, seeming to feel that by an hour's rest the blessing might be lost.

"Two months have passed since that precious day and night, and each day has given us increasing evidence that the prayers then offered were armed by a faith which moved a heavenly hand, full of blessings. We look upon no past season of revival with deeper interest than the present one. There has been less tendency to excitement than formerly, but, we believe, no less deep feeling. We saw no diminution of interest to the last day of our term, which occurred about a week since. The uniform and increasing spirit of prayer, which has prevailed during the entire two months, has surprised us all. Prayer was invariably the last sound of the evening, the watchword of the midnight hour, and the early call of the morning. In one instance, two individuals spent the whole night in supplication. I could distinctly hear their voices from my bedroom, and will you wonder that, *when* I slept, my visions were of the richest spiritual blessings? One little girl of nine years would pray two whole hours before retiring; and then she was willing to retire only with permission to rise and pray in the night, if she should wake. And she was *very sure* to wake. About three o'clock, every morning, that little one's earnest pleadings would rouse me from my slumbers.

"We met our pupils every day for an hour of social prayer, and the seasons were always those of melting tenderness. We often almost forgot, at such times, that we were tenants of mortality, as we heard these children pleading *within* the veil and close by the mercy-seat. In these meetings, our school, the parents, brothers, sisters, and friends of the girls, were remembered with overflowing hearts. The hour allotted for this purpose was always too short, and made us long for that better world, 'where congregations ne'er break up.' With the following and kindred expressions, our last prayer was almost always closed: 'If we have not been heard here, we will go to our closets; and oh, if not heard there, we will return here; and from here we will go again to our closets; and so we will continue to plead for salvation for these dear, dear ones, till we drop into our graves.'

"The scenes of these little meetings were varied, but always of thrilling interest. Sometimes a large portion of the little company, including the hopefully pious, would seem to be overwhelmed with a view of sin, as committed against a holy God; and, oh, such touching confessions of guilt, I never heard from mortal lips! They would seem to be thrice slain by the law, and then, as if a ray of hope darted across the mind, a weeping voice would entreat 'the Holy One to walk about among the hills of Judea, find Golgotha, and let them live.' But again, the sight of God's holy law, and their multiplied sins, would lead the same one in bitterness to cry out, 'But, oh, we are afraid that our sins have risen so high that they have covered Golgotha, that it is hidden from thy view, and, oh, then we are lost, forever lost!' During the same meeting, we would again hear one approaching the eternal God with this touching entreaty, 'Lift not the mercy-seat from off the holy ark to behold the law we have broken; but look into Jesus' grave and let us live.'

"At another time, with a deep sense of the guilt incurred by the neglect of gospel privileges, the one who led the petitions would say, 'We had almost said, blessed rich man in hell! He has not, like ourselves, to answer for the privileges of three revivals, the pleadings of the Spirit, and a host of Christian friends. Oh, when we look at ourselves, we can hardly refrain from saying, 'Blessed rich man, *burning* in hell!' Again, the Lamb slain on Calvary would seem to stand in our midst, and draw, if not all, many to himself.

"Little family prayer-meetings, as they were termed by the girls, were held almost daily in each room. These we seldom attended ourselves, but they were seasons which will ever be remembered by those who participated in them. Each room-mate was then especially and tenderly remembered. Having occasion, once, to enter one of these meetings, I found them pleading most fervently for one who had manifested but little feeling. Each petition seemed to rise higher, as a Saviour's groans and dying strife were urged before the eternal throne, till, at length, every countenance was turned upward, as if to behold the dying Lamb, and the one who was praying involuntarily stretched forth both hands, as if to seize and apply the dying sacrifice, saying, at the same time, 'Oh, come, Lord Jesus, and save our perishing sister.'

"The efforts of the older girls for the salvation of the younger ones, and for the scores of women who were constantly resorting to our dwellings, were of a deeply interesting character, and such as heaven could bless. The hour after supper and before the evening meeting was usually spent in going from room to room, and warning every one with tears. The entreaties, sighs, and prayers, which were heard at that hour in every corner of our apartments, were enough to melt the hardest heart, and to make the Christian rejoice that he was a stranger in a strange land for his Saviour's sake. Scarcely less affecting were those seasons when, in the seclusion of the closet, the hoary-headed, superstitious grandmother, the worldly-minded mother, and the thoughtless sister, were constrained to weep as their sins were set in order before them, and they were tenderly entreated to seize the passing hour to secure their salvation. Meetings were held, three days of the week, for the benefit of the women in our vicinity, which were usually attended by from twenty-five to forty. In these the girls always assisted us, leading in prayer, and addressing 'the beloved mothers,' as they termed all who were older than themselves, in fittest words and in the tenderest manner.

"The last days our dear girls spent together were their best ones, and seemed to bind them very closely to each other, and we hope to the dear Redeemer. Their separation was deeply affecting. When all were ready to go, a prayer-meeting was held in each room, which was prolonged, by these praying ones, till they were compelled to leave. Those who felt that they had no interest in Christ, clung to their praying sisters with tears and sobs, which seemed to say, 'We cannot part.' The interested part of the school went forth with apparently holy, chastened feeling, thanking the Lord for what he had done, as well as seeking grace and blessings for the future.

"This revival extended to several villages. In Geog Tapa a goodly number were hopefully converted; and those already Christians were, as John said in his imperfect English, 'very much firmed.' The girls were very abundant in labors of love during their vacation, holding frequent meetings, and pleading with their friends to seek the salvation of their souls. In some instances their anxiety for their parents led to scenes of touching interest. One had often, with tears, besought her mother to love the Saviour. At length the mother said to her, 'My daughter, why do you weep for me? I do not wish you to be blind. Have mercy on yourself. Why will you make yourself blind with weeping for me?' The child quickly replied, 'O mother, I would gladly be blind, and see no more with my bodily eyes, if you might be a Christian, and see the way to heaven!' The father of another, who was urging him to pray, said, 'I cannot, my child, but you may pray for me. She immediately knelt by his side, and with many tears entreated the Saviour to soften his heart. The hoary-headed man of more than threescore years was deeply moved. He, too, knelt, and a flood of tears gushed from eyes unused to weep. When, closing her prayer, the child arose, the father's strength was gone, and for more than half an hour he lay weeping under the stings of a guilty conscience."

The next term of school continued until the 6th of June, when it was dismissed for the summer. "Those last weeks," says Miss Fiske, "were happy weeks. The Saviour was with us, and our loved charge seemed to improve more than I had ever known them to in twice the time. They prayed more and studied better than usual. We were particularly interested in seeing their improvement in writing compositions. They would come from their closets to write not only some of the sweetest, but some of the best, things in the Syriac language. The Spirit of God taught them what we, for years, had labored in vain to teach them."

The close of the school this year was a memorable occasion, constituting a marked epoch in the history of the institution and of female education in Persia. At the close of this term, the first public examination of the school was held, the parents and friends of the pupils, and some of the leading Nestorians, being invited. Miss Fiske was deeply interested in preparing for it, and highly gratified with its results. This is her own account of it: "It was an occasion of deep interest to us, and to all who were present. The day was as fair a one as ever shone on the earth, and everything seemed to conspire to make it pleasant. About two hundred guests were with us, and listened with unabated interest to the exercises, till the sun went down. The pupils were examined in ancient and modern Syriac, Bible history, geography, and natural philosophy. They sang two pieces which they had practised for the occasion, and joined in several hymns, with the whole congregation. More than twenty of the girls had prepared compositions to be read; but the day was too short for all. The exercises commenced at nine o'clock in the morning, and continued till twelve, when we took a recess of an hour and a half, in which time we had a dinner in the yard. One hundred and seventy-five sat down at one long table (the others at shorter ones), at one end of which was the school, and next the mothers of the girls. The meal passed off pleasantly, and at two we all found our places again in the school-room, which we had enlarged for the occasion by removing a partition. The examination continued till six o'clock, when Mr. Perkins gave a most interesting address. After the address, diplomas were given to Sanum, Sarra, and Moressa, who, by their scholarship and good deportment, have richly earned them. These three girls will be in the school no more, unless as teachers.

"John's blind old father was led from Geog Tapa, nearly six miles, to be present. As he learned that the day was well-nigh spent, he said, 'I wish Joshua was here.' 'What do you wish of Joshua?' was the inquiry. 'I want to have the sun commanded to stand still for two or three hours; the day is too short.' As the crowd passed away several old men came, and, taking Miss Rice and myself by the hand, said with tears, 'Will you forgive us that we have not done more for your school?'

"We thanked the Lord for the Ebenezer, — the stone of help, — which we were permitted to rear June 6th, 1850."

CHAPTER XV.

JUNE, 1850, TO JULY, 1851.

Women learn to Read. — Dismal Night-ride. — Moressa's Marriage. — Exegesis. — Study of English. — Religious Interest. — Sickness of Miss Rice. — Sister's Death. — Mr. Stoddard's Return. — Examination.

One of the cheering results of the public examination in the seminary, described in the preceding chapter, was a strong desire awakened in scores of adult women to learn to read; and all who made the attempt persevered in their efforts till they were able to read their Bibles with facility. The pupils, also, seemed inspired by the occasion with new desires to be useful, and went to their homes resolved to do more than ever for the elevation of their own sex in Persia.

"One of them," writes Miss Fiske, "is teaching a school of eleven scholars; and as many as sixteen are Sabbath-school teachers. Some of them have regular meetings with the women, and others are employed in teaching mothers, brothers, and sisters to read. We feel that many of them are doing a good work, in which our hearts rejoice."

In August three missionaries — Rev. Mr. Marsh, of Mosul, Rev. Mr. Sandreczki, of Smyrna, and Rev. Mr. Bowen, of the London Church Missionary Society — spent a short time at Oroomiah. Miss Fiske did

16

much for the entertainment of these guests, and says, "Their visit was a rich treat." With other members of the mission she accompanied them on their departure as far as Gawar. The Sabbath was spent at Baradost, where, in the evening, hearing that a large company of Koords were meditating an attack on their party, they deemed it advisable to go forward four miles, and lodge in Turkey. That night-ride Miss Fiske thus describes:—

"After dark our camels were loaded, and we proceeded again in solemn procession. Oh, how I wish my pen could portray the scenes of that night! Think of the string of fourteen camels, sixteen horses, with their riders following, and a dozen men, a part of them armed, walking by our side. Then think of the night, dark as could well be; our guide misleading us; the road dreadfully rocky, and in some places almost impassable for loaded camels, the loads often falling from their backs, the animals still oftener falling, and ourselves stopping at every such occurrence, till, after six hours of weary plodding, we reached the end of the four miles, and pitched our tents to take a morning nap."

The school was reassembled the last of October, commencing the seventh year of its history.

"We long to see," writes Miss Fiske, "the Spirit again with us, by his special influences. Oh, pray for us, that we may not be left one year without a revival! We have the children of the mission in our school, and, in all, they number forty-four. This is a large family, and our hands are full, but not too full. I never had better health than now.

"Moressa, one of our oldest girls, was married a

few weeks since, but is now with us as a teacher. I was not present at the time of her marriage; but when, an hour after, I lifted up the veil of the young bride, I found her reading from her little hymn-book some of Zion's sweetest songs. It was pleasant to see this, so different from the mirth and thoughtlessness usually prevalent on such occasions. . . .

"I have now a class of our older girls reading Isaiah. I wish I could convey to you some of the lively impressions I receive from reading with Orientals. I intended to take notes for you, but have failed to do so. I may here allude to thoughts new to me on one or two passages. 'Men of strength to mingle strong drink.' Isa. v. 22. Not, to mix spices, etc., as some commentators suppose, but to mingle strong drink (arak) with wine, by drinking both at the same time. The words of this verse are a common expression in reference to hard drinkers who drink both wine and arak. Another passage speaks of 'sowing a city with salt.' Judges ix. 45. There is a plant here called the 'salt plant,' which is sown where it is designed to root out everything else; and it does it most effectually. I have often seen it. I give you these native interpretations, and I am interested in thousands of thoughts which come up in reading the Scriptures with the class. I spend two hours every day in this delightful employment."

The English language was not taught in the school generally; but the missionaries were convinced that a knowledge of it on the part of some of the pupils and native helpers was very desirable. "I feel more and more," writes Miss Fiske, "that we can accomplish much by teaching our best helpers English.

Moressa spends most of her time in teaching such men as Priest Eshoo. We already see rich fruits of her teaching. Both she and Yonan greatly need a good dictionary. My own — Webster's — is kept in such constant use that it is fast going to pieces. 'Holiness to the Lord' is written on it, and I feel that no one of my books is doing more in the good cause. An extra copy of this large dictionary was placed in my hands some time since, which I gave to John, writing in it, 'Preach the Gospel;' and preach it does, and preach it will."

This winter did not pass without witnessing in both seminaries a state of more than usual religious interest. Miss Fiske thus refers to it: "During the first part of the term we had a pleasant, orderly school, each day being delightful, and since the last of December we have had the special influences of the Spirit. The work has not been as powerful as it was last year, and yet the season has been one we shall ever delight to remember. Most of the older girls had been deeply affected in previous seasons of interest, and their readiness this winter to rise at the Master's call has filled our hearts with gratitude. I cannot speak confidently in regard to those who have recently begun to inquire for the heavenly way, yet I can but believe that some lambs have been added to the Saviour's fold."

During all these months, Miss Fiske was feeling constant solicitude in regard to a loved sister, of whose increasing illness she was from time to time apprised, and to whom she sent frequent letters of tenderest sympathy, from which a single brief extract is given.

"*December* 8. — I cannot let a letter go without a word to you, my suffering sister. Oh, my heart is with you, and often my soul almost bursts its tenement to fly to you. I ask my Father every day to relieve your pains; but I remember that he knows best, and that when I plead for health for you, I may be asking to have the brightest part of your eternal crown taken away. 'Not my will, but Thine be done,' was a sweet prayer when it was first uttered, and so it is now. But we may ask to have the cup removed and not sin, if we can close with those words. Again be assured that my heart is with you. Yes, I do bear with you a sympathizing part. To our faithful God I commit you."

In the month of April Miss Fiske was called to one of the severest afflictions of her missionary life, in the severe sickness of her loved and efficient associate, Miss Rice. By day and night she watched by that sick-bed, with anxious heart and unwearied care. The very pang of separation was at one time experienced when the sick one seemed to be actually passing within the veil. When the girls in the school were informed of her condition, they all, with tearful eyes, retired to their closets to commit their loved teacher to the compassionate Jesus, and then were admitted to her room to look once more upon her face, and receive her few touching farewell words. But prayer in her behalf was heard, and she was mercifully brought back from the very borders of the grave, and still lives to carry forward the good work among the Nestorian women from which her associate was afterwards removed.

"For a month," says Miss Fiske, writing to her

mother, May 7th, "I did not go into school at all; leaving it entirely with Yonan and the older girls. The Lord was their helper, and the school did well under their care. I now teach four hours each day, coming in and sitting with Miss Rice a little while between the lessons. . . My own health has suffered some, but I am now feeling pretty well. I feared, after I wrote last, that you would be anxious about me. But, my dear mother, I trust, has remembered that the Lord always keeps Fidelia when others are sick. Yes, he always gives me strength equal to my day."

A note from Miss Rice to Miss Fiske's mother will show how completely the missionary and the teacher were, for the time, merged in the nurse.

"OROOMIAH, June 23, 1851.

"MY DEAR MOTHER FISKE: — I wish to tell you what an invaluable blessing your dear daughter has been to me, especially during my late illness. I know not with what words to express the degree of comfort she gave me in those days, when reason was dethroned. She could interpret my strange speeches; she could quiet my imaginary fears, and her presence was always enough to bring order out of confusion. I think I never felt more grateful to any human being than to her for her *motherly care* during those days. Even then I dreaded nothing so much as being separated from her, and I delighted to look upon her when I needed less her anxious care, as I was recovering. No one else could bring me such relishing drinks and food as she. Others were very kind; but a mother's heart will understand me, when I say, that no one seemed like Fidelia. She could soothe my aching head, and arrange my pillows so nicely, and calm my restless frame to sleep. I rejoice that you have such a daughter, and that I have such a sister. May she be rewarded a thousand-fold for her unwearied kindness and love."

During all this time, while Miss Fiske's sympathies and energies seemed taxed to the utmost by the sickness of her associate teacher, she had to bear daily an almost crushing weight of anxiety in regard to that tenderly loved sister, who, in the far-off home of her childhood, was, by slow and painful stages, going down to the grave.

In reply to a letter from an older sister, telling her that the dear sufferer had, apparently, but a little while to remain on the earth, she wrote, June 30th, "I have tried to control my feelings, and God has given me grace in a good measure to do so. Still my heart is full. I have prayed earnestly and often that I might be prepared to hear the saddest intelligence in regard to our dear sister; and yet I found that I was not prepared to hear that she was so low, and probably just about to leave you. I would not weep for her, but I cannot refrain from weeping when I think of our broken family circle. The thought of our aged mother being thus tried is almost too much for me. I do, and will try to be ready for the tidings, which, I fear, may be on their way to me. I will try to say, 'My Father's will be done,' though it will be with streaming eyes. Oh, my mother, my mother, how will she bear it? What can I do for her? Shall she be written childless before called to her own rest? Must she see her children, one after another, go from her, till she is left alone? My thoughts of her are the bitterest pang in my trial. Oh, you will do, I know you will, all that you can for her. But *I* may not give her one comforting word in this hour of trial! O my sister, there is a deep meaning in giving up all for Christ; in forsaking father and mother, — yes, an aged widowed mother, — which affliction alone can explain to us. I have never had anything take such a hold of my feelings, since I left you, as do thoughts of my dear mother."

"*July* 1. — I wrote thus far yesterday, and my feelings would allow me to go no farther. To-day I take my pen more composedly. Yes, I trust I can now say, better than yesterday, 'I know in whom I have believed, and Him will I trust,' who is so worthy to be trusted. The coming weeks will be weeks of deep anxiety to me, but my hands will be full, and I hope I shall, with my feelings of sorrow, labor more and better for my Master. I feel that I need trials, and my prayer is that they may not be lost upon me."

Already the "sad tidings" which were to extinguish the last ray of hope were far on their way to her, and called forth the following: —

"OROOMIAH, July 17, 1851.

"MY DEAR AFFLICTED MOTHER: — My spirit flies to thee to-night, and gladly would my tears mingle with yours at this hour. But I may not be with you; and I am comforted even in this, for I can commit you to your Father and mine, and feel that all will be well. . . . 'Even so, Father, for so it seemed good in thy sight,' is, I trust, the language of my heart; but of a deeply wounded heart. I cannot doubt that the dear departed one rests with her Saviour; and this reproves me when I am ready to repine. When I turn to myself and feel how great my loss is, I am sad; yet, with streaming eyes I can say, 'I am ready to be alone, deprived of her words of comfort and sisterly affection, that she may tune her harp of gold a little while longer than it is my privilege to do.' But, when my thoughts turn to my precious mother, I am again almost inconsolable. O my mother! my mother! how is it with your soul? Are you comforted in this sore bereavement? Can you rest all on the compassionate Jesus? Can you rejoice, when the billows are rolling over you, that you are the mother of a daughter passed into the skies? Many have been your cares and anxieties for the dear departed one; but they are all ended now. She has gone to the world where sin and sorrow have no place. Oh, how ought we to be comforted in this, though our hearts must and will bleed at every pore! I cannot express to you, dear mother, what I feel for you in this bereavement. I will not cease by day, nor when evening overshadows me, to plead with Jesus to remember you. And will not he who remembered his own afflicted mother remember mine? Will he not take care of her till he is ready to give her a place with her dear husband and loving children above?"

During these days of anxious suspense in regard to her sister, the arrival of a new reinforcement to the mission afforded Miss Fiske a measure of relief. "Mr. Stoddard's return," she writes, "was to us all a season of chastened joy. We thanked the Lord for bringing him back to us, and one with him whom we can and do tenderly love; but still the recollections of the past were almost overwhelming."

The school continued in session till about the middle of July, and closed with a public examination similar to that of the previous year. Mr. Stoddard thus speaks of it: —

"The examination was highly creditable to the pupils and their indefatigable teachers. Indeed, I doubt whether I have ever, in any place, attended one of greater excellence. The pupils were thoroughly acquainted with all their secular studies; and their familiarity with the Scriptures was truly wonderful. In the historical parts of the Old Testament, in describing the minute arrangements of the tabernacle, in the analysis of the Epistle to the Hebrews, and other similar exercises, they exhibited a clearness of mind, a tenacity of memory, and a readiness of speech, which might put to the blush many a theological student in our native land."

CHAPTER XVI.

JULY, 1851, TO JUNE, 1852.

Vacation in Gawar. — Visit to Ishtazan. — Mar. Shimon's Visit. — Gawar occupied. — Letters to Mrs. Coan. — Condition of the School.

WORN with the labors of the school-room and the sick-chamber, Miss Fiske was glad to escape from the heat of the city, and to find a vacation-retreat among the Koordish mountains. With Miss Rice, Mr. Stocking and family, Mr. Coan, and several native brethren, she passed five weeks most delightfully in Gawar. The company dwelt in tents, in patriarchal style, moving from place to place. It was a season of rest; but not of inactivity, as will appear from a few extracts from letters which Miss Fiske sent to her missionary sisters at Seir: —

"*August* 7. — Let me write you of our recent visit to Ishtazan. The morning we started was delightfully cool, and our good mules, without a thought or a care on our part, carried us safely *up* the mountain, and *down* also. Will you wonder that we have learned to love the 'stubborn mule'? I never felt so much like kissing a beast as I did my mule when he so carefully and patiently carried me down that long, steep stairway. I will not stop now to tell you of the way; of the loving embraces of the clouds, and of those lofty mountain-tops with their changing smiles and frowns; of the overhanging rocks, asking leave to make the traveller's destruction sure, and of the firm rocks, giving shelter in a weary land; or of other pleasing sights in that peaceful valley: of the sweet waterfall; of the ribbon stream threading its way down from those lofty heights, even from the tops of the 'everlasting hills;' of the smiling groves; of the cultivated patches; of the choice fruits, and of that variety of flowers, which makes you feel that spring, summer, and autumn reign together there. As we noticed in turn each flower, and some which for long years we had not seen, we were glad that our feet had been directed thither, and that those sweet things might, for once, 'blush' not 'unseen.' We crossed the river, and reached the village of Ooregа a little after noon. Here we found a good resting-place on the top of one of the houses, beneath the shade of one of the finest walnut-trees we had ever seen. The people brought us mulberries, apples, etc., and then sat down to talk with us till they had made our supper ready. After supper we moved to the church-yard; and, while you were praying for us, and for the world, we were seated in the midst of a large company of men, women, and children, who were listening to the truth. The moon shone brightly upon us, and it was a sweet silence that reigned in that valley, broken only by the preacher's voice, and those echoes of the gospel message which the hills that evening gave back. The little company who had listened with so much interest soon went to their homes, and we lay down to rest in the church-yard. The sand-flies allowed us to sleep but little, and we were glad to see the light breaking from the mountain tops. Tuesday forenoon we spent in Ooreya and Moosperan. Almost every moment was occupied with religious conversation. After dinner we again mounted our mules and rode out to see the fearful road that leads to Upper Jeloo. There was much of sublimity, I dare say, in those scenes; but to me there was so much of the awful that I was glad to leave the place and wend our way down to the quiet village of Boobawa. Here we had a meeting in the open air, and the attention to the word preached was more deep and fixed than on the previous night."

"*Darawa, Aug.* 16. — We came to this place day before yesterday. You can hardly imagine in what a Sodom we are. It is the '*Gulpashan*' of Gawar. Those of you who have been in Gulpashan, and heard the revilings, and boisterous, fiendish talk of the women there, can have some idea of our present situation. The men are not a whit behind the women; and, I doubt not, they speak just as they feel when they say, 'We would not receive a priest, or deacon, in this village who could not swear well, and lie too.' It was with difficulty we could get a place here to pitch our tent, or obtain anything for ourselves or our horses to eat, the first night; but the people are now becoming more civil, many lingering about our tents at time of prayers, and we are encouraged to try to do them good. We had a great many visitors yesterday from the regions above, this being a highway. Among them were two young men from Jeloo. Seeing our tents, they left their mules and came running towards us with great apparent delight. Recognizing Yonan, they first embraced him, and thanked him for his preaching last year, and then poured floods of 'peace' on us all. We had a very pleasant interview with them, and learned that they had seen Mr. Coan. They spoke of his preaching in the highest terms, saying, 'It was just what we needed.' As these words fell from their lips, one of the women on the opposite side of the tent called out: 'Have you heard these deceivers preach?' He replied, 'Yes; both last year and this, and hope I shall again.' On hearing this, she drew her brawny arms into the form of a deadly instrument, and, giving an awful thrust, cried out at the top of her voice and in fierce anger, 'The blood of thy father smite thee, thou Satan!' The young man laughed, and said, 'My mother, these men are right, and it is in my heart to go to their school this winter.' Dreadful was the volley of oaths which now fell from the enraged woman's lips. She is a fair specimen of the women of this village; and the young man of those who call to see us here."

"20.—We had hardly finished reading your letters when Mar. Shimon was announced as at hand. He rode up to our tent, saying to his attendants, 'I shall first go and inquire after the health of the gentlemen and ladies, and then I will go to my tent.' The old man put on his pleasantest airs and stayed with us an hour and a half. After his noon-day sleep we all went over to his tent and called on him. He was surrounded by some sixty or seventy of his 'makoole,' as he calls them. He came out of his tent to meet us, and, for some reason which we cannot quite understand, seemed very desirous to show us all honor. He took pains to bring our school into notice, in the presence of all, by saying, 'I am afraid Miss Fiske is not happy here. She does not look well.'

I assured him that I was very well and happy, and rejoiced to see him looking so well. He then said to those present, This lady is happy only in having a great company of Nestorian girls about her, teaching them, eating care for them, and trying to do them good.'"

Miss Fiske enjoyed exceedingly this tour in the mountains, and returned with invigorated health, though she soon after suffered from an attack of ophthalmia, and subsequently from an attack of erysipelas. Owing to the prevalence of fever, from which several of the pupils were suffering, the school was not reassembled till about the close of October. A fresh burden of care and labor was every year imposed upon the teachers by the new scholars who were received. "Our school," writes Miss Fiske, "numbers forty. Several of the girls are very wild and rude. They give us a great deal of anxiety and care. You can hardly conceive how very low these girls are when we take them. They are as filthy as the beasts, and will lie as fast as they can speak. Grace, and grace alone, can subdue them." Yet she adds, "Our school is very pleasant. I do not know that I ever had more pleasure in my duties. I am very well; but I find that I cannot confine myself as closely as I used to do. I mean to be very careful; for I feel that it is a duty to take care of the body as well as the soul."

Whether absorbed in her work among the mountains, or in her school, the grief occasioned by the death of her loved sister remained fresh and keen. Her letters to her family friends disclose a degree of mental suffering of which her incessant labors in her Master's service gave no indications. Her sensibilities were too delicate, her social affections too strong, to recover quickly from so deep a wound, while her love for souls, and her conscientious devotion to Christ would not allow her to fold her hands and yield herself up to the sorrow that was flooding her soul. With apparent cheerfulness, and with untiring zeal, she labored for her degraded Nestorian sisters; but when she took her pen to address any of her distant kindred, the pent-up feelings of her smitten heart found full expression. From this bitter experience she did not fail to gather precious fruit. To her only surviving sister she writes, November 12th: —

"I had never really expected to hear of the death of either of my sisters, and I think that my prayers had been comparatively few that I might be prepared for such tidings. I now desire very much to be ready and willing to give you all up, and to be *alone* in the world. It is sweet to love and to be loved, but we must give our Saviour the first place; our dearest earthly friends must have a second place, or they will certainly be taken from us. I feel that I have always been prone to set my heart too strongly upon my friends. Not that I have loved any of you too tenderly, but I have always felt that I could not spare one of my family friends. I do hope and pray that I may, henceforth, be ready at any moment to have any earthly tie broken; and I hope you will feel the same when you think of me. Since hearing of L——'s death my feelings of grief have been so intense, I have almost wished that, in death, the rest of us might not be divided. But let our Father's will be done. If he helps us, we can bear all things. . . .

"And has our dear mother suffered so much! Oh,

that I could have added one drop of comfort during those sorrowing days! She was in my heart almost all the time last summer; and if I have ever prayed for her, it has been since hearing of our sad bereavement. It must be a great privilege, which I know you will prize, to have her with you. My heart swells, and my eyes fill with tears, as I think what a comfort she would be to me. I sit in my little room many hours, my hands filled with work, but my heart longing for my mother's company. If I may never see her, I will try to comfort her by frequent letters."

The establishment of a permanent missionary station in the mountains of Koordistan, for which Dr. Grant had so earnestly labored, was not lost sight of by the mission after his death. The way had gradually been prepared, and the time, it was thought, had come, for some members of the mission to make their home in Gawar. Mr. and Mrs. Coan, and Mr. Rhea, were appointed to this field, and removed thither in the autumn of 1851. Miss Fiske felt a deep interest in the undertaking, which her vacation visits had done much to render practicable at this time. She followed with the tenderest sympathy those who went forth to brave the rigors of a winter in the mountains, and to endure the privations and hardships incident to a life among such a rude and degraded people. Her letters to Mrs. Coan were frequent, extracts from which will help complete the picture of her own life at this period: —

"*Nov.* 25. — I have felt, and do feel, so much interest in Gawar that my thoughts are very often with you. I know that you have a trying field, and I feel for you in all your perplexities. Yes, my heart will always be with you, and I shall love to commend you, as often as I do myself, to heavenly guidance. I hope and expect that you will this winter see precious fruits of your labors."

"28.—I sympathize with you in all your trials about getting your daily bread. We were troubled just so last summer. I wish we could do something more for you. Can we not? Would you not like to have me make your butter? I can, just as well as not, and the footman can carry it."

"30.—In our women's Sabbath school I have those who cannot learn to use a book. I commenced with the creation, and purpose to go on giving them the history of the Old Testament. If we can only find something to arouse their dark and stupid minds, I shall hope that they will be prepared for the Spirit to affect them savingly. Our older girls help us so much this year, that I find more time than ever before to labor for the women. I feel that I have been so much engrossed with my school the last two or three years, that I have not done my duty to my poor sisters. They must live forever in happiness or misery. How should this thought urge us on to labor for those who seem so unpromising! They are probably no more superstitious and wicked than was the one our Saviour met at the well; and his power is not less now than when he caused her to sit in sweet penitence at his feet."

"*December* 1. — We had our first missionary meeting this year, with the girls, to-night. We took the missionary map and went over the world, telling the religion of every nook and corner. I was surprised to find the older ones so perfectly familiar with the general religions of the world. I thanked my God for it, and resolved, if life and health are spared, to have a meeting of the kind once a week during the winter. Ten of the girls will probably never return again after this year, and they ought, when they leave, to be good missionary scholars. I feel so well this year, that labor is a precious privilege."

"12. — I feel for you most sympathizingly in all your trials. I know that you are blessed with a sensitive nature, which keenly feels such things as you are now exposed to; and I could not wish that you might not feel them; but I rejoice that grace enables you to bear them cheerfully. We shall not be rewarded for *not feeling*, but for *bearing*, when every tender and delicate feeling is sorely tried."

"22. — Do you know, my dear sister, that the winds, the clouds, and the falling snow come to us this winter with a voice they never had before? Yes, they remind us of those who are now far away for Jesus' sake. True, these messengers speak to us in some sweet tones, for they bid us thank our God for the grace given you to go up and possess the land; but they make some hearts deeply anxious for you. . . . I am afraid you are trying to do too much. What seems to us but little may be more in the eye of Omniscience than what we count the success of months or years. How very little we know of the Lord's ways, or of what we are doing for him! I have been exceedingly happy in school this winter, and have felt that our pupils were rapidly improving; but a sadness has often stolen over me when I have thought that perhaps we were not blessed in reality. Those days, when, with weeping eyes and a broken heart, I felt that all was going to desolation, and prayed accordingly, may have been better days than these. Those of our pupils who have appeared to love the Saviour in past days are very consistent in their daily walk, and are very often at the throne of grace; but we do not see new cases of interest, and I sometimes fear that we may fill our precious winter months with labor, and yet not win souls to Christ.

"Our classes in the Bible are deeply interesting. The only one into which I go daily is now reading the book of Ezra, and in connection with it the books of Haggai and Zechariah. We were so much interested this afternoon in the fourth and fifth chapters of Zechariah, that the sun went down before we could leave them, and for half an hour we had candles. We have never read the prophets much together, and the interest of the girls is intense."

"*January* 15, 1852. — You ask advice in regard to teaching those women. I fear, with you, that they may not all learn to read; but if they do not, your labor will not be lost. A woman who knows her letters only, respects herself the more, and feels an interest in her children's learning to read, which you do not see in others."

"30. — Whoever undertakes to do anything for women and girls here, has a trying work. They are more degraded and more difficult to raise than they can realize who have never labored expressly for them. I very seldom speak of what I consider the great obstacles in the way of benefiting them. I feel so much on this subject, and in reference to my own deficiencies, and the want of a blessing on my labors, that my heart is too full to talk. It is a comfort to water one's couch with tears, and then commit all to Christ."

"*February* 14. — I know too well how you feel when your women quarrel, and say they will come no more, etc. My first years here were full of just such trials. Sometimes, when all was going on quietly in our little school-room, an angry mother's voice would be heard at the door, and she would come in to storm and rave because her child had no better clothes or food. How many times, as day after day such trials come, have I asked, 'Shall I *ever* see any fruit of my labors?' I have cried and worked, and worked and cried, and stooped down and written my sorrows in the dust. I write freely to you, but I do not speak of my trials to others, because they do not understand them. I often think of dear Miss Lyon's words, 'The more degraded those for whom you labor, the more blessed are you in laboring for them.' Is it so? Then, dear sister, let us take a strong hold of our work. We will try to go onward and look upward. The work, though a trying one, must be done, and shall not we rejoice to labor in such a cause? One poor woman or girl in glory will make us count each trial for her a precious privilege."

Miss Fiske made frequent visits to Geog Tapa to aid and encourage in the work of teaching the women. Of one of these visits she thus wrote: "I spent yesterday in Geog Tapa. We visited Moressa's school, and were delighted with it. Moressa is a more than ordinary teacher, and she gives her whole mind and soul to the work. Her little girls are taught to govern themselves, and to try to do good as well as to learn to read. The women in Geog Tapa are doing better than ever. Poor ones! they make a desperate effort to learn to read, and many of them are reaching the desired object. We found three in a yard yesterday with their wheels, spinning, being taught Scripture history by one of the girls. While their wheels were buzzing, the girl's voice was raised above the noise, telling of Israel's wanderings in the wilderness. Do you think that Solomon's wise woman, when she laid her hands to the distaff, did better than these? My heart is full when I see such things, and I want to bring our dear American friends to us on eagle's wings, that they may rejoice with us."

The school was dismissed for the summer, June 1st. The next day Miss Fiske writes: "The last winter has been a season of more than usual care, and I can hardly tell you how it seemed last night to sit down in my little room and feel that I need go neither this way nor that, but could rest. In a fortnight we expect to go to Gavalan to spend the summer, and to take our first class — ten in number — with us."

Of the condition of the seminary, during this year, Mr. Stocking says: "It never gave more gratifying evidence of intellectual and general improvement than at present. It has been found practicable to bring the schools under as strict regulations, in all respects, as are introduced into similar institutions in America. Their time is regularly divided into hours for study, exercise, and recreation. Accounts of delinquencies for not observing the rules of the school are regularly given; and it is seldom that one is found tardy in retiring, rising, at meals, etc. It is an important fact, showing the disposition of the pupils to conform to our wishes, that for the last four months there have been but five communications during study hours, both in school and in their own rooms, either by whispering or other outward signs; and those were made by girls who had been but a short time with us.

"Though there has not been, during the present season, that special religious interest which we have reported in former years, we can speak of a decided growth of religious principle. The piety and benevolence of the scholars find scope for exercise, on occasions set apart for the use of the needle, and for the teaching of numbers of their own sex who are eager for instruction."

CHAPTER XVII.

JUNE, 1852, TO JUNE, 1853.

Vacation at Gavalan. — Entertainment of English, Russian, and Persian Commissioners. — Cholera. — Death of Gozel, of John's Parents, and of Judith Perkins. — Question of Return to America Considered. — Domestic Department of the School. — Religious Interest. — Ophthalmia.

Mr. Stocking and his family, having, for sanitary reasons, removed to Gavalan early in the summer of 1852, Miss Fiske and Miss Rice, with their class of oldest pupils, joined them about the middle of June. Teachers and pupils alike were interested in doing something for the poor ignorant women there. "We gathered them together," says Miss Fiske, "on our first Sabbath in Gavalan, and gave each girl her charge. For two Sabbaths all went on finely; but, on the third, the women and children were nearly all missing. On inquiry, we found they had heard that we were teaching them, preparatory to sending them to America. The poor mothers were greatly alarmed, and not only withdrew their children, but absented themselves. During the following week we visited them all in their homes, and the next Sabbath they were found in their places in the Sabbath school."

Not many weeks passed before Miss Fiske was

summoned to Seir, by Dr. Perkins, to assist in entertaining the English, Russian, and Persian commissioners appointed to fix the boundary between Turkey and Persia. Although regretting to be absent so long from her pupils, she cheerfully obeyed the summons, and highly enjoyed meeting those distinguished persons; contributing not a little to their pleasure and entertainment while they were the guests of the mission. Her long residence among a rude and uncultured people had not disqualified her for those duties of courtesy and hospitality, which prevail in refined and polite circles. She could one day sit on the mud floor of the Nestorian hovel, instructing ignorant and degraded women; and the next, preside with grace and dignity at the entertainment of princes and nobles. In his funeral sermon Dr. Perkins thus alludes to this trait of her character: —

"Her rare versatility of power was sometimes conspicuous in the entertainment of large European parties as our guests, whose visits here have, indeed, been few and far between; but, whenever they have occurred, as in the case of General Williams and his large party, while surveying the boundary, and of the British Ambassador, Mr. Murray and his suite, when leaving Persia for Bagdad, she has shown herself equal to any position in the social circle, and quite prepared to fill and adorn any sphere of female duty and responsibility; and she never failed to command the high respect of all such guests, as an accomplished lady, as well as the peerless principal of our female seminary."

This year the city of Oroomiah, and many of the villages of the plain were again visited by that fearful scourge, the cholera, which swept the people into the grave by thousands. Among the early victims was one of the pupils of Miss Fiske, of whom she thus writes: —

"Gozel was the daughter of a most pious and devoted father, who for a long time seemed to desire nothing so much as her conversion. She had taught both her parents to read when they were more than forty years old, and had given them a great deal of valuable instruction. Their heart was bound up in their 'teacher,' as they always called her. The Saturday evening preceding her death she prepared her lesson for the Sabbath school; but when the school assembled, Sabbath noon, she was at the bar of God. Her parents looked back on that last evening of her life with peculiar delight. They were a happy family, studying the Bible together. When they had finished their lesson, the father said, 'Gozel, my daughter, will you pray with us?' They knelt with her in gladness, not knowing that it was the last time. After prayer, she again took her Testament, read a chapter, and then retired for prayer. Her father noticed that she remained longer than usual in her closet, and he was also struck with the fervency of her devotions. He waited till she was ready to retire, and then the happy family separated all in good health, and in the hope of many years of happiness. But at midnight the angel of death passed that way, and called for the loved daughter. Before noon she died, and before the setting of the sun she was borne to her long home."

The next messenger brought them the sad tidings that John's blind old father, more than ninety years of age, had been smitten down by the cholera. "For several years," says Miss Fiske, "this good man had given delightful evidence of piety. After his conversion he seldom passed a whole night without rising and going into his closet to pray, and each member of our mission was at such times remembered by name. He followed all the young preachers with his prayers. When a company returned from the mountains last year, he said to them, 'God is my witness, that three times each day I have asked him not to allow you to come back with heads bowed down.' Many a time, after he became sightless, have we sat by his side, and heard him thank God that he had taken the gift of sight from him. 'My blindness is the greatest blessing of my life,' he would say. 'I am now entirely cut off from the world, and I have nothing to do but to pray and praise.' Just before his death he roused himself from a stupor, and called for his children and his children's children to the fourth generation to stand beside him. With uplifted hands he blessed them, and then fell asleep.

"The next Sabbath John's mother was prostrated by the same disease, and, after a few hours of suffering, her joyous spirit was released also. When almost gone, John said to her, 'Mother, where are you?' 'I am walking after Jesus,' was her sweet reply. At the time of John's conversion she violently opposed him. For years, when he attempted to have family prayers, she would engage in some kind of work to disturb him. During all this time, John labored and prayed for her; but his heart often sank within him as he looked at her hardness of heart. The winter of 1848, however, brought comfort to John and to us also, as we heard her in agony, inquiring, 'Is there mercy for such a sinner as I am?' She came to me one day, the big tears rolling down her cheeks, saying, 'I am not now that self-righteous woman I used to be. There is no such evil heart in this village as mine. It is a cage of everything unclean. There is in it a serpent of a hundred heads, that has pierced every part of it.' She was pointed to the Friend of sinners, and seemed, during that winter, to take hold of him; but her wicked heart was still her theme more than her Saviour. She used at that time to take the women of the village with her into a stable, and there, where the 'horned oxen' were feeding, tell them of their sins; but was seldom heard to speak of future punishment. When asked in regard to the justice of God in punishing her, she replied, 'If I must atone for my sins by suffering, God cannot make too hot a hell for me.' She continued in this state mourning over her sins, for a whole year, with only a trembling hope in Christ. The winter of 1849 was one of peculiar blessings here, and to her it revealed a Saviour in all his sufficiency, and in all his loveliness. Speaking of the change in her feelings at that time, she remarked: 'Last winter Christ was in heaven, but now he sits all the time by my side.' From that time till called to her rest, she was a growing Christian. If, when we entered her house, she was occupied for a little while with household duties, she would come afterwards and say, 'I have been Martha, but I will be Mary the rest of the time you are here.'"

The raging pestilence, after having numbered among its victims several of the warm friends of the mission, was permitted to come still nearer, and to snatch away one from the mission circle. JUDITH GRANT PERKINS, the eldest of the missionary children, whose memory parental affection has embalmed in that interesting volume, "The Persian Flower," was suddenly transplanted to bloom in the Paradise above. Besides the afflicted parents, none felt the death of this lovely child more keenly than did Miss Fiske. All the children in the mission had a large place in her heart, and she was a great favorite with them. To visit "Aunt Fidelia," or to receive a visit from her, was one of their richest treats. Judith loved her with almost filial love, and was ambitious to be like her. When quite young, observing one day a small mole on Miss Fiske's face, she desired a "spot," as she called it, to be made on her own face, and tried various expedients to produce one herself. Miss Fiske mourned for her as for an own child; and for many days was with the bereaved parents, occupied with those offices of sympathy, which she so well knew how to render.

After returning from Gavalan, Miss Fiske superintended certain necessary repairs in the walls of her school building, which delayed the reassembling of her pupils till past the middle of October.

Owing to the illness of her only surviving sister, and the improbability of her recovery, Miss Fiske was led, at times, during this year, seriously to consider whether it might not be her duty to leave her missionary work and return to America to be with her aged mother. "My attachment to my home here," she writes her sister, "and to my labors, is such that I am sure that I am in no danger of wanting to go home unless duty calls. I know that my danger is on the other side. I have thought and prayed much over the subject the last year, and, while I have come to no definite conclusion, I think I am ready to go wherever my Father calls, and I cannot but feel sometimes, that I ought, at least for a season, to leave my Persian home. Would it be any comfort to you to have me with you for a year or two, were I afterwards to return? I only want to know what my duty is."

To her mother she wrote November 19th: "I long to see you more than I can express. When I think of my native land, there is nothing in all its length and breadth on which my eyes would so gladly rest, as *my mother*. I do long once more to sit by your side, and beg your forgiveness for the many times I have injured your feelings, and made you sigh as you looked on your wayward child. I want to thank you also for all your tender care of me before I knew the mother that loved me; and for all the wholesome discipline bestowed upon me in my early years. If I have ever been useful to any one, I feel that I owe it, under God, to my mother, and my sainted father. My feelings have been very strong and almost overcoming of late, when I have thought of you. I cannot tell why, but I have seemed to feel afresh that I had left you. 'Behold thy mother,' has often come to me in gentle whispers, and I have been carried to you in the hours when 'sleep stealeth over man.'"

"We have now," she writes early in December, "about fifty scholars, and have our arrangement so that they do all of their work. This is no small care, but we get along very well, and feel that it is doing the girls much good. They never studied better, and the quiet and prayerfulness of the older girls is delightful. . . . It is pleasant to see them shaking off oriental indolence, and trying to move quickly and to do work well. I am often tried by their inefficiency, but pity towards them is the prevailing feeling of my heart."

"*December* 17.—It is now early morning. I have been up more than an hour, and have time to write a line before breakfast. It is Saturday, our washing day. Were you here you would soon see the girls washing dishes, cleaning knives, rubbing candlesticks, sweeping, bringing wood, washing towels, making fires in the wash-room, etc. We expect all this will be done at quarter before eight; when, were you to come in, you would see our large family assembled in the school-room in their wash-room dresses, with their clothes-bag and soap in hand, ready for action. First you would hear me go over the list of articles which they ought to wash, to ascertain if some careless one has not forgotten something. Then you would see twenty of the girls wending their way to the wash-room. I think you would recognize Fidelia there in a tall figure crowned with an old black hood; you would hear her call the roll, and then see two good managers distribute the water to their companions. The water flies, and the clothes come out clean. Then another set comes. We expect that all will be done before noon. Then all are assembled to comb and braid their hair. You will think this queer; but I have still to look after them, to keep them free from what 'moves and has a being' on them; and it is easier to do it when all are together. The girls try to keep themselves clean; but it is very difficult for them to do it, coming in contact, as they often do, with their friends. It is impossible to have to do with this people and not share their vermin. But to return to the girls: their heads all combed, and the wash-room cleaned, they again meet with their sewing and knitting, and we assist them in preparing their work for the afternoon, remaining in the school-room till half-past twelve, when all go to their rooms. The dinner is soon prepared, eaten, and the dishes washed, and then all sew in their rooms. At half-past three all assemble again in the school-room, where we 'take their accounts;' give them their Sabbath lessons; see if all the arrangements for the Sabbath are complete; and then, after singing a few hymns, we feel that the work of the six days is done. The Nestorian Sabbath begins with the setting sun."

During the opening weeks of 1853 there was much sickness among the girls of the seminary. "My little room," writes Miss Fiske, "has been a hospital, and my time almost all consumed with nursing. You know how anxious I always am if any one is sick. I often feel that in this I do not cast my cares on Him who careth for me.

In February and March, the seminary was again visited by the special influences of the Holy Spirit. "For more than a month individuals have been affected to tears in almost every meeting, and at almost every season of family devotions. At sunset we see many going regularly to their little prayer meetings, which have been opened by themselves, without any word from us; and our house is at that time a 'house of prayer;' still the blessing seems, in a great measure, withheld. Why is it so? This is a question I cannot answer. 'Lord, is it I?' comes home with peculiar force just now."

Subsequently Miss Fiske wrote: — "In our school, the season was one of delightful interest, though there were but few conversions. We see in our pupils from year to year stronger proofs of attachment to the Saviour, and greater capability of working in his vineyard without direction from us."

While the religious interest was in progress, Miss Fiske suffered severely from an attack of ophthalmia, and by using her eyes at night while they were still weak, the optic nerve was so affected that for months she suffered much, and was scarcely able to use her pen at all. For this reason the school was dismissed for the summer earlier than usual. Mr. Stocking and family, with whom she had found a pleasant home for ten years, having left for America, she spent her summer vacation mostly at Seir, in the family of Mr. Stoddard, hoping by entire rest to regain the use of her eyes. "How great this trial is," she writes, "I cannot tell you, and a kind Father grant that you may never know by sad experience. The apple of the eye, — how dear it is to us! but not so dear as is the Christian to his Saviour. He will 'keep us as the apple of his eye,' but in love he may deny us the blessing of sight. I hope, by being very careful, soon to be able to use my eyes pretty freely; though I can hardly expect again to use the midnight lamp after a day of cares in and out of school. But I have the very sweet comfort, that I shall see in just the way that will best advance the Redeemer's kingdom. And shall I ask for anything more? Is it not enough that God uses us as he wills?"

CHAPTER XVIII.

JUNE, 1853, TO JUNE, 1854.

Report of the State of the Seminary. — Religious Interest. — Examination of School at Geog Tapa. — Sabbath School. — Counsel to a Young Convert.

DURING the long summer vacation of 1853, Miss Fiske, though obliged by the state of her eyes to be comparatively idle, was able, in connection with Miss Rice, to prepare, at the request of the mission, a full report of the condition of the seminary, which was forwarded to the Missionary House in Boston. From this report the following extract is taken: —

"The school is in every sense a family. They meet together daily for morning and evening devotions; they come to the dining-rooms for their meals; they are subject to the same rules, enjoy the same privileges; and all are required to give some aid in the domestic work of the great household. Every one understands her specific work, and she is expected to do it promptly and faithfully. If there is a failure, it is searched into, and, if the cause prove to be ill health, her teachers care for her with a parental interest and anxiety. Her companions are ready to take her place, and they gladly give every needed attention to the sick one. If their teachers are ill, it is gratifying to see with what eagerness their affectionate hearts plead for the privilege of ministering to them; by night as well as by day they show not only their willingness, but their ability to render very essential aid in the sick-room. They are constantly with us during term-time, and seldom ask to visit their homes, except in cases of sickness or death of friends. They are generally very prompt in returning to us after vacations.

"Once might have been seen here a company of untutored little girls, fresh from their village homes, with uncombed hair, in filthy, tattered garments, rudely jostling each other as they passed; conversing aloud, or in a whisper, as they pleased, and studying their lessons in loud concert in school hours; when dismissed, clambering over the seats, or making the school-room ring with their shouts of noisy mirth, and sure to engage in some mischief, unless in their teacher's room, or under her watchful eye; dishonest, untruthful, ungrateful scholars; objects that awakened compassion, and required patient, unceasing care.

"To the praise of God's grace, with grateful hearts we record the visible change,—a change all the more beautiful, regarded as the result of moral power. When the bell calls to school, our pupils, with books in hand, hasten through the spaceways without a word of conversation, and in two minutes are all seated at their desks. A deep silence pervades the room, while prayer for divine guidance is offered by one of the teachers. After this, the classes move quietly to their places for recitation; and, during the whole day, no loud studying is heard, no whispering is seen, and there is a near approach to non-communication even by signs. When we are addressing the whole school, they give their respectful, earnest attention. At recess, some of the girls may be seen walking in the yard; others have taken their knitting from their pockets; some are reviewing their lessons, to be sure of not failing in the next recitation; a group of younger ones are learning the outline maps from an older scholar; another is aiding her companion in ascending some acclivity in the rudiments of science, which she has just climbed; while a few have gone to their rooms to seek communion with the Holy One. When the school is dismissed at night, each girl takes her books, passes noiselessly out, and arranges them in her room, where she will want them for the study hours.

"We are rejoiced to see among those pupils who have been longest with us a strong regard for order, honesty, and truth, which has enabled them to exert a controlling influence in school, and which they carry with them when they leave us. They often write us letters full of expressions of warm attachment, and deep gratitude for our instructions and reproofs.

"Some years ago a course of study was fixed upon in our school, which, it is hoped, most of those who come to us will complete. More than half the course prescribed is biblical. If this seem a large proportion, we have only to say that, in training our pupils, we should seek not only their greatest good, but the greatest good of the Nestorian community. There is, at present, a most interesting spirit of inquiry among the females in regard to the sacred writings. Many of them bake their bread, spin their cotton, weed their fields, etc., asking what these things mean. We can personally reach but few of these dark minds constantly; we must do it through our girls, and we are sure that all who look carefully at the subject will feel as we do, that those who go out from us must be women of 'one book.'

"Our reasons for entering on our present domestic arrangements are these: First. To dispense with native women in the house, whose influence is far from being good; to teach the girls to depend on themselves, and to leave no room for fault-finding with others. Secondly. To give the girls more exercise than they can get in their walks in the yard, to which they are confined for recreation. Our school being in the midst of a Mohammedan population, our pupils cannot go beyond our premises unaccompanied. Thirdly. That the pupils may keep up, to some extent, their early habits of labor. They have worked in their homes, and they must work when they return to them. We have feared that they might suffer from being so many months of the year exclusively engaged in study. Fourthly. To give more stability to their character, and especially to their Christian character, and so better fit them to labor for inquiring souls in their villages. Those girls who have made the greatest effort to help themselves here, have best met trials on going out from us. Those seasons of religious interest, in which some time each day has been given to secular employment, have produced the most lasting and happy results. If people are converted in the villages, they will be converted in the midst of hard work, and it seemed desirable for our pupils to realize that the sinner can give his heart to God in such circumstances."

"The hours of the day are so closely occupied with

duties connected with the school and family, that our pupils could find little time for extra labor with their needles, were the demand and pecuniary inducements for such a kind of industry far greater than they now are. They are generally inclined to be diligent, and to fill up all their leisure moments with some useful employment. They cut and make all their own clothing, and do considerable sewing and knitting for others. They earned about six dollars in this way last year, which they will devote to some benevolent object. It will be seen that they can have but few idle moments, when it is known that they knit more than a hundred pairs of stockings and gloves, in their recreation hours, during the winter term. Our pupils now furnish their own clothing in part. This, with the greater economy of the girls in domestic management and saving the hire of help, enables us to reduce the expenses of each pupil to about eighteen dollars a year. This sum includes rent, repairs, board, clothing in part, fuel, lights, etc.

"For several years after the establishment of our school, we often lost promising pupils by their early marriages, either through the influence of friends or from their own choice; but now we see little disposition to make any engagement till the course of study is finished. Our older pupils place a very high value upon piety and a good education in their future companions. The refusal of one of them to allow the time of her marriage to be fixed by any one but the superintendents of the male seminary, saying of her intended, 'When Mr. S. says that he has studied enough, I am ready,' expresses the feelings of many others. Those who have contended against the evils of early marriages in years gone by, when an unmarried girl of fourteen years was scarcely to be found, could but shed the tear of gratitude over our last graduating class, ten in number, and all between seventeen and nineteen years of age.

"In reviewing the past, and in looking for the results of labor expended on our school, we find much to humble us, and much over which to mourn. Still, when we look on those females to whom saving mercy has, as we trust, been extended; when we meet, as we go out, those wives and mothers who have been made better by instructions gained while with us; when we see our pupils teaching scores of little girls in the villages, not only to read, but to love the Saviour; when we meet a large number of adult females whom they have taught to read the word of life, and whom they now often gather into Bible classes and prayer-meetings; — when we see and hear these things, we cannot feel that our labor has been altogether in vain, nor can we refrain from sending up notes of thanksgiving to Him who has given his rich blessing to what we in weakness have sown."

Owing to the prevalence of cholera, the school did not open in the autumn of 1853, till the first of November. Miss Fiske's eyes still troubled her, and she could use them only to a limited extent in teaching. Other duties, however, pressed upon her. January 17th, 1854, she writes: "Since the school assembled, my heart and hands have been full of labor and care. Our large family of fifty is a delightful charge, and I become more and more attached to them every year. For the last few weeks there has been some religious interest among our pupils. We hope and pray for a rich blessing."

"*March* 17. — The past six weeks have been a season of much religious interest in our school. Several girls hope that they have passed from death unto life; and others, previously pious, have been much quickened. They have been so anxious to become the Lord's that it has been a delightful privilege to lead them to the 'fountain of living waters.' The girls who went out from us a year ago have been faithful helpers in their villages. Six of them have taught girls' schools, which have been centres of strong religious influence. Two of them, Nargis and Khanee, teach in Geog Tapa, where they have had a school of fifty girls."

Of an examination of this school on the first day of June following, she thus writes: "It was held in the church. Some six hundred were present to listen to the girls, who were arranged in the middle of the church. The exercises continued for three hours, and I never saw a company of Nestorians listen with more interest. The singing, particularly, charmed them, and 'Our daughters can learn as well as our sons,' was heard from many a parent that day. One of the teachers was the first little girl I took under my care after coming to Oroomiah. As I saw her manage her little flock, I thanked the Lord that he had spared me to see 'children's children.' In the afternoon there was an examination of the Sabbath school, or the adult part of it, in the grove back of the church. There were probably a thousand persons present, and the clear Persian sky over our heads was only an index of what was passing below.

It would have done you good to see those old men and women reciting the word of God, with the ease of little children. You would also have thanked the Lord, when a large company, of both sexes, came forward, who had learned to read."

Miss Fiske received, about this time, intelligence of the conversion of a niece, which called forth the following response: —

"MY DEAR C.: — You have written me many letters which have been a great comfort to me; but over none have I rejoiced so much as over the one just received. You have, as I trust, sincerely given yourself to the Saviour, and begun the Christian life. Bless the Lord for enabling you to do this; but renew the consecration every day. It is only in this way that you can retain the blessedness you are now tasting. Give yourself daily to the Saviour, as you did when light and peace first dawned upon your soul. When I look back upon my own life as a Christian, I feel that I have lost many years from not having realized that I must give my heart daily to the Lord. I trust that you have begun the Christian life with much prayer, and that to your dying day you will love to hold frequent communion with your Saviour. If you do, you will not go into his presence as a stranger; but will feel that he is yours, and that you are his, and you will go to meet him with joy."

CHAPTER XIX.

JUNE, 1854, TO JULY, 1855.

Making Maps. — Visits to Ada and Supurghan. — Death of Mr. Stocking. — Political Disturbances. — Askar Kahn. — Account of School, for Mr. Stevens. — Letter to Holyoke Seminary.

DURING the summer vacation of 1854, a large class of the older pupils were retained under the care of the teachers, for the purpose of receiving special instruction designed to qualify them to teach and to labor among the women.

"We rather feared," writes Miss Fiske, "the effect upon ourselves of such a care in the summer; but we have been kindly kept by our Father, and have much reason to thank him for the improvement of our pupils. Besides giving considerable attention to study, during the two months they were with us, they made one hundred and eighty maps. Were you to see these, I think you would pronounce them beautiful. A part of them are designed to accompany our Geography in Syriac, and a part are for Sabbath schools, — such as maps of Canaan, in Old Testament times; of Palestine, in the Saviour's time; of the journey of the children of Israel, etc. Those for Sabbath schools have been widely circulated, and are doing great good."

About the middle of August, Miss Fiske visited

Ada and Supurghan. At the latter place she spent the Sabbath with one of the graduates of the seminary, now married and laboring there with her husband.

"I met Moressa's Bible class," she writes, "in the yard of the church. There were more than usual present; but she says she has had as many as twenty-five every Sabbath, all summer, and often as many as forty. She wished me to question them on those parts of the Bible they had been over. I did so; and to say that I was gratified, expresses but little of what I felt, when listening to those women, who, when I was last in the village, were so rude that it seemed hardly possible to speak a word of instruction to them. They had been over the first six books of the Old Testament; and those who had been pretty constant in their attendance appeared quite as well as did either of the classes of old people at our late examination in Geog Tapa.

"While absent, I thought much of the talk which I had with you, about doing less for our seminaries and more abroad. We must try to do more in the villages, but I do not believe we can afford to do less at home. It is through our pupils that what we do for the people generally, will be done. In Ada and Supurghan I was asked many times to send home quickly the girls that I have. They said they wanted them to teach; and I believed them. I always come home from the villages feeling that I will labor more and pray more for my dear pupils. What blessings all our scholars would be to their people, if holy, active Christians!"

In July, intelligence was received of the death of

Mr. Stocking. This excellent missionary, after sixteen years of faithful and exhausting labors among the Nestorians, returned with his family to America in 1853. His death carried sorrow to the hearts of all his missionary associates, by whom he was greatly beloved. Miss Fiske, having been so long a member of his family, was most deeply afflicted by the unexpected news of his departure, and thus wrote to Mrs. Stocking: —

"My dear, dear Sister: — I have scarcely ever, in my whole life, felt so much bereaved; certainly never by a death out of my own father's family. I loved Mr. Stocking as an own brother, and I feel for you as I should for my only sister if she were in your circumstances. . . . Oh, it would be such a relief to this aching heart to be with you for one short hour, and learn the particulars of my dear brother's last days, and once more press those orphan children to my bosom! They were not orphans when I so often embraced them. Dear ones! my heart is full when I think of them! And what shall I say of my feelings when I think of you, dear sister? Would that I could fly to you! I know that the grace of God is sufficient for every trial, however severe, and to that grace I try to commend you. I trust that you are able submissively to bow to your Father's will; but I know that the world must look very desolate to you. When I think of never again seeing you in Persia, my heart well-nigh breaks. Your house and everything in it wear a strange sadness to me. How much comfort have I taken in thinking of your return, in keeping everything for you, and in planning to arrange each nook and corner so pleasantly for you! How many times, in imagination, have I seen you all coming back to us, on some bright June day, and have thought how I would stay at home while others would go out to meet you, and how I would try to have your home seem unchanged to you! But *all* is now changed. Your home here would now be a sad one to you; it is to me. I think of you so constantly that everything wears the garb of mourning, and often, before I am aware of it, my tears are falling thick and fast."

In the spring of 1855, there were some tokens of the Spirit's gracious presence, but the season passed without any such manifestations of his awakening and converting power, as had been earnestly desired, and as former years had witnessed. It was with the mission a time of great anxiety, on account of the disturbed state of the country, caused by the Crimean war, and on account of new indications of hostility to the labors of the missionaries, on the part of the Persian government. Miss Fiske's letters at this period make frequent allusion to the troubles which encompassed and threatened the mission.

"*March* 17.—The past winter has been one of more than usual commotion in our field. Orders from the king, designed to cripple us in our labors, and perhaps to stop them altogether, have been issued; and, though they have not yet been carried into effect, they have caused no small stir among the people. We feel that we are in danger of having our work interrupted. The war question is likely soon to be a practical one in Persia. We can hardly expect this summer to pass without seeing the country involved in the conflict. But we can do nothing in regard to it, except pray 'Thy kingdom come,' and labor for souls as long as we can. We have nothing to fear if we are only found faithful."

"*April* 19. — A Persian nobleman, Askar Khan, sent by the king to see the firman enforced, has been in Oroomiah for nearly a month. He has directed our press to stop, and made sundry requirements in regard to the education of females which show that he is ready to do anything in his power to stop our labors. Our press, however, still works, and no order of his has been heeded. You know that we enjoy the protection of the British ambassador at the Court of Teheran; and we have been directed by the English Consul at Tabreez to go forward till otherwise instructed by the British ambassador. The influence of this embassy in Persia is less than in former years, and they may not be able to do for us what their liberal hearts would prompt them to do. We feel that our present situation is a critical one. The clouds that hang over us are very dark. Oh that they might be charged with blessings! The coming months may drive us from Persia, or they may make our position here more favorable than ever before. We believe we are ready to follow the leadings of Providence, whatever they may be. We have strong hope that our enemies will themselves fall into the pit they have digged for others. We can join in some of David's prayers for his enemies, and in so doing heed, I trust, the admonition, 'Be ye angry and sin not.'"

"23. — Askar Khan visited our school just before the term closed, and expressed in the strongest manner his disapproval of everything done for females. 'Their work,' he said, 'is to cook for their husbands, and to labor in the fields. They need no other knowledge.' Such are the feelings of those who now set themselves against us; but we trust in the Lord, and if we may not labor for our sisters in one way, we will seek to do it in another, if allowed to dwell in the country. We cannot believe that our work here is to cease, though it may be temporarily interrupted. We remember the signal blessings of the past, and take courage. The work is the Lord's. He loves it better than we do; and if he helps us we will not forsake him nor his work in the hour of trial."

"*June* 4. — We have been permitted for the last month to go on with our labors with less disturbance. The panic excited among the people by the appearance and course of the Khan has somewhat subsided, and we find our meetings again full, while but little outward opposition is manifested. The Khan says he has made his report of our labors and forwarded it to the capital, and now awaits farther orders."

While in the midst of these disturbances and dangers, Miss Fiske prepared an account of the labors among the Nestorian females for the use of the English Consul at Teheran, from which a brief extract is given: —

"OROOMIAH, May 1, 1855.

"R. W. STEVENS, ESQ., H. B. M. CONSUL AT TEHERAN:

"DEAR SIR: — I have been requested by our mission to write you, giving an account of the school for Nestorian girls in Oroomiah, of which Miss Rice and I have the care, and of other labors for females in connection with the school. I do this, not with the expectation of inciting you to greater efforts to aid us in our labors, since it would hardly be possible for you to do more than you have done during your residence in Persia. My only object is to put you in possession of such facts as will enable you to answer those who charge us with doing that which is unlawful, or, rather, that which is not for the best good of the Nestorian community.

"The design of the school is to so educate Nestorian girls that they may be better daughters and sisters, wives and mothers, than are those usually found among the people. Unless a change, and a very great change, can be wrought in the females here, all the efforts in behalf of the other sex will fail of producing permanent good. We aim to give the members of the school such a training, physical, mental, and moral, as shall best fit them for a happy and useful life among their own people. . . .

"Aside from the various duties of the school-room, kitchen, and wash-room, the pupils are taught to cut and make their own clothing. They also give attention to other plain needle-work, and ply their knitting whenever they find a few leisure moments. Some ornamental needle-work is taught the older girls. This has not a very prominent place in our instructions, though we deem it important. It tends not a little to soften the asperities of these wild girls. The same hand, however, that skilfully uses the worsted needle, is found in summer among the golden wheat holding the sickle, and in autumn gathering the vintage." . . .

At this time Miss Fiske's thoughts often turned with tender interest to her Holyoke friends. "There is but one spot in favored America so dear to me as your home, and were I to return, there is but one person I would long to embrace before seeing you: that spot is my early home, and that person my own dear mother. And am I not right in believing that you pray for me and mine? When I see rich blessings descending on my Nestorian sisters, I am wont to believe that Holyoke's sisters are praying for us. Your prayers may do more in this interesting work than our labors can. Those whom I have called *my* children in the Lord, may in the last great day be found to be *your* children, — the children of fervent, prevailing prayer."

The younger pupils were dismissed early in the season, the elder ones being retained till July, when entire rest from school duties was found necessary for the teachers. It had been a busy and trying year, and Miss Fiske had become greatly worn by her school labors and the care of the sick. Yet, in reply to expressions of solicitude in regard to her health, she could say, "I am generally very well. Sometimes I feel as though I must soon give up, but rest makes me ready to begin my labors again. I would acknowledge the special goodness of the Lord in giving me so much of health for twelve years. During this time I have not required, nor had any missionary sister to watch by my side for a single night."

CHAPTER XX.

JULY, 1855, TO JUNE, 1856.

At Gavalan. — The Girls as Missionaries in the Mountains. — Native Converts at the Lord's Supper. — Domestic Labors. — "If you love me, lean hard." — Revival. — Sanum's Children Poisoned. — Baptism at a "Fair."

During the summer vacation of 1855, Miss Fiske made a short visit to Gavalan, whence she wrote, August 14th: —

"Our pupils are now busy in their homes, and some of them, we hope, are doing a great deal of good. John recently made a tour in the mountains, visiting our girls in Tergawar, Marsheboo, and Gawar. We have a girl married in each of these places. John speaks of them as 'light-houses in the great, dark sea of iniquity which covers the mountains.' His first remark on returning was, 'What blessed seed you have sown in the mountains! Wherever a man goes he finds his own house, and strengtheners of the feet of righteousness.' It is pleasant to hear such reports from our dear children. Mr. Rhea, who has been in Gawar the last nine months, says, 'It requires as much self-denial for one reared in Oroomiah to go to the mountains, as for one to come from America to Oroomiah.'"

"OROOMIAH, September 17.

'I returned to the city a few days since, and now am busy in preparations for the winter. Our annual meeting was held on Wednesday and Thursday of last week in Seir, at which all were present. On Friday the mission met some seventy of the natives in the city, and with them celebrated the Lord's supper. It was a season of deep and tender interest. There are many more, who, in the judgment of charity, should come to this ordinance, and we hope at some future time to meet them at the table of our Lord and Master."

The first communion to which native converts were admitted was in September, 1854. After the service, some of the men were observed to withdraw, and sit down together in silence. Fearing lest they might have been disappointed at the absence of those forms to which they had been accustomed, Miss Fiske ventured to approach and speak to them on the subject. "'Is it always so when you commune,' asked one of them, 'or was this an unusual occasion?' 'Why do you ask; did you not enjoy it?' Not enjoy it! Jesus Christ seemed to be almost visibly present; it was difficult to realize that it was not the Saviour in person who presided at the table. It must have been just such a scene when the ordinance was first instituted at Jerusalem, and I could not get rid of the inquiry, 'Shall one of us go out like Judas to betray him?' The very simplicity of the forms gave the ordinance great attraction for them. One woman travelled sixty miles through snow to attend the communion in January, 1858."

After the departure of Mr. Stocking for America, Miss Fiske and Miss Rice kept house by themselves; though nominally belonging to the family of Mr. Breath, whose house was connected with their own. This arrangement often devolved upon them the pleasant, though sometimes onerous, duties of hospitality. In the absence of other missionary families from the city, their guests were numerous. Thus, Miss Fiske writes, under date of September 18th: "We are the only family here, and consequently have much company. I have been here eighteen days, and in that time we have prepared one hundred and forty-one meals for others. Those of the brethren connected with the press go to their work in the city, and stop with us. Those who attend the Sabbath services do the same; and others, for various reasons, are often here, so that we are seldom alone. But you will remember that I always liked to have company better than to visit; so it is no burden to me."

Let us now take another view of the secular labors of these missionaries, given by Miss Fiske in writing to her sister. "We are now laying in stores for our great family, and for ourselves. I have sometimes thought that I ought to tell you more particularly just how we live. You would like to know what we eat, as well as what we do. Now that we keep house, we think most of good bread and butter, both of which we make. As I looked at my churning to-day,—it was about a pound and a half,—I felt very rich, and thought it looked about as yellow and good as your butter. Our bread is always of wheat; no other grain being raised here. We buy a load (five bushels) for a dollar and three-quarters. As it is not properly winnowed, we are obliged to have it washed and picked over. Then the mills here do not bolt it, so we have it sifted through a muslin sieve. The flour is very good when all is done. We have no fresh fruit for winter, but we dry a good deal, and cook, as we want it, in molasses made from the juice of the grape. We use but little meat. To-day I have made some squash pies. The squash was from American seed and the pies taste home-like. Oh, how much I thank our dear mother for teaching me so much, and so well in the kitchen! The Nestorians honor my mother for this. It is no undesirable thing for a missionary lady to be acquainted with domestic economy. Much depends on having good food, that is, such as we can relish. The native dishes are, for the most part, very greasy, and consequently unhealthy; and I have no doubt that there has been a great loss of health, not to say, of life, among missionaries, for want of such food as they had been accustomed to eat. We would be as free from 'serving tables' as possible; but I feel that health and, consequently, usefulness are so dependent on nourishing food, that I am as sure that I am doing missionary work when providing this, as when holding a prayer-meeting."

On assembling her school early in November, Miss Fiske could say, "I never entered into my work with more gratitude, and I do earnestly hope and pray that rich spiritual blessings may this year be ours."

The incident alluded to in the following extract from a letter to a friend, written in December, contains a sermon from which others may, perhaps, profit as much as did Miss Fiske.

"I have learned here, as I never did in America, that He who fed the five thousand with the portion of five, can feed the soul, and richly feed it, too, with what I once thought were *only* the *crumbs*. May I give you one of the Master's sermons? A few Sabbaths since I went to Geog Tapa with Mr. Stoddard. It was afternoon, and I was sitting on a mat near the middle of the church, which has no seats, and only a floor of earth. I had been to two exercises before going to the church, one the Sabbath school, and the other a prayer-meeting, with my girls. I was weary, and longed for rest, and, with no support, it seemed to me that I could not sit there till the close of the service; nor could I hope for rest even when that was over, for I must meet the women readers of the village, and encourage them in reading their Testaments. I thought how I would love to be in your church; but God took the thought from me very soon, for, finding that there was some one directly behind me, I looked, and there was one of the sisters, who had seated herself so that I might lean upon her. I objected; but she drew me back to the firm support she could give, saying, 'If you love me, you will lean hard.' Did I not then lean hard? And then there came the Master's *own* voice, 'If you love *me*, you will lean hard;' and I leaned on *Him* too, and felt that He had sent the poor woman to give me a better sermon than I might have heard even with you. I was rested long before the church services were finished; and I afterwards had a long hour with the women readers, and closed with prayer. A little after sunset we left, to ride six miles to our home. I was surprised to find that I was not at all weary that night, nor in the morning, and I have rested ever since, remembering the sweet words, "If you love me, lean hard."

The hostility of the government still continued, and there seemed reason to fear that the schools would all be broken up. But in this time of trouble the Lord interposed, and another precious season of revival was enjoyed in both seminaries. The work in the female seminary was one of peculiar interest. Extracts from different letters of Miss Fiske will give a connected account of it.

"Another cloud of mercy has passed this way, and my own dear school has shared richly in the blessing. We assembled our school last November, little expecting to retain the pupils many weeks. It seemed as if earth and hell had combined to destroy the tender vine. But the Lord has not allowed the 'boar out of the wood to waste it.' He has 'purged it, that it might bring forth more fruit,' and rich have been the clusters drooping from the branches. It was not till the eighteenth of February that we saw any very marked indications of the Spirit's presence among our dear children. There was more than usual seriousness early in February, but it was like the morning cloud. Sabbath evening, February 17th, I returned from our English prayer-meeting, with an unusually heavy heart. The thought that our term was rapidly passing away, and not a soul converted, was peculiarly saddening. The girls had retired, and I was alone. I thought, and thought upon our state, but I seemed to have no strength to rise and carry those precious souls to Christ. Sleep had forsaken me, and I so shrunk from meeting the duties of Monday that I almost wished for a long night rather than for the morning. It was eleven o'clock, and I supposed all were asleep, when I heard a gentle knock at my door. Could I open the door? Must I see a face again? Yes, I could and did open the door, and there stood one of the dear girls whose heart was not as cold as I had thought. She said, 'Are you very tired?' 'No, not very tired,—why?' 'I cannot sleep; our school has been resting on me all day, and I thought perhaps you would pray with me.' How changed were my feelings now! I was ready to say, 'Come in, thou who art sent of the Lord.' As an angel from heaven the dear child strengthened me that night. She knelt by my side, and, while we felt that God was near, we carried our precious family to him. She did not leave me till the midnight hour, and then I could sleep. The work I had vainly sought to do was left with the Lord, and there was peace. Jesus said at that hour, 'Peace I leave with you;' and when the morning came there still was peace. It was hardly light when I went in to morning prayers. 'Could ye not watch with me one hour?' was the word that Jesus spoke to me that first waking hour, and so I carried it to our family devotions. I had hardly repeated it when I saw three in tears. They were in different parts of the room, and their manner indicated tender feeling. I said little, for it seemed safer to pray. Is the Lord with us? I asked again and again; and as I knelt in prayer so strong was the assurance that he had indeed come to bless us that I could but say, 'We thank thee, thou long-neglected Spirit, that thou art indeed with us.' All day there was a tender, subdued feeling manifested by some, but no one asked us to point out to them the way to heaven. There was quiet at the tables, quiet in the rooms, and prayers in the closets. Tuesday was a deeply solemn day. In all parts of the room could be seen those whose studies seemed a burden, and who longed to be alone with God. Before leaving the school-room Tuesday afternoon, I said, 'If there is one of our dear family who feels that she must make her soul her first care, I should be glad to see her in my room at the ringing of the half-past eight bell this evening. That bell rang; I sat alone in my room; the door opened, and one came in, then another, and another, till I could no longer say, 'and still there's room,' but could only say, 'In my Father's house there still is room.' Twenty-three were there with bowed heads, and never, while I remember to pray for the dear Nestorians, shall I forget the solemnity of that meeting. The next day it was very difficult to go forward with our lessons, and, when recess came, not a few silently withdrew to their closets. At eleven o'clock Mr. Perkins came from Seir, to sing with the school. I went out to meet him, and told him that we had reason to feel that God was with us. He said, 'Shall I sing with the girls, or pray with them?' I thought it best to sing, as usual. He went in, and gave out 'Blind Bartimeus.' Each book was opened, and all began to sing, but some voices faltered on the first stanza, more on the second, and before the close of the hymn our brother's clear voice was heard all alone. He reached out his hand for my Bible, and, opening it, said, 'There is a time to sing and a time to pray, and perhaps some wandering child would be glad to go to her heavenly Father now.' He read the parable of the Prodigal Son, and prayed. It was affecting to see those wanderers turning their faces, that day, towards their Father's house. The intermission at noon was lengthened, for we could not feel it right to draw the girls so soon from their closets.

"The girls are now — April 7th — away for a vacation. The morning of their departure will long be remembered. I was awakened from sleep by the voice of prayer in the school-room, and soon found that a few girls, who lodged in that room, had arisen from their beds, and, without putting up their bedding, had knelt down to pray together before the dawn, lest they should have no other time. They had six prayers before the rising-bell rang. After breakfast, all set about their usual domestic work; but prayer-meetings soon followed, and some of them were called from their closets when their friends came for them.

"I look back on those few weeks as, perhaps, the greenest spot in all my earthly pilgrimage. I thank the Lord for giving me one more such sweet foretaste of heaven, before giving me a place among his redeemed ones above. I thank him, too, for remembering so many of my dear girls. I have long loved them, and now Jesus loves them. What more could I ask for them?

"There has been some interest in several villages, and many have come to us for religious instruction. Could you have seen these loved Nestorians, sitting down by us, and asking, with tearful eyes, for the way of life, you would not wonder that I could not find time to write. For two months I did not write a single letter.

"One cold morning, soon after the revival began, a woman, who had walked three miles through the snow, called at the seminary, with the inquiry, 'Is there any interest in the school?' 'Why do you ask?' replied the teacher. 'I have thought of you continually,' she said, 'for two or three days, and last night, after falling asleep thinking about you, I dreamed that God was visiting you by his Holy Spirit. So, when I awoke, I arose and baked, and hurried here. I am so anxious about my daughter! Can I see her?' When informed that the Holy Spirit was there, and that her daughter was among the inquirers, she sank down, weeping for joy. She soon met her daughter, in an adjoining room, and, in her earnest intercessions with her, was overheard to say, 'This is more than anything I have seen in Persia.' Once it was only pious daughters in the school wrestling in prayer for their unconverted mothers; now it is also pious mothers wrestling for their unconverted daughters in the school."

The opposition, which could not prevent, seemed to be intensified by this interesting work of grace. It manifested itself especially towards the native helpers, and in one case came near being attended with fatal results. Miss Fiske refers to it in the following letter: —

"Our helpers have been reviled and insulted, and, to crown all, an attempt has been made to take the lives of Joseph and Sanum, who have been located three years in Dizza Takka. This was done by putting arsenic into their supper, while it was over the fire.

Joseph was away, attending a meeting, and thus escaped. Sanum, and their two little children, ate of the soup, and in about five minutes were taken seriously ill. They suspected what had been done, and, Joseph being called, emptied the pot and found arsenic at the bottom. Remedies were used, and they were apparently out of danger when Dr. Wright reached them. There is little doubt as to who did this work, but they are not yet brought to justice. The authorities oppose proper investigation, and would evidently be glad to clear the guilty, and have probably taken bribes for this purpose. We feel that in the present state of things our own lives are in jeopardy every hour."

The poisoned mother fully recovered, but the children, after lingering some months, both died.

"Yesterday was our last school day this year. The girls had, for some time, been very busy in knitting, etc., for benevolent purposes. A Sabbath-school class in Boston had given us five dollars' worth of tidy cord, woollen yarn, cotton yarn, etc., which we thought the girls might make into various articles, and then sell them. Accordingly the last day of the school was fixed upon for the purpose. Mr. Coan, being about to leave for Gavalan, proposed to have his little girl baptized in the morning, and Mr. Breath also wished to have his child baptized at the same time. We had invited all the mission and several natives to be present, and at eleven o'clock all met in our school-room, which the girls had previously prepared with some taste. The exercises were mostly in Syriac, and lasted till about twelve o'clock. After dinner we repaired again to the school-room. The girls' work was first sold, nearly seventeen dollars being realized from it. This done, each member of the mission said a few words; a hymn was sung, and the exercises were closed with prayer. The girls propose sending their money to Aintab, to aid in teaching the one hundred and fifty women there learning to read."

CHAPTER XXI.

JUNE, 1856, TO JUNE, 1857.

Maternal Association. — Repair of Seminary Building. — Health Impaired. — Tour in the Mountains of Koordistan. — Wedding of a Pupil in the Mountains.— Mission Schools.— Hostility of the Government.— Assassination of Askar Kahn. — Sickness and Death of Mr. Stoddard and Harriet. — Religious Interest in the School. — Thoughts of Heaven.

At the close of her school in 1856, Miss Fiske greatly needed rest and change of scene; but she felt that duty required her to spend most of the summer in the city; and scarcely any period of her missionary life was more crowded with exhausting labors than those months of vacation. In the following autumn she suffered from the first development of that disease which finally caused her death, and she always attributed it to the fatigue, anxiety, and exposure attending those vacation labors. June 20th, she writes: "All the families of the mission have now left the city for the summer, and Miss Rice and I are left here alone. Unless there should be unusual sickness here, we shall not both be away on the Sabbath, or on Friday, for we have a flock here still, to whom we are tenderly attached, and for whom we feel that we must labor."

During the year she had formed what might be called a Maternal Association, — meeting a number of Nestorian mothers every Friday, to instruct them in regard to their duties. In this meeting she felt a deep interest, and regretted even an occasional absence from it. Still another reason for remaining in the city was the necessity of repairs in her school-building. The house being built of mud, the walls and roofs often needed the attention of the mason and carpenter. She preferred to superintend this work herself, and while it was going forward, endeavored with characteristic zeal, to do something for the spiritual good of the workmen employed.

Her description of the work will be read with interest: —

"*June* 20, 1856. — For a few days our house has presented such a scene as you will probably never witness, unless your home shall be in Persia. Some parts of our mud tenement were in danger of falling in, and we feared that a serious accident might be the result, if it were longer left in this state. As soon, therefore, as our pupils left, we brought together a goodly number of masons and other workmen to demolish, and then rebuild. Miss Rice is at Seir, and I am glad to enjoy the dust and care of a dozen men alone, for there is danger of ophthalmia to those who must be in the dust. To-night I can feel that the worst part of our work is done; the pillars being raised, and the heavy timbers resting on them. The workmen have been very willing to do as I wished, and I feel that I have great reason for gratitude that no harm has befallen any one. Every morning the motley group of workmen have met in our schoolroom, and we have read the Bible to them, and questioned them with reference to it, and one of the masons, who is pious, has then led in prayer. We feel that all who come into our house must hear enough of the gospel to enable them to secure life eternal, and when we have no missionary brother with us, we are sure that our Father would have us lead these darkened minds to the light."

"*July* 4. — My sixteen women have been in again for a maternal meeting. One of our older pupils, who is with me, had a meeting with the children. I took the names of the children of these mothers, and found that they had forty-three children living, and had lost fifty-six. This is perhaps not a larger proportion than usual, of the native children who die in infancy."

Amid her cares and labors in the city, she found time for flying visits to Saatloo, Saralan, Barandooz, Degala, and Wazarawa, to hold meetings and attend Bible classes with the women. In August, hearing of the illness of Mr. Coan's children in Gavalan, she hastened thither to aid in caring for the little sufferers, filling up every moment, when she could be spared from the sick-room, with efforts for the good of the women, who were glad of her instructions and prayers.

The effect of these incessant labors began to appear in her impaired health. "Since my return from Gavalan," she writes, "my eyes have almost entirely refused to be used. During the spring I thought they were better; but a succession of nights of watching has brought the trouble back again, and I am obliged to be very careful about exerting myself much in any way, as any effort affects my eyes the same as writing does. I am sometimes quite discouraged in regard to them, and then again I am hopeful."

In October she made a tour in the mountains, going to places which had never before been visited by any ladies of the mission. Of this tour she writes, soon after her return:

"You will be surprised to know that I have been over the most trying roads in Koordistan, and you will thank the Lord that I am safely home. We were absent from Oroomiah three weeks. I enjoyed much in seeing my poor sisters in those mountain fastnesses, but I cannot conceal the fact that the journey was a trying one. For weeks after my return, I dreamed every night of the dreadful precipices, and waked, finding myself holding on to the bed-posts in great fear of falling. I rode a mule from the time of leaving Gawar, and once was thrown over his head, the animal falling on me. One man seized his tail, and another his ears, and so I was unharmed. In going from district to district we were obliged to pass mountain ridges, parts of which were so steep that it was not possible to hold on to the animal in ascending, and on reaching the top we would find a corresponding descent to the next valley. Walking over Mt. Tom would be an easy task compared with some of these walks. Sometimes I felt as though my last resting-place would be on the mountain side; but strength was given for each day; and at evening, when surrounded by listening ones, I never regretted any effort I had made. I enjoyed much the wild scenery on the banks of the Zab; but it was not pleasant often to feel that a single mistep would plunge me hundreds of feet below, to be dashed in pieces on the rocks, or to meet death as certainly in the foaming torrent. But the Lord was my Keeper and the Keeper of all our company. I am feeling well since my return, and think the change of air and scenery did me good. During the summer, neuralgia was my almost constant guest; but I am now quite free from it. I really feel that I have five times as much strength as I had three months ago. Had my tour been months instead of weeks, I should probably have become quite robust."

In the valley of Tekhoma the tourists attended the wedding of one who had been for a short time a pupil in the seminary. Miss Fiske thus describes it: —

"As we came in sight of the bridegroom's house, all was noise and confusion; some were playing on the drum and fife before the door, while others, fantastically tricked out with marigolds, were engaged in the most wild and boisterous dance I ever saw, and singing rude and wicked Koordish songs. Several of the dancers were brandishing drawn swords, as they danced in imitation of the Koordish war dance; and others were, at intervals, discharging pistols. I know not when my feelings were more shocked than by seeing such a profanation of the Sabbath by those who were nominal Christians. It soon became evident that we could accomplish but little good by our presence, especially as so many of the people were under the influence of wine. We however sat down for a time and conversed with a few persons who were willing to listen. As we sat by the door, the bride was brought in by a noisy procession, amid the music of drums and fifes, the firing of guns, and the shouts of the rabble. When she was about entering the house a quantity of walnuts and raisins was poured on her head; which were scrambled for by the boys and girls. Before leaving, I had an opportunity of talking a little with the poor girl, who was forced to act a part, no doubt greatly against her will, in such heathenish proceedings, and of reminding her of the truth she had heard in days gone by. It may be that she will hereafter remember our visit with interest and profit."

Miss Fiske, having received a letter which alluded to the Report made by the Deputation sent out to India in 1855, to examine into the condition of the mission schools there, thus replied: —

"*Nov.* 4, 1856. — You refer to the education question before the American Board. I have read with much care everything that has come from the press in regard to it; and you will perhaps be surprised when I tell you that I most cordially approve the views of the deputation to India, so far as I understand them. I do not think they intended to interfere with schools, where the first and great work was to save souls. . . I deeply feel that the missionary who has the care of a seminary is in great danger of allowing the study of English, or science, to come in and rob God of his dues. Oh, I have felt this, and have made it my daily prayer that I might be kept from it! We must strive to make our pupils intelligent; but if they do not become Christians our labors are in vain. It is not my impression that Dr. Anderson, if he had visited us, would have wished to change essentially our seminaries; but I am inclined to think that he would have wished our village-school system somewhat reduced, and I think it will be reduced without directions from home. These schools have done great good, but as our work progresses changes are called for, and one, I think, is that there be fewer schools and more preaching of the word."

Miss Fiske, having reassembled her school, writes, Nov. 13th: "Our present number of pupils is a little less than forty. The government agent here is very busy trying to excite such fears as will keep girls away from the school. He threatens to fine every parent who shall presume to allow his daughter to remain with us after about the twentieth of this month. The parents seem but little intimidated as yet, but we are not without considerable anxiety. The Lord reigns. This is our stay and comfort."

Again, Dec. 18th, she writes, in regard to the opposition: "Our helpers have been imprisoned, beaten, and threatened with being sent to Tabreez in chains. They are forbidden to preach in the churches, and bonds have been given by evil-minded men, in which they pledge themselves, in the sum of one hundred dollars, to report if they go to the church, break the fasts, etc. Our village schools are almost all broken up, and we hourly expect the pupils of our seminaries to be taken from us. We awake to the fact that the Persian government is determined to break up all our operations, and to drive us from the country. We look in vain for help from any earthly source. We are tried, but we do not despair, feeling that God will appear for us in due time. I had a most pleasant dream a few nights ago, in which I thought my dear father sent my departed sisters to ask me to come and stay with him until the storm was past. I leaned on him once more, and asked him if he was sure the enemy would not come to his dwelling. He replied, 'My child, rest here with me. I want you to stay with me, and you may be sure the enemy will never cross the river.' I said, 'My father, the river is very shallow.' He looked at me most tenderly, saying, 'I know it, my child, but the enemy were never known to cross it.' I then rested sweetly with my dear father. I waked to find it all a dream; but I have loved to dwell on it in my waking hours. If we ever reach the blissful shores of heaven no enemy can come after us."

The enemy *did not* cross the "shallow stream," in this instance. A divine hand held him back, though his feet were allowed to advance a little farther into the waters. Late in the autumn the agent of the government, Askar Khan, again visited the female seminary, exploring with an inquisitorial eye every part of it. In the school-room he paused, and began to question one of the girls who could speak Turkish. Some of the questions and answers were as follows: —

"Are you allowed to follow your own customs?"

"We follow all that are good. We have some very foolish customs which you would not wish us to follow."

"Do these ladies let you see your friends?"

"Certainly; we always see them when they come here, and we go home three times a year, and once we stay three months."

"What do you do when in your villages?"

"We go out into the fields and work, and do everything our friends do."

"Are your teachers willing?"

"They tell us to help our friends all we can, and are sometimes displeased because we do no more for them."

"When here what do you do?"

"We study and learn all wisdom."

"Are you allowed to use your own books?"

"Certainly. The book which is the foundation of

our religion they have printed for us, and we use it more than any other."

"Do you fast?"

"One day at the beginning of the year, and several other days."

"Have you not forsaken your father's fasts?"

"Not any that are written in that book. I am careful to keep all those."

"Would your teachers be willing that you should fast?"

"They would be willing; but we do not wish to fast more than our book requires."

"What are your prayers?"

"Such as our book teaches us."

The examiner was baffled by the discreet replies of the girl; yet in a decided manner condemned female education, and told the girls that their former condition was the only proper one for them.

But the time had come for this "enemy of all righteousness" to be taken out of the way. His removal was sudden, and in an unlooked-for manner. Askar Khan was assassinated in his own tent by a Koordish chief, Dec. 18th, and the next day his corpse was carried past the very door of the missionaries whom he had sought to oppress.

But a sorer trial than persecution was soon to befall the mission in the death of "that disciple whom Jesus loved,"—Rev. D. T. Stoddard. For many reasons Miss Fiske was deeply afflicted by this event. She and Mr. S. joined the mission at the same time, and they had been intimately associated in the educational department of the work,—had made frequent tours together in the mountains and among the villages, and were in full sympathy in their general views of the missionary service, and in the spirit of elevated and ardent piety which so well fitted them for that service. While together scaling the mountains of Koordistan in October, they little thought that, in three months, his feet would stand on Mount Zion above, and that she was inhaling vigor from those mountain breezes for watching so soon by his sick and dying bed.

Mr. Stoddard was attacked with typhus fever on the 22d of December, 1856, and died January 22d, 1857. During that month of severe sickness, Miss Fiske was with the afflicted family. "You will perhaps wonder," she writes to a friend, "that I should be away from my school for twenty days. I stayed, not because I was able to do so much, but because I could not bear to leave. I felt that I was hanging over the dying-bed of one of the last of my early missionary friends. I could not tear myself away, and, for the last four days, I was never, for more than two hours at a time, away from his bedside till he had gone from us."

When the sad event took place, Miss Fiske immediately announced it to her associate Miss Rice in the following note: —

"Thursday, Midnight.

"MY DEAR SISTER: — 'It is finished; the conflict is past.' As you gather our precious family around you for morning prayer, read this hymn, and think of our dear, dear brother as a happy spirit before the throne. At twenty minutes past eleven, he passed away so gently that we could hardly tell when he was gone. Peace, oh, such sweet peace sits on his countenance!

Let the girls also sing this morning, 'How blest the righteous when he dies;' for its sweet words comforted our hearts when we felt sure he was gone. My heart is full, I want to see you all once again, and with you pray, as our dear, departed brother did, Monday night, 'Let us be thine in life, thine in death, thine in judgment, and thine when an abundant entrance shall be ministered into thy kingdom.'

"Your affectionate sister,

"F. FISKE."

Only one short month had passed after Mr. Stoddard's death, before his eldest daughter, who, on the previous November, publicly confessed Christ, and, with her father, sat, for the first time, at the sacramental table, was attacked by the same disease which had just made such a wide breach in the missionary circle; and in twenty days another grave was made in the little cemetery at Seir. Father and daughter slept side by side on that green, sunny slope to which the thoughts of many, both in Persia and America, turn with tender interest.

March 21, 1857, Miss Fiske writes: "When Harriet was first taken sick, I supposed it impossible for me to reach her, as the roads were so blocked up with snow, that they were only passable to footmen. But Mr. Perkins' great anxiety to have me with her dear mother, to aid and comfort her, led him to come down for me; and I was drawn to Seir on a hand-sled on the 4th instant. I was thankful for this privilege of going to see dear Harriet, and thankful that I could remain with her as long as mortals could do anything for her."

Only for brief seasons of rest did she leave the little one till her sufferings were ended. "I can never forget," she writes, "my feelings, as a missionary brother said to me, when her gentle spirit had passed away, 'Will you close her eyes?' My thoughts went back to the same evening of the same month, thirteen years ago, when I passed the evening and night with Harriet in my arms, or standing by the sick mother. Now, mother, father, and child are gone, and I alone am left of those who watched and suffered in that sick-room, March 16, 1844. As I placed my hand on dear Harriet's eyes, for a few minutes I could not close them, but rested my head on the pillow beside her, and wept bitter tears. . . . We knelt by the bed of the departed one, and prayed; and tried to trace the spirit's upward flight, and to think of the joyous meeting of father, mother, and daughter, and of their being forever with the precious Saviour. It was such a sweet vision which passed before us, we felt that we would not, if we could, bring back either of the three to be with us. Blessed family meeting! Separation will be 'known no more.' Such were our feelings as we looked upward; but when we turned our eyes again to earth, sadness stole over us."

Before Miss Fiske was called to Seir by the sickness of Harriet, there were indications of unusual religious interest in her school. Her first thought was, that she could not be absent at such a time, but finally concluded that if duty called her elsewhere, the Lord would take care of his own work without her help. "When I left to go to Seir," she says, "several of my dear girls were inquiring for the way of life. Their impressions were greatly deepened by the call of Harriet to go up higher; and others were added to the list of inquiries. When I returned, I had a most affecting meeting with a little band, who hoped that they had begun to love the Saviour during my absence."

From that hallowed spot at Seir, where she had seen the gate of heaven open twice within a short time, Miss Fiske returned to her school duties with a body worn and weary, and with a spirit chastened and filled with heavenly longings.

To her mother she writes, May 21st: "Is it not pleasant to think of being almost home? Will you not enjoy the 'communion of the saints' made perfect, as you cannot that of frail imperfect beings on earth? Will you not again clasp your long-lost children there? The dear babes, whom you gave to the grave more than forty years ago, are not lost. You shall see them again, little ones before the throne; and I hope you will find your other children there, or that they will soon follow you to your sweet rest. How glad will papa be to see you, and to see all his dear family! In my sleeping hours I often see him, and he always comforts me, and wipes away the falling tear. It will be delightful to meet our friends in heaven; but, when we look on our dear Redeemer, I suspect we shall almost forget our friends. To see Jesus as he is; to grow in likeness to him every hour; oh, will it not be delightful! We shall sin no more when we reach heaven; will not that, too, be delightful?"

A little later, writing to her sister, she says: "We must not dwell too much on our losses, nor on the closing scenes in the life of dear friends. We must look away to the world of life and lŏve, and there behold our dear ones free from all sin; sick no more; every hour learning something new of the Holy One; satisfied in a Saviour's love, and serving him without weariness. If I could sing, I am sure I should often sing, 'Oh, I want to be there!' But I am willing and glad to stay here just as long as my Father wants me to stay. I only pray that I may become so much assimilated to the holy ones above, that I shall *feel at home*, if permitted to reach the heavenly land."

CHAPTER XXII.

LAST YEAR IN PERSIA.

Counsel to a Young Christian. — Death of Mrs. Rhea. — Revival. — Sanctified Sorrow. — Decides to return to America. — Last Communion Season in Persia. — Last Prayer-Meeting. — Farewell. — Journey. — Voyage. — At Home Again.

CIRCUMSTANCES again made it expedient for Miss Fiske to spend the entire summer vacation in the city and at Seir, and she was too busily occupied to find the rest she greatly needed. Her eyes protested against such incessant use, and for several weeks she was obliged to give them an unbroken holiday. But weak eyes did not prevent her from rendering the sympathy and aid so much needed and so fully appreciated by that stricken missionary sister, from whose desolated home she had so recently witnessed the departure of two whom she tenderly loved.

As the season advanced she was able to resume her pen occasionally. To a niece she gives the following excellent advice: "Whatever Providence gives you to do, do it with all your heart. If you are a housekeeper, keep house well; if you are sewing, sew well; if in the sick-room, strive to do everything in the most quiet and acceptable manner for the sick one. You will, probably, never meet a person of whom you may not learn something valuable. I have never known a person so faulty, that he did not combine with his faults some excellences. I think you will find the same true. Dwell as little as possible on a person's faults; speak of them less than you think of them; and let them never hinder you from imitating what is truly excellent." . . . .

To her mother she sent the following tender expression of her filial devotion, on the seventeenth anniversary of her father's death.

"September 27th, 1857.

"MY DEARLY LOVED MOTHER: — I know that your thoughts have turned to your far-off child to-day; and my first thoughts were certainly given to my lone widowed mother. You, probably, sometimes feel that your lonely pilgrimage is a long one, and that it would be good to be at rest with the dear Saviour, and the departed loved ones. And, my mother, you will go home just as soon as your work is all done. It is a great comfort to your surviving children that you still live. I know that you have more in heaven than on earth, but there are hearts on earth which cling to you very closely. They pray not only that your life may be prolonged, but that your last days may be very peaceful and happy, and that, walking quite on the verge of heaven, you may have very rich foretastes of your eternal rest. The Saviour stayed not in this world till old age; but I know that he loves his aged disciples, and sympathizes with them most tenderly. The loving John leaned on his bosom in old age, as truly as in youth, and I doubt not that the Saviour loved him more tenderly than when the glow of youth was on his cheek. 'Paul the aged' was not forsaken of Him, by whom he had been called in early manhood. His last words show that he was still the object of his Redeemer's tender love and care. Feel not, my mother, for a moment, that your dearest Friend is not as near and as compassionate, as on the day when you gave him your young heart.

"'When age with gray hairs shall their temples adorn,
Like lambs they shall still in His bosom be borne.'

"When we cannot do for our Lord and Master we can 'lie passive in his hands;' and perhaps he never loves us so well as when thus we show that in him we have believed."

The month of September brought another sore bereavement to this mission. Mrs. Rhea, whose lovely character and missionary zeal had greatly endeared her to her associates, died, after weeks of acute suffering, at Gawar, where her husband was stationed. Miss Fiske was denied the privilege of being with her suffering sister; but did all she could for her through others. To Miss Rice, who was at Gawar, she wrote: "I am not only willing, but glad to have you with them. Our missionary work is our first work, and if we can do anything to contribute to the precious life and health of our brothers and sisters, it is missionary work in the highest sense."

Miss Fiske entered upon, what proved to be, the last year of her connection with her loved school, with but partially recruited energies.

"We have," she writes, November 5th, "a large number of new scholars this year, but they seem a pleasant company, and, if the Lord condescend to dwell with us, we may hope for a year of blessings. I sometimes feel much worn under my labors and cares; but I have great reason for gratitude for so large a measure of health as is granted me. I want to live better, and to be prepared for my eternal home."

She labored on through the long winter of twenty weeks with diminished strength, but with undiminished zeal. "I have generally felt very well," she writes, "and school duties have been a pleasure, and they are a pleasure still, when strength does not fail. The feeling will sometimes steal over me that I may become unfitted for missionary work, and be a burden, rather than a help, in the blessed cause. But I will not despond; my times are in my Father's hands." Her earnest desire for another revival in her school was granted; and the spring months of 1858 witnessed a repetition of those scenes which had so often gladdened her heart in former years. We give her own account of it: —

"*April 7th*, 1858. — Since writing you, we have seen some delightful days; delightful, because the Saviour was with us to seal precious souls for himself. The interest in our school commenced early in February, and continued to the close of the term, about the 20th of March. The number of hopeful conversions was not so large as it was two years ago, neither was the number of the impenitent so large at the commencement of the year. I look back on the season, as, on the whole, one of the most precious I have seen in my missionary life. I have had less of health and strength to engage in active labors, than during some previous seasons of refreshing; still, I have been permitted to point many never-dying souls to the Lamb of God that taketh away all sin. Oh, how thankful I am for the privilege of doing so! What are we, that it is given us to be co-workers with our dear Redeemer?"

The state of Miss Fiske's health was becoming more and more precarious, and the question of duty in regard to it, a more serious and pressing one. "You ask me," she writes, "if I do not hope to see Shelburne Hills again. It has not been my general expectation that I ever should. When I gave up my American friends it was with the feeling that I was doing so for Christ's sake, and that I should not see them again till I should see my Saviour. I have been *perfectly happy* in this feeling, and still am; but the last year has made me feel that I cannot expect to labor many more years without such a change as I cannot find here. It may be my *duty* to leave for a season, and that, too, before very long. I wait to know my Father's will."

After a brief vacation, the school was reassembled, and Miss Fiske resumed her duties in connection with it. But it soon became evident to the members of the mission that she could not long continue her missionary work without a prolonged season of rest. Indications of the disease which terminated her life had appeared, and, in the judgment of the mission physician, were of too alarming a character to be longer neglected. It was hoped that a voyage at sea would benefit her; while in her native land she could receive such medical treatment as her case required. And, as Dr. Perkins and Mrs. Stoddard were expecting to leave for America the following summer, it was decided that she should accompany them. This decision she thus announces in a letter, under date of April 28th: —

"MY DEAR SISTER: — You will perhaps be surprised by what I am now about to tell you. After fifteen years of unceasing labor in the missionary field, it is thought by my good friends here that I *must* seek a change for a season, in order to prolong my life and usefulness. A few months more may find me on my way to my native land. If spared to reach you, will you again give me a place in your family? I feel confident that you will give me a sister's welcome, and that I may pass a year with you, comforting and being comforted. I shall feel like a stranger, and my heart well-nigh bursts as I look forward to the future. I leave my own home here to be homeless." . . .

Further expression of her feelings in regard to this step is given in extracts from subsequent letters: —

"*May* 13. — I have given up my school, and am making preparations for my long journey. While I do not, and cannot, doubt that it is best for me to plan for this, still I often have very sad feelings. The future looks dark, very dark. But I seek to trust my dear Father who has always led me so gently." .

"29. — Very few missionaries can leave with such pleasant recollections of their life on missionary ground as I shall carry with me. I have been laid aside from labor very little, and more than half of the years I have spent here, the gentle dews of heaven have distilled upon my precious school, and upon those about me. When I came here there was no Nestorian female whom I could take by the hand and call a sister in Christ.

"How rejoiced was I when I saw one such! A few weeks since, on our communion day, I was allowed the privilege of taking ninety-three by the hand, and give them seats in our chapel previous to coming to the Lord's table. Forty-two of these had been my own dear pupils; several others were detained from being present."

The communion season in May was one of peculiar interest, and was the last which Miss Fiske enjoyed with the Nestorians. An account of it, and of a prayer-meeting which she held with her pupils on the same day, can best be given in her own words: —

"The day was one of the finest of those charming May days in Oroomiah. Most of the communicants were able to be with us. Those who had been our former pupils came at once to our school, while others were distributed among the families of the mission. I had asked this, that I might gather my scattered children around me once more in a prayer-meeting, before going to the Lord's table. As many as sixty or seventy of our pupils were with us. They had come from distances varying from one mile to sixty. As they gathered in our Bethel, on which at different times we had written 'Bochim,' 'Ebenezer,' 'Jehovah-nissi,' their tenderest feelings were called forth. As yet they knew nothing of my intention to leave, and, as I did not wish to turn their thoughts from Christ to me, I did not tell them. I found that I could say little to them, and that I must ask the Lord Jesus to stand in the midst of us. He came and whispered peace. After singing a hymn I read the words, 'Looking unto Jesus,' and many seemed to realize that he was with us; their eyes were not holden. After singing, I said it would be pleasant to have them tell of their joys and sorrows in the Christian life, and then together to carry them to Christ. Hardly a moment passed before Khanee, one of the two little girls first received into my school, spoke. She had recently buried her only child, and with a full heart said, raising her arms as if still holding her little one, 'Sisters, four months ago, you saw me here with my babe in my arms. It is not here now. I have laid it into Jesus' arms. I have come to-day to tell you that there is a sweet, as well as a bitter, in affliction. When the rod is laid upon us let us not only kiss it, but press it to our lips. When I stood by that little open grave I said, 'All the time I have given to my babe I will give to souls. I have tried to do so; pray for me that I may be faithful.' We had all followed the dear sister in what she said, and were all weeping. I could only say, 'Who will pray?' Sanum (whose children were poisoned), understanding well the bereaved mother's feelings, knelt at once, and carried us to the Saviour, who surely wept with us. I can never forget how she prayed for bereaved mothers, nor how she pleaded for those still folding their little ones in their arms. As we followed her in her earnest entreaties there was perfect silence, except as the sweet voice of her own little babe seemed sometimes to add to the tenderness of the petitions. A child in heaven! What a treasure! and what a blessing that the heart may be there also! As we arose we saw that Nazloo, who had just come from the banks of Jordan, had a word for us. It was this: 'Sisters, I have just come back from the grave's brink. I am here to-day, to tell you that it is a very different thing to be a Christian in this pleasant school-room, from what it is when standing with one foot in the grave. Let us all examine and see if our hopes will stand in the hour of death.' A tender prayer followed, in which it seemed that all must join in the petition: 'Search us and try us.'

"The next to speak was one of our early pupils. She had come many miles that day, and said: 'Sisters, I could think of but one thing all the way this morning, "Freely ye have received, freely give." We have certainly received freely, have we given anything? Can we not do something for souls? I am afraid the Lord Jesus is not pleased with us.' They were then asked if they were ready to enter into direct labors for souls, and if they would not like to keep the names of those for whom they should labor, and when they should come up to the feast of the Lord in September, bring them and pray over them. I was not with them in September; but the first letter I opened on reaching Boston, in December, gladdened my heart, for there fell from it some thirty lists of names that had been brought up to that September communion, and for whom they would have me pray.

"We spent nearly two hours in this prayer-meeting, and each moment was full of interest. Twelve or fourteen of the girls said a few words, and more prayed. Afterwards we all went to our large dining-room, where, seated on the floor, they partook of a single meal, with 'gladness and singleness of heart.' I then told them that I had made arrangements for them all to have 'class prayer-meetings' if they desired it. I can never forget the pleasure they manifested when this was announced. All retired to rooms designated, and soon the voice of prayer went up all over our house, and there was a sweet and affecting fellowship of hearts before the mercy-seat. The bell rang for going to the chapel, but it seemed to be unheard, and I was obliged to say to each little company, 'The Master calleth for you.' As we moved towards the chapel, we were joined by other women, and, when I went in, I took each by the hand and gave her a seat. When all were arranged, I took my seat back of them. At a glance I could see the number of seats occupied, and found that there were ninety-three sisters before me. Do you wonder that my heart was full at that hour, as I looked at so many sitting with us in heavenly places in Christ Jesus? There was but a single one of the ninety-three, with whom I had not prayed, and who had not prayed with me. There were more men than women at the table. Thirty came for the first time, and six of these were our own dear pupils. As they took the covenant we all stood with them; and there seemed a deeper meaning than ever before in being 'forever the Lord's,' and there was a reality in meeting Christ at his table."

It was cheering to Miss Fiske to see, during those last weeks in Persia, such precious fruit from the seed she had sown. June 9th, she wrote: "Yesterday, four of our former pupils, with their husbands, left us, as missionaries to the dark mountains of Koordistan. It was a day of deep interest. I do thank my Father for allowing me to live to see my dear children thus take their lives in their hands and go forth for Christ's sake."

The party about to leave the missionary field for America consisted, besides Miss Fiske, of Dr. Perkins, Mrs. Stoddard, and her only daughter, and two daughters of Dr. Wright. The day fixed for their departure was the 15th of July, and on the afternoon of that day they began their long journey. On the 17th, Miss Fiske wrote to her mother an account of the parting scene: —

"It was the most trying day to my feelings that I have seen in Persia. I have been able to bear trials, but to be surrounded by loving, weeping friends, from whom I was literally tearing myself, was too much for me. There was agony of soul in it, and it seemed sometimes as though the flesh could not bear it. For many days before I left, our house was thronged with visitors. My loved pupils came and sewed, and did everything they could to aid me in my preparations, although they often said, 'We cannot see very well, the tears so dim our eyes.' On the night of the fourteenth, more than thirty were with us, and they continued to come till the hour of our departure. They gathered around me, and I gave them last words, and prayed with them, as well as my feelings would allow. At noon our whole missionary circle met at Mr. Coan's, and after dinner sang, 'Blest be the tie that binds;' read the one hundred and twenty-third Psalm, and united in prayer. It was an hour of deep and tender feeling for those who left, and for those who remained. From Mr. Coan's we repaired to our chapel to meet our native friends, and to pray with them, for, perhaps, the last time. Mr. Rhea conducted the devotions, Mr. Perkins adding a few words. The great congregation followed us to our house to bid us farewell there. This scene over, we moved away, accompanied by scores of friends."

On the morning of the departure, about seventy of Miss Fiske's pupils gathered about her. They asked for the privilege of one more prayer-meeting with her in her room, 'the Bethel,' as they called it. She told them that she could not lead their devotions. They replied that she need not, for they would carry her that day, and she found it good to be carried at that hour to the throne of grace by those native sisters. Six prayers were offered, all tender and comforting; one of them particularly so; and left so deep an impression on Miss Fiske's mind that, after leaving them, she recalled and wrote out the substance of it the same afternoon. It was offered by one of the pupils about seventeen years of age: —

"She first prayed for themselves, asking that when Elijah should go up they might all see the horseman, and the chariot, and catch the falling mantle, and not sit down and weep, nor send into the mountains to search for their Master; but arise, and, taking the mantle, go smite Jordan, and, passing over, go to work. She then reminded the Saviour that he had promised not to leave them comfortless, and entreated him to come and abide with them. When she turned to the departing company, having in mind the heat of the day, and their prospective night travelling, she asked that the sun might not smite them by day, nor the moon by night. Thinking of the narrow precipitous roads, she prayed the Lord to give his angels charge concerning them, to bear them up in their hands, that they might not dash a foot against a stone. Remembering the streams, she asked that when they passed through the rivers, the waters might not overflow them; and that the Lord would spread a table for them through all the wilderness. They were to sleep in tents on their land journey, and she entreated that the angel of the Lord might ever encamp round about their moving tabernacle. Knowing that they would go a short distance in a steamer, and then in a sailing-vessel, she prayed that when on the 'fire-ship' the flames might not kindle upon them; and that when on the 'winged ship,' where the waters would go up to heaven and down to hell, they might be kept in their Father's hand, and brought to their desired haven. She then asked that, if it could be the Lord's will, all her teacher's friends might be spared till she should reach them, especially that her aged mother might live to see her, and that when she folded her child in her arms, she might say, like Simeon of old, 'Now lettest thou thy servant depart in peace.' The closing petition was, 'May our teacher's dust never mingle with a father's, nor with a mother's dust; but may she come back to mingle her dust with her children's dust, hear the trumpet with them, and with them go up to meet the Lord, and be forever with him.'"

Miss Fiske had frequent occasion, in the course of her long journey, to remember this prayer; and she always felt comforted and encouraged by it.

The progress of the party was slow. Children and invalids could not travel rapidly over rough roads under the intense heat of a Persian sun in midsummer. They reached Trebizond, the terminus of their land journey, August 20th, and, after resting a few days, took the Turkish steamer "Brandon" for Constantinople, where they remained till September 18th, when the English steamer "Africa" bore them thence to Smyrna, where, after eight days, they embarked in the "Andrew Carney" for Boston.

In one of her last letters, written before going on board, she says to her associate teacher, Miss Rice: —

"I feel to-night as though I should love to fly to our parlor, and, sitting down by your side, tell you how sadly I sometimes feel. It is not best for me to tell any one all that I feel. I do so dread reaching Boston, that I sometimes think I shall have to pass through severe trials to make me feel just right. I dread meeting the world again. Oh, if I could only fly away to my quiet Shelburne home without looking at a face, how glad I should be! I was never made to meet the world. I cannot do anything acceptably, and I shrink so from being a 'gazing-stock.' But I will not dwell on this; it does no good. Let me, rather, seek to strengthen you for your labors, and not draw upon your sympathies.

"I must now say farewell to Asia, and farewell to the dear friends here. I wish I had lived better, and had done more for Christ these fifteen years. As I look back on my missionary life, filled up with loving kindness and tender mercy from my Father's hand, oh, how I loathe myself! I have never done what I might for the poor Nestorians; for my missionary brothers and sisters; for the children; for anybody. It is a great thing to live for Christ alone."

Of the voyage Dr. Perkins thus speaks: —

"It was eighty days in duration, and in roughness altogether unparalleled in all my experience of several times crossing the ocean. During the whole month of November we made not a foot of progress;

not being becalmed for a single day, but tempest-tossed, and tempest-bound in the middle of the Atlantic Ocean, and often in gales so awful that the stoutest heart might well quail. In one instance in particular, for twenty-four hours, our vessel, without an inch of canvas spread, lay balancing and quivering on its side, kept so under the simple force of the tempest on its bare hull."

The following extracts are from a journal-letter to her school in Oroomiah, written during the voyage: —

"*October* 12. — We went to bed last night as usual, and I was soon asleep. I slept till after two o'clock, when I was suddenly waked by a stream of water pouring down on me. I got out of my box as soon as I could, and found Miss E——, who sleeps in a little box above me, quite soaked. It was raining very hard, and the water had collected in a little hollow place in the roof, and, running over, had come into our little window, though it was shut, and after filling, or partly filling, the first box, had come down on me. We did not wish to waken any one else, so we took all our things from the little room that they might not get wet, changed our dripping clothes, wrapped our shawls about us, and lay down on some little narrow seats in the cabin. Before we got quite arranged, the first mate came in, and laughingly said, 'Are you going ashore?' I replied, 'We have been washed up, and have come on shore.' . . . I do not know how many yards of rope there are to the sails, but I never see them tangled. All are kept in order and beautifully oiled. It would, of course, greatly endanger our lives if everything was not done well on the ship; but, perhaps, by neglecting little daily duties we do more harm than a sailor could do by pulling the wrong rope. I love to remember how much pains you all took last winter to do well, and I trust you do much better this winter."

"*November* 1.—Since last writing you we have had a very angry sea. It has not allowed us to be quiet by day or night. Our chairs walked from side to side so much that we had to put them all away, and sit on seats screwed down to the floor. Our table is fastened down, but we cannot fasten down our dishes, and they walk about in a wonderful manner. Sometimes a dish of meat empties itself on to one of our plates. Again, plates come over into our laps, our water is spilled and runs over the cabin in streams. Yesterday the molasses-cup came over to see me from the other side of the table, and emptied itself at my side. Do you understand why all this is? If you will read the one hundred and seventh Psalm you will know."

"8.—In my sleep last night I saw you all, and I thought I was with you. You were all so good and pleasant,—everything made me glad. I arranged all your lessons for another year, and saw you begin to study with all your hearts. I prayed with you, and my heart was very joyful. When we had finished, you all went out into our pleasant yard, and you were so still that I thought there were no scholars in the wide world so good as mine. While you were in the yard, I had my little boys and girls of the Sabbath school come in. While I was talking with them I waked, and, lo! it was a dream! But it was a dream I love to remember, and it moves my pen to-day, though old ocean remonstrates."

The following extracts are from a journal-letter, written during the voyage, to Miss Rice: —

"Did I follow my feelings I should be writing you half the time. My heart will be with you in all your labors. I have carried you, and I will carry you to the dear Saviour. It is sweet to leave you there, and to believe that he will make all grace to abound toward you. I understand something of your cares and anxieties, but Jesus understands them far better, and you will always find it sweet to pillow your head on his compassionate bosom. Oh, may you rest there! He wills that we not only lie on his bosom, but rest there."

"20.—I have not been sea-sick much of late, and really feel very well. The captain says I weigh fifteen pounds more than when I came on board. I do not quite believe this; but there is some ground for his remark.

"I long with exceeding longing to know of you and of our dear school. Oh, may you be greatly blessed this year! Spare yourself just as much as you can, that you may live to care for the dear children. When I was in Constantinople, I felt more than ever that it is a great blessing to have had *many* years to labor for the same interests. I pray earnestly that your precious life may be spared; and, if my Father can so delight in me as to give me back to labor with you, I will love him for his very tender mercy."

The long and stormy voyage at length ended, on Friday, the 17th of December; and, about sunset, Miss Fiske was welcomed to the hospitable home of kind Christian friends in Boston, who had for weeks been anxiously awaiting her arrival. The next day she went to Newburyport, and passed the Sabbath with relatives residing there. Some difficulty in getting her things from the vessel, together with the desire of the senior Secretary of the Board to confer with her in regard to the affairs of the mission, detained her in the vicinity of Boston for a week. During that time she visited also the friends of her associate, Miss Rice, at Lincoln. On the 24th her eyes again greeted her native hills, mantled with snow as when she last looked upon them at the same twilight hour. Mother and daughter, after a separation of nearly sixteen years, were folded in each other's arms.

Three days later she wrote: "And now you will ask, 'Are you at home?' Yes, I am 'at home' with my own dear mother and my only sister. I came to Greenfield on Friday, safely and easily. There I found my sister and her husband, and other friends. We came immediately out to Shelburne, and were here early in the evening, — an hour earlier than my mother expected me. Sister allowed me to go to her room without telling her that I had come. I opened the door so gently that she did not notice it. She was just asking some one in the room to move something. I said, 'Mother, Fidelia will do it.' You can imagine, but I cannot tell you, what followed. It is my mother, but she is more changed than I had been led to suppose. I am sure you will feel, when you see her, that she must soon go home. If I ever return to Persia I shall, doubtless, be spared the trial of leaving a mother."

The same day she wrote Miss Rice: "Yesterday I

attended church all day, and stood, after the morning service, a long time to shake hands, and exchange a few words with old friends. The old people all came, and, throwing their arms around my neck, wept there. The younger ones came and asked me, 'Can you remember such a little girl, or such a little boy?' I can remember many, and those I have never known I feel a deep interest in, they meet me with so much tender cordiality. The blessed revival of last spring has made Shelburne a delightful place. I met a Bible class at noon by special request. They were all pious young ladies, most of them mothers. It would have done you good to see how they listened to every word, wiping away the tears. Several other Bible classes came for me, and I told them I would go to them in turn."

CHAPTER XXIII.

JANUARY, 1859, TO DECEMBER, 1860.

Letters from Nestorian Pupils. — Letters to her Nestorian Pupils. — Visit to Mount Holyoke Seminary. — Visit to Oxford and Painesville Seminaries. — Invited to give Religious Instruction at South Hadley. — Revival. — Visit to Montreal.

WE are now to contemplate Miss Fiske in a new sphere of Christian activity. But, before doing so, let us take a further glimpse of her missionary life through a few of the many letters which followed her to America from her Nestorian pupils.

"September 25, 1858.

"O MY BELOVED MOTHER! — I begin to speak to you with a full heart, for it is a long time since I have talked with you. My heart longs to tell you of the change in our beloved school. We came together on the first day of October. Our return was much like that of the Israelites from Babylon to Jerusalem. They came and saw their city laid waste, their temple in ruins, and their holy things, which they had loved, scattered. Every time they looked on the spot where the temple had stood, their hearts were crushed. So, when we came back to school and did not see you, and went not to take your hand nor to be kissed by you, and saw not your ready feet coming to the door to bring in each girl and make her happy; and when we went into the school-room and saw the work of your hands, our hearts were broken, and we could not restrain our tears; and especially did my tears flow when I remembered the times that we, the daughters of the church, used to assemble in your room to mingle our prayers, our tears, and our joys together. I thought, also, of the time when you used to throw your arms about my neck and entreat me, with tears, to be a lover of the Lord. Oh, how do these remembrances leave an aching void which cannot be filled! It seems to me that the ways of your room mourn because you come not to our solemn feasts. Perhaps you will say, 'Oh, it is not so.' But I think if you were to come into your room this moment, and see the curtains fallen, and the doors and windows closed, you would say, 'It is true, the ways do mourn.'

"If the prophet Jeremiah were here, I think he would say, 'How doth Miss Fiske's room sit solitary, that was full of inhabitants! How do the daughters, the virgins of the Oroomiah school, mourn, and their eyes run down with water, because Miss Fiske is far from them!' Our school has always been such a pleasant place to me, — I have been so happy in it, and in its heavenly employments, that not even the death of my friends could take away that joy. But now I seem surrounded by dark clouds, and, sometimes, to be sinking in the deep mire. Yet I will try to say in all this trial, 'The will of the Lord be done.'

"Give my love to my blessed grandmother. 'Blessed is she among women,' the mother of a daughter of whom the whole Nestorian nation give testimony, that like Deborah she is a mother in Israel."

"Affectionately yours,
"KHATOON, of Geog Tapa."

"OROOMIAH, April 7, 1859.

"DEAR MOTHER OF MY SOUL, MISS FISKE!—Though high mountains and wild oceans separate us, yet your love and kindness are ever before my eyes, and fill my soul with such love that I cannot forget you. I can never forget the mother who has taken so much pains, and eaten so much trouble for me. How I remember those melting seasons when you used to put your arms around my neck, and talk with me about my soul, and tell me of my lost state, and how Christ poured out his blood, and humbled himself, and became obedient unto death, even the death of the cross, for my sake! Especially do I remember how you used to speak of the love, the measure of which no creature can reach, which saw a remedy in its own blood. At that time I did not understand the sacrifice for sin. I was going on in the road to destruction. I knew nothing of everlasting life, of the love of Christ, and of the forgiveness there is in him. But you pointed me to the cross; you showed me the fountain of Siloam where all may wash and see; and I do not know how to express my gratitude to you. The more I think of your labor for me and your love to me, the more I feel that I can never reach to its greatness or its bounds.

"You will wish to know of your loved school. We have had pleasant times, for we have been visited from above. We missed you greatly, but the Teacher, who is better than any earthly teacher, came and taught us this winter. The Lord Jesus has been the Gardener of our school. He has come down and watered it with heavenly rain.

"Would that I might sit by your side again, hear your counsels, and look in your face. Receive peace in large measure from my father, mother, and all our friends.

"Your loving daughter,
"SELBY OF WAZERAWA."

"SARALAN, May, 1860.

"MY BELOVED MOTHER: — I received your letter just before I received a bitter stroke from the never-erring hand of my heavenly Father. Many thanks for your loving remembrances of me. They are abiding tokens of your true motherhood. I have many thoughts of you and of those blessed days we passed together in that blessed school. I am very sad when I think that perhaps I may never, in this house of my pilgrimage, see your face.

"Dear mother, I have much to write, but you will excuse me from it because of my great weakness. Like a daughter distressed, who would find a little rest by falling into the kind arms of her mother, I come to tell you what has pierced the heart of your child. Beloved, you used to write me that I must take good care of my dear and tender babe, Aweshalom. Perhaps I did not fully do as you told me. I am not sure in regard to it. But one thing I know: the Lord who loves little children was not willing that I should keep him. And I believe he will take better care of my dear child than I could. You must know that I am deeply wounded and crushed by this stroke. My tears cease not. His first birth was October 14th, 1858; his second and spiritual one, April 23d, 1860. His life with us was a pleasant one, and he made our lives very sweet and delightful; but now he has gone to heaven, while we remain on the earth. He lives the new life, while we die daily. He is strong, while I am weak. He has grown beautiful in the light and image of our Saviour, while I am pining away. It seems sometimes as if our comforters were far from us; but our Saviour stands very near to help and to comfort.

"Your true daughter,
"HOSHEBO."

As the absent teacher was followed by such expressions of tender interest from her loved pupils, so from her native land she sent back to them words of unabated affection:—

"SHELBURNE, Jan. 27, 1859.

"MY OWN DEAR GIRLS:—When this reaches you it will be spring, and oh, how I should delight to see you in your pleasant school-room! I love to think that the Holy Spirit is with you, and that souls are turning to God. I am glad to know that some of you talked and prayed with so many women last summer. Continue to do so, and pray much for them alone. You will never be sorry for any labor for Christ. Thanks for all the letters you have written me. They are a great comfort to me, and I love to read them to my friends; my dear mother, especially, loves to have me sit by her side and read them to her. She thinks of you a great deal and prays for you.

"I am happy in seeing my friends, but not happier than when with you. I think of you by day and by night, and often see you in my dreams, and try to do something for you. The Lord bless you and help you all to live near to him.

"Your affectionate teacher,

"F. FISKE."

"SHELBURNE, Feb. 19, 1859.

"MY DEAR GIRLS:—I have received the names of those for whom you labored, and with whom you prayed, between the May and the September communion. They were given to me the evening I set foot on land. It did me good to receive them, and I thanked the Lord that you had cared for so many souls. Have you seen them brought to Christ? Will you not labor for them till you see them loving him, and then help them to be holy, working Christians?

"As you meet together to-day, perhaps you will remember the last communion day that I was with you. I often think of it, and of all my dear pupils, who came to the Lord's table. I trust that you grow in grace; that you live nearer and nearer to God from month to month. It is a blessed thing to be included in Christ's family. Let us all try to be the true followers of the Holy Jesus, such as he can love and allow to rest on his bosom.

"My mother wishes me to tell you that she loves you as her own children. She is very glad to see me, and wishes me to be close by her side; but says,

'If God calls you to go to Persia again I must not say no.' She is very weak, and I do not think she will live to see me go away again. In heaven you will know her, I trust; and there I hope to meet you all, if I do not on earth. But I do hope to see you in Persia, if our lives are spared. Accept much love for your children, fathers, and mothers, and all your family friends, and believe me

"Your affectionate teacher and friend,

"FIDELIA FISKE."

After resting some weeks with friends in her native town, Miss Fiske spent a few days at Mount Holyoke Seminary, South Hadley. The visit was one of deep interest to herself and to others. While there, she wrote: "I am enjoying my visit here far more than I supposed possible. Things move on very quietly, and I think there is a good standard of scholarship maintained. They say there is less missionary interest than formerly. This may be so, but the young ladies certainly gave me their warm sympathies. Their eager countenances and tearful eyes have made me quite forget my early determination to be silent. I have met the whole school several times, and I have no doubt that I have received more good than I have imparted.

"I was not allowed to feel myself a stranger there, but sat down just as I used to do, and could not realize that I had been away sixteen long years. On going to my room, the first thing that met my eye was dear Miss Lyon's Bible on the table. Can you imagine my feelings as I again took the precious book in my hand? Her sofa, chairs, and mirror were also in the room, and were recognized at once, and helped to hallow the spot.

"The first hymn sung in the seminary after my return was the same one sung when I was leaving in 1843, — 'Go, ye messenger of love.'"

The effect of this visit upon the young ladies was very great. Says an eye-witness, "It seemed as though the whole seminary must go in a body to the heathen, under the impulse of their intensely excited interest." Another says, "Many of the young ladies had never seen her before; but her simple, earnest words, and the wonderful magnetism of her face, gained their hearts at once. While she spoke, her youthful audience seemed moved by a common impulse, and more than one was heard to say, 'If Miss Fiske would ask me to become a Christian, I believe I should do so.'"

A second visit to the seminary in April only deepened the interest which the first had awakened.

In June she visited, by urgent invitation, the seminaries for young ladies at Oxford and Painesville, Ohio, — those worthy offshoots of Mount Holyoke. The daughters of the West, not less than those of the East, felt the strange charm of her presence and the power of her words, and in many a heart was kindled a missionary interest which never died out.

The trustees and teachers of Mount Holyoke Seminary were very desirous of securing for their institution the services of Miss Fiske. She was invited to act as a kind of chaplain, conducting the daily devotional exercises in the hall, and religious meetings, and in a general way caring for the spiritual interests of the seminary.

Of this invitation she writes to her associate, Miss Rice: "I said to them that I could not do what they desired as it should be done, and that I was not willing to attempt it. The idea pleases my mother very much, because she thinks that I shall be near her, and shall not be going hither and thither. She does not, of course, realize that, if I do it, I shall do it as a *barbarian*. I write you this, that you may know how to pray for me."

Again she wrote to the same, after she was persuaded to reconsider her decision: "I felt that I could not, and ought not to give religious instruction there; I still feel so, and I think those good trustees and teachers are greatly mistaken in supposing that I can. I feel that all that I have said about missionaries being incapacitated for labor at home is true; and I am sure that I can never expect to do anything more in the world, unless permitted to be again among the Nestorians. I am allowed to make my *home* at South Hadley the coming winter, or, rather, am invited to do so. I shall probably avail myself of this invitation to some extent, and shall thus hope to get some good for our own dear school. I wish to know more of the present modes of teaching, new books, etc."

Having thus, with characteristic modesty, accepted the position, she entered on her new duties in December. She found the situation a delightful one, and the spiritual magnetism of her presence was speedily felt throughout the entire school.

She soon found herself in that revival atmosphere which she loved so well to breathe, whether in Persia or America. Writing to an early and fast friend of the seminary, January 3d, 1860, she says: —

"The Spirit of the Lord is with us, and our prayer is that he may not be grieved away. You probably know that there have been several hopeful conversions since the year commenced. Last week there seemed to be an increase of interest, but it was not general. The feeling manifested yesterday was such that I thought it best, at evening, to invite those anxious for their souls to meet in the north wing parlor. Thirty-five were present. Some eight or ten of these, we hope, are Christians. Others seem deeply anxious, while some evidently know little of the plague of their hearts. The meeting was a deeply solemn one. We are encouraged to labor and pray; and we know there are many who pray for these dear young ladies. I never felt more the importance of having this dear seminary wholly devoted to the Lord. It was early given to him. *It cannot be taken back.* The last few days have been very pleasant to me, because my leisure hours have all been filled with conversing and praying, either with young Christians, or with those who would find Jesus. Oh, it is good, for it seems like being engaged in the same work I had in my Eastern home!

"Nothing seems to interest the young ladies more than to hear about Miss Lyon. I wish that a part of the furniture of every room might be Miss Lyon's memoir. Can it not be so? I am afraid not half of the pupils read it now."

To the same she again writes, March 2d:—

"There is so much of holy interest concentrated here, that those who early loved Holyoke must love it ever. It does me a great deal of good to meet those old familiar faces, which must ever be associated with the remembrances of dear Miss Lyon. There are not a few, I am sure, who thank the Lord that, while new friends have been raised up, there are those left who helped lay that first stone, and who went down with Miss Lyon into the quarry to find it, and who, with her, consecrated it to the Lord with many tears.

"I trust you will never wonder that your life is spared, while you can pray for Holyoke. You may do more for it on the bended knee than active hands and feet can ever do in its service. One of the excellent missionary fathers, in his first letter to me after reaching Oroomiah, said, 'Always be ready to *do* the work, and let others have the name of it.' I felt as though it was a word from my Saviour, spoken through him, and I have loved to dwell on it all these long years. If we can only have the privilege of doing and praying, will we not be satisfied? Now that I am away from my precious children it is doubly sweet to pray, — to carry them and lay them right in my Father's arms. He loves them better than I do. He planted the vine in the wilderness, and he will take care of it. My only fear is that I shall not be found in full sympathy with my Saviour in all his designs of love towards it. . . .

"There are some cases of deep interest in our family now. The Spirit is still with us, but we long to see a more powerful work which shall bring in all. We would not, however, choose the particular mode of operation, if we can only be sure that God is with us, and that his work will not cease nor be retarded through our negligence. In the series of revivals which I was privileged to share in Oroomiah, God's workings were varied. If I looked for a particular mode of blessing it always came in some other way. There were seasons when all seemed to bow as in a day, and we stood still to behold our God passing by. There were other years when the work of conversion extended over months, and the Lord called his children to do much in leading and guiding."

In February she went to Boston to be present at the embarkation of a band of missionaries destined to the Nestorian field. Her great joy at their departure was mingled with deep regret that she could not accompany them.

In a letter to a friend, dated May 23d, speaking of her mother, she says: "It is a comfort that I can do some of the last things for her, though I may get home first. I sometimes long to fold her in my arms and fly away to Persia. But we shall both have a fairer land, and stronger arms of love about us soon. I will leave her with Him who loves her. If I could have her with me in my Eastern home, I should be too free from earthly care. I need more of trial than most of God's children do. I know it and sorrow over it, but still I keep needing it."

Again she writes: "I have been happier in America than I supposed it possible for me to be, but this does not make me wish to linger here longer than is necessary. I shall be glad to be back in Oroomiah in my Father's good time."

And again: "I am encouraged to believe that I may safely return next year. There now seems to be no hindrance, if I can leave my mother. In regard to this, I shall try to know my Father's will. I regret the tendency there is among missionaries to come home, and *stay* at home. It does harm to the cause. If I am told not to go, I shall try to be satisfied, but I tell you just what I feel, when I say that no place in America seems as desirable to me as to be again with you."

Of her Persian school she writes: "As I look at it from an American stand-point, I have no desire to change materially the plan of study. Let it be as much Bible as ever, and we will try to have all the helps to the study of it that we can. I am pained to find the Bible so neglected here."

In July Miss Fiske had the pleasure of being present at the embarkation from Boston of another company of missionaries for Persia; and again she felt it to be a sore trial that she could not join them. Her parting tears were tears of joy that they were going, and tears of sorrow that she must be left behind.

In the autumn she visited Montreal, Canada, at the invitation of friends, who had become deeply interested in her work in Persia. One object of the visit was to meet the young ladies of Miss H. W. Lyman's school. The interest which she awakened, both among teachers and pupils, found expression in valuable gifts, which were accompanied with the assurance that the donors would remember her stay among them, "not only as a time of much enjoyment, but also as the starting-point of a higher Christian life."

CHAPTER XXIV.

JANUARY, 1861, TO DECEMBER, 1862.

Visit to New York. — Parlor Meetings. — Letters of Sympathy. — Missionary Meetings in Maine. — The War. — Commemorative Anniversary at Mount Holyoke Seminary. — Memorial Volume. — "Woman and her Saviour in Persia." — "Recollections of Mary Lyon."

AFTER her return from Montreal, Miss Fiske, by special request of the trustees, resumed her duties at Mount Holyoke, and remained there during most of the seminary year. In January and February, the institution was again visited with the special blessing of Heaven, and her hands were again full of that revival work in which she so much delighted. Her room was often thronged by those who sought her counsel and prayers; and some fifty or sixty of the young ladies were hopefully converted during those few weeks.

In April, 1861, Miss Fiske, by invitation of ladies interested in her missionary work, spent a short time in the city of New York. One who enjoyed the privilege of listening to the story of her labors thus writes: "The parlors of several ladies in New York and Brooklyn were opened to her, and filled to overflowing with attentive and delighted listeners. In some cases lecture-rooms were opened that larger numbers might come within the sound of her voice; and whenever Christian friends were privileged to meet her, they felt a new bond of attachment to the mission which she represented, and a profound respect and love for one who had been so untiring in efforts to elevate and save the hitherto neglected daughters of Persia. The opportunity of an acquaintance with a missionary of such experience, and such glowing love for souls, as Miss Fiske manifested, was regarded, by many, as a rich privilege, and the impression left on every mind was, that God had chosen, and peculiarly prepared, her for this service."

As the year at South Hadley drew to a close, Miss Fiske felt a degree of the same solicitude for the spiritual welfare of the pupils about to leave the seminary, which she so often felt when dismissing, for vacation, her pupils in Persia.

July 19th, she writes to a friend: "To-night I meet the Christians; Sabbath evening, those who are not Christians; then I meet them twice all together; and then turn from them. There is something so solemn in closing up labors, — in leaving the last impress! How could we do this, if we might not afterwards go and ask our Father to take care of it? Is it not comforting to fall back into the arms of our Eternal Father?"

Miss Fiske still felt herself so closely bound to the members of the missionary circle in Persia, that she continued to "bear their griefs, and carry their sorrows," no less than when with them. To the bereaved mothers, especially, did her heart turn with tenderest sympathies, as shown by the following letter to one of them:—

"SHELBURNE, August 2, 1861.

"MY DEAR SISTER: — I have heard none of the particulars of dear Julia's leaving you; but to know that she has gone makes me long to write you. I feel afraid to speak, or to write you, when the Lord has come so near you. I know full well that it is easy to make the wound still deeper, or, rather, to open it all too rudely. I would not do this, my precious sister, for my heart tenderly sympathizes with you in the hour of sorrow. We had asked the Saviour, who loves you so tenderly, if he would not allow you to retain dear Julia a little longer. We had thought that your dear Edward and Lillie might be all that you would need to give for the infant choir of heaven for the present. But there was surely a want in that band that none but Julia could fill. She was not taken till He, who knows every little child, had looked over all, and seen that no other could fill just her place among those little ones. She surely lives; she is with Christ, and has her work. Yours has been a precious privilege to watch her for more than five years, and to lead her to love the Saviour. She is in his arms now. There is no mistake in this; and I feel, my sister, as though you were a great deal nearer to heaven than those who have no little ones there. I know that you can be happy in what God has done; and are you not thankful that you may weep unrebuked by Jesus? How thankful I should have felt to be with you at the time of your giving dear Julia to the Lord again! Pleasant, very pleasant, are my memories of the angel-child, and it would be a comfort to me to have seen her last look on earth, and to have done for her some of those last things. The

Lord comfort you, my dear sister. Does he not abide with you?

"In tenderest love and sympathy, your sister,

"FIDELIA FISKE."

A few months later another and deeper sorrow came upon this stricken missionary-sister, which called forth another, and, if possible, tenderer letter of sympathy. We anticipate and give it in this place:—

"SOUTH HADLEY, Feb. 8, 1862.

"MY DEAR, DEAR SISTER:—You are in my heart continually, and tenderly do I bear you and the dear children to the Lord Jesus. How much I thought of you all, during that week of Mr. B.'s death! I had an unusual longing to be with you; and, had I known what was passing, I should have desired it still more. We thank the Lord that he comforts you in this hour of trial; but we do not forget that great comforts are only given where there has been deep sorrow. I know that your soul has been, as it were, riven, and that you can never go back to the place where you stood three months ago. You must ever walk in such a shadow as had not before fallen upon you. It can never be lifted from you till all shadows flee away; but there is a loving voice that you will hear more distinctly than heretofore, and there is a hand that will not fail to lead you. I know that, in your deep sorrow, you find much for which to thank the Lord. You must thank the Lord that your dear husband was spared to you so long; that you had a happy home with him so many long years; that you had his help in the divine life through such a portion of your pilgrimage. You are grateful, too, that he comforted so many others, and that then He who loved him *best* took him, and glorified himself in his death."

The interest which Miss Fiske's "parlor talks" awakened caused invitations to pour in upon her from every direction, many of which she accepted; and in some cases her "talks" became almost public lectures, being held in the church instead of the parlor. In regard to speaking to ladies, of her missionary work in Persia, she says: "I have often done it, and I am willing to do it, when judicious friends feel that it is best. I have been accustomed to speaking in my school, so that it is easy for me to do it, in my own informal way. I sometimes meet ladies several times in a week, and am able to do this because I do it so informally. In a few instances gentlemen have come in with ladies, but not by my arrangement. I love to tell Christian friends of what the Lord has done for our dear Nestorians; but I shrink from everything that would give an impression that I am a lecturer."

In October, 1861, she accepted the invitation of Rev. W. Warren, one of the District Secretaries of the American Board, to visit Maine, and hold a series of meetings under his direction in several of the principal cities and towns of that State. Of this visit, Mr. Warren has kindly furnished the following account: —

"Miss Fiske came to Maine at my request, partly for the benefit of the journey and change, and partly to address the mothers and children in my district. Her coming was as an angel's visit to us. It was just after the decease of a beloved daughter, and at the time when my eldest sons, since gone, were sinking in a decline. She exactly appreciated our case, and was truly a daughter of consolation to us. 'In all our afflictions she was afflicted.' I never knew one better fitted to impart sympathy and comfort to the tried. Her quick insight into the sensibilities of others helped her to measure accurately their griefs. Her nature was disinterested and responsive; the action of her mind intuitive. She knew when to speak, and what to say, and how to say it. She brought you very near to the Saviour's heart, or brought the Saviour's heart very near to you. She was in no sense a stranger in the family, but was as one of us. She chose to be her own servant, and declined attentions that cost others the least inconvenience.

"Her Christian cheerfulness was remarkable. She was trustful and hopeful. The night was never so dark, but *she* could see a star; the way never so hedged up or crowded, but *she* could find a path. Her smile was an inspiration; a sweet welcome of the gospel; an imprint of pure love. If there is such a thing as making religion attractive to the impenitent, she had the art of doing it. Who could but be happy in her society, or delighted with her conversation, and charmed by her influence and presence?

"Miss Fiske addressed fifteen audiences in Maine. She was naturally diffident; and it was often a severe trial for her to appear in public. An appointment was made for her in Portland; but it was very difficult for her to bring her mind to meet such a responsibility, and she spent a part of the night previous in prayer, as a preparation for the service.

"She declined to address mixed assemblies. Her

Christian modesty shrank from it. It was contrary to the refined instincts and sensibilities of her nature. She was a representative woman in this regard; a model of Christian propriety as touching things doubtful. In one or two instances, however, the notice of her lecture had been liberalized somewhat by the pastors, so that *stalwart men*, with their wives and children, had ventured to take possession of their pews. She recoiled from the task of encountering such a presence. I told her to *ignore* the men, and not to regard them as present, for they were contraband, in the circumstances! I also told the gentlemen that they must not regard themselves as present; and, while they had a right to sit in their pews, they would not be regarded as listening, as the lady present did not address gentlemen publicly. They nodded assent, and seemed to say, 'That is all we want!' In one case, she began her lecture by speaking to a mother in the audience who had brought her little babe with her: 'I am glad to see that mother here; and I am glad she has brought her baby with her. It will not disturb me in the least, even if it cries. The Nestorian mothers used to bring their babies to meeting, and this mother is here, no doubt, because she feels an interest in the poor mothers in Persia.' By this time the stout-hearted men, even though not permitted to listen, were feeling for their handkerchiefs to remove their tears.

"In another place, where several men of distinction had gotten into the assembly, one of them said to me at the close, 'What does this mean? Why did you not let us know about this? I should have taken *four* pocket-handkerchiefs with me if I had dreamed of her power. I saw, indeed, that his one handkerchief was ruined before the lecture was half through; and no artist could have recognized his face, though he himself was a dignified D. D.

"I will not trust myself to give a description of the power of her 'talks,' as she termed them. They took the assembly at once into captivity. The interest ran from the little child up to the strongest, stoutest intellect. Her discourses were a vision of what she described. She translated you at once to the scene of her delineations. Call this art, if you will; genius, eloquence, — but there was something higher and purer, which art and eloquence cannot reach. The whole was irradiated by the spiritual; a moral splendor sat upon the scenes of her descriptions, and upon her lighted, radiant countenance meanwhile."

Miss Fiske was by no means indifferent to the fearful civil war which was shaking the whole country, and in which was involved not only our existence as a nation, but the stability of republican institutions. But she looked upon it not simply with the eye of a patriot, but with the eye of a Christian, and of a Christian missionary. To her associate teacher at Oroomiah she writes: —

"*February* 22, 1862. — I should be so glad if you could have our telegraphic despatches; but I trust you have better ones, even from heaven. There are joy and sorrow too, in our nation. I realize more and more what the struggle is costing. It costs money, and it costs the deepest affections of the heart. When it is over, will not Christians know better how to give of their treasures to the Lord, and their sons and their daughters to the holy warfare? But the end is not yet."

Again she writes: "The awful scenes in our country are enough to make us feel that we must be hidden under the shadow of the Almighty. I sympathize with the general principles held at the North; but, oh, this glorying, this boasting, this forgetting of God! He will punish for this. We cannot prosper till we are humbled. It is North and South together that must bow. The feeling and the struggle now are desperate."

To a friend in Montreal she writes: "I suppose you still feel a deep interest in all that is passing in the States. Shall we come forth from this struggle a better people? Shall we be 'pure and then peaceable'? Shall we be better soldiers of the cross? I can never speak of our country's welfare here without bringing tears to many eyes. It is heart work, as well as work of the hands, to which we are called. The young ladies have just sent off a valuable box for the soldiers. A text of Scripture upon a card was put upon each article. We did this last summer, and have had some very pleasant returns from those texts."

It was proposed to celebrate, this year, the twenty-fifth anniversary of the Mount Holyoke Seminary, by a reunion of all the graduates and early friends of the seminary, and by a commemorative address. The preparation for that anniversary involved a vast amount of correspondence and other labor, into which Miss Fiske entered with her characteristic zeal and efficiency; contributing in no small measure to the success with which everything passed off on that interesting and pleasant occasion; and others perhaps thought, what one clergyman expressed, when he said that he believed she was "brought home to arrange for that celebration, if for no other reason."

After the anniversary, it was thought desirable to have some permanent record of the exercises of an occasion so full of sacred interest to the pupils and friends of the institution, and Miss Fiske was charged with the duty of collecting and arranging for the press the materials for such a record. The result was the publication of a volume, entitled, "Memorial. Twenty-Fifth Anniversary of the Mount Holyoke Female Seminary."

While thus occupied with labors connected with that commemorative anniversary, her hands were full of other work which made a large demand upon her time and strength. Many persons who had listened to the story of her missionary life, and of the wonderful work of grace wrought among the women of Persia, had often urged her to prepare the same for the press. She, however, instinctively shrank from such an undertaking; but at length so far yielded as to consent to furnish the material for such a volume, if the right person could be found willing to digest and prepare it for publication. The right person was soon found in Rev. T. Laurie, of West Roxbury, who very kindly offered to render the desired service; and the friends of missions were laid under great obligations to him for the publication of that most excellent and useful volume, "Woman and her Saviour in Persia."

"I feel that God has sent him to do it," writes Miss Fiske. "It is a great relief to me to feel that the responsibility is another's. He will do it a great deal better than I could. I should have made a book *all self.*"

While thus busily at work upon two volumes the design of a third began to take definite shape in her mind. In preparing for the commemorative anniversary, she was led to collect many notes of Miss Lyon's religious instructions to her pupils. Her first plan was to include some of these in the "Memorial;" but afterwards it was thought best to publish them in a separate volume, and to connect with them some new and interesting incidents in Miss Lyon's life, which had come to light. The materials accumulated as she proceeded with the work, and it was left unfinished at her death, having been committed by her to the hands of a dear friend and former missionary associate, by whom it was subsequently completed, and given to the public as "Recollections of Mary Lyon." When considering what was the best use to be made of the materials which she had collected, she wrote to a friend: "I do not want to write a memoir; and I do not want anybody to write another memoir of Miss Lyon; but I do want some of these things to do good in the world. I think very highly of Mrs. Cowle's memoir of Miss Lyon. Every time I read it, I value it more and more."

The "Recollections" are not a new memoir, but they give some new lights and shades to the excellent portrait which other hands had drawn of that wonderful woman.

CHAPTER XXV.

1863.

Invited to be Principal of Mount Holyoke Seminary. — Invited to assist at McLean Asylum. — Letter to Miss Jessup.

Dr. Wright, of the Nestorian Mission, being in this country, and expecting to return to Persia during the summer of this year, 1863, it was the confident hope of Miss Fiske that she should accompany him. Her aged mother was comfortable; her invalid sister's health was improving, and it seemed to her that the Lord was at length opening the way for her to go back to her loved missionary work. She laid all her plans accordingly; made many purchases for her outfit; and wrote to her friends in Oroomiah that she hoped to keep Thanksgiving with them.

It soon, however, became evident that Dr. Wright, who was superintending the printing of the New Testament in Syriac, would not complete his labors in season to leave the country till the next spring. When informed of this, Miss Fiske wrote, "I was more disappointed than I supposed I should be; still I am happy in what the Lord directs. If he keeps me here a few months longer, I have only to ask that he will use me in his service."

Her detention in this country led the trustees of Holyoke Seminary to inquire whether it were not a providential indication that she should be permanently connected with that institution. She had before been repeatedly solicited to take the position of Principal, or of Associate Principal there; but her reply had uniformly been, "Persia!" The matter was now more formally brought before her, and she was urged to take the position, for at least one year, if not permanently; and to allow her name to appear on the catalogue. She heard all the arguments in favor of such a course; but her purpose remained unchanged. Alluding to the subject in a letter to Dr. Wright, she says: "I am afraid to consider any question of this kind, unless it is *certain* that I cannot go back to Persia. I do not think so much of what I can reasonably expect to do there, as of giving up the work. It seems to me that there is much in *abiding in our work*, even if we can do but little. I think of the influence upon others; and more, I trust, of what my heavenly Father desires. My four years in America have been very pleasant, and I should go back with the feeling that there is before me more of self-denial and trial than I should be likely to meet here; but I am afraid it would not be right to stay here; and, if not right, I could not be happy in staying. This is what I have said to these proposals, and I do not feel satisfied with any other view. If I am wrong, I trust I shall be set right."

To Miss Rice she wrote, in reply to expressed apprehensions lest she might be induced to remain in America: "It is not strange that some of you feel as though I never should go to Oroomiah. I may never go, but if so, it will not be because I think the work at home more important, nor because I am not ready, and glad, again to find my work where I have felt it a privilege to labor. We will ask that the Lord's will may be done."

The Trustees of Mt. Holyoke, being every year more and more convinced that Miss Fiske's services at the seminary were invaluable, and that she was really doing as much there for the cause of missions as she could do in Persia, were very reluctant to acquiesce in her decision. One of them said to her, "I have done talking with you, but I shall continue to talk with the Lord about it."

She was glad when the question was definitely settled. "It is an inexpressible relief to me," she writes, "to have the subject of a change in my relations here given up. I will do anything I can to stay up Miss Chapin's hands, and comfort her heart; but I do believe I can better do this by keeping just where I am; and my missionary friends will be far happier to feel that I am doing nothing to cut myself off from them. I have assured them that there is no change in me; that I am only resting here, waiting for my Father's leading; and he will lead and guide me, for he knows that, —

"Oft in my quiet resting-place,
I hush my hastened breath,
To hear the blessed guiding words,
His loving Spirit saith."

Other attempts were made to induce Miss Fiske to remain in her native land. It was proposed by a friend, who appreciated her rare qualities, to open a school for young ladies in Boston, to be under her care, and to be of that high literary and religious character, which, it was believed, she, better than almost any one else, could give it. Gladly as she would have accepted the proposal under other circumstances, her convictions of duty in regard to the missionary work forbade her doing so.

Having occasion to visit a friend in the McLean Asylum, at Somerville, her kind, sympathetic nature so won the hearts of the unfortunate inmates, and so drew them about her, as interested listeners, that the superintending physician, deeply impressed with her power over them, was very desirous that she might have some connection with the institution. "I was surprised a few weeks since," she writes, "by a call from Dr. T——, and an invitation to connect myself with the asylum, in caring for the suffering ones. I told him I was not at liberty to do any such thing while there was any prospect of my return to Oroomiah; and more, that I did not think my health sufficient for it. My sympathy for the class gathered there might lead me to such a connection, were there not reasons against it."

In September, 1859, Miss Fiske visited the Asylum for the Insane in Trenton, N. J., and there, too, her kind and sympathizing manner drew the unfortunate inmates confidingly towards her. She says: "In one of the wards they insisted on my sitting down with them, kissed me, and begged me to stay, saying, 'How glad we are to see Miss Dix!' I wished that I could comfort them as she had done in her visits. You know how much I feel for this class, and they read my feelings. 'God bless you!' were their parting words."

In October she writes from South Hadley: "We have about three hundred and forty pupils, and you can conceive that this brings a very great pressure upon the teachers. More than two hundred applicants were refused admission during the fall vacation. There is a growing improvement in the religious character of the school, and this gives the people confidence in placing their daughters here. This year we have more than one hundred who are not Christians. A few have, we trust, begun to love the Saviour since we came together. Only four weeks remain of this term, but time enough for a rich blessing. Oh, pray that it may be given us!"

The religious interest increased, and, in the absence of two of the teachers, an amount of labor devolved upon Miss Fiske, to which her strength was scarcely equal. It was her joy, however, even in weakness, to lead inquiring souls to Christ, and she was ever studying how the better to do this. "We have," she says, "yet much to learn, I doubt not, of the way to Jesus, and how to tell that way to others. We need little children to talk to, that we may realize the simplicity of the way."

To one of the recent associate principals of the seminary, at this time a great sufferer, unable to walk, and with no hope of recovery, the following letter was addressed: —

"South Hadley, Nov. 9, 1863.

"My dear Miss J.: — As I have thought of you of late, confined to your seat or bed, I have been asking my heavenly Father to help me to prize my limbs as I should, and to walk in his ways.

"I remember, when, twenty-three years ago, I had not for many weeks had my reason, I used, when better, to wake in the morning, exclaiming, 'I am here, and I know where I am. Bless the Lord, O my soul!' I thought, then, that I never could wake with other than heartfelt thankfulness for reason, and for every blessing. But alas! I have waked many times without the offering of a grateful heart. As I read your letter, it seemed to me sent from God to remind me that I need to go to Bethel and renew my vows of consecration, and get my heart filled with grateful love. Dear, precious friend, you are suffering for us; and will you not pray for us, that we may bear life's burdens more joyfully, doing what we can more gladly? I have never so longed for the rest which heaven gives as during the last year. O my friend, there is a 'need-be' in all that our God does! Some must be laid aside in mind, and some in body, that others may better study God's will. He takes those in whom he will be most honored. You wanted to do us good. You asked your Father a great many times that you might be a blessing to *all* your friends. Did I not hear you thus pray? Did not the Spirit of God indite those petitions? You used to say, 'In thine own way, Father;' and I know you are not sorry that you left it with God to choose the way. He has chosen, and we would all learn of you. I want to learn so well that Jesus will not feel that you have suffered in vain for me."

CHAPTER XXVI.

LAST LABORS AT SOUTH HADLEY.

Health Failing. — Revival. — Right Hand. — Parting Prayer-meetings.

MISS FISKE entered upon, what proved to be, the last year of her earthly life, with greatly enfeebled health. The disease which compelled her to leave the missionary field, though so long held in check, was soon to have a fatal termination. In the autumn it gave signs of increased activity, which, from week to week, grew more and more alarming, although she did not speak of them until January. She remained, however, at South Hadley through the spring term, which closed about the end of March. Her last work there was the work, in which, above all others, she most delighted.

During those last months, the seminary was blessed with another revival of great power; and her labors amid those scenes of thrilling interest were indeed a fitting close to her life's work. After the first of January, she was seldom able to attend the general exercises of the school, or even to take her meals with the family; but in her own room she welcomed many who came to her for religious conversation and prayer. That room became a hallowed spot, as the invalid teacher there pointed inquiring ones to Jesus;

urged thoughtless ones to seek the Lord while he might be found; or, kneeling with them before the mercy-seat, breathed forth the tender and earnest prayer in their behalf.

Many of the details of these closing months of labor may be learned from her own pen.

To a friend in Montreal, she writes, January 8, 1864: "A thousand thanks for all your thoughtful love, for your words of cheer, and for your prayers. You tell me that I am not free to speak of my feelings. I thought I was; but if it be true that I am not, it is because words cannot tell what I feel. I love to tell some dear friends of soul conflicts, and of sweet assurance of pardon of sin, and of the rest which Jesus gives. I should love to-night to talk with you of these things, and to thank you for letting me know so much of your own heart. You say that you long for more grace. Did you ever *long*, and not receive? You will tell me soon that you have had very gracious visits from the Saviour. If you do not feel that you are what you should be, you will feel that Jesus is all; and the more you feel your sins the more sweetly you will trust. I have been taking a great deal of comfort the last few days in a little book, by Wm. Ried, of Edinburgh, 'The Blood of Jesus.' I feel very much as Miss Lyon said she did, a little while before she died; 'I can only bear milk;' and this I find here.

"You ask concerning the religious state of the school here. About twenty indulged hope last term, and some ten more have begun to hope within a few days. But, oh, how much greater blessings we need! We long especially for a thorough work among Christians.

I suffer less from my cough than in the autumn, but I cannot bear the cold, and can make but little effort. I think I shall feel better when the cold weather is gone. Now you will not think that I am sick, for I am not; but you know I am exceedingly careful, expecting to be very well some time, and hoping then to do a great deal."

"*January* 11.—We had a good Sabbath yesterday. I had a precious meeting with the dear young Christians. This morning I had a delightful time with the senior class, in their Bible lesson, which was the ninth and tenth chapters of Jeremiah. I prepared a literal translation from the old Syriac, which greatly interested them. This gave a freshness to every word, and they are greatly delighted with the poetry of the Bible.

"'Would that my head were waters,
And mine eyes a living fountain of tears;
I would weep by day and by night
For the slain of the daughter of my people,'

seemed to come home to them very much, as we spoke of Jeremiah's deep feeling and elevated language. If young ladies would be more familiar with the Bible, how chaste their language would become! This afternoon I have been using for the young ladies, the article on Abyssinia, in the December number of the 'Christian Work.' And here let me tell you, that we have had this work the last year, and value it exceedingly. How true that we Americans have nothing so good!"

Again she writes to a friend in Boston:—

"27.— . . . I am enjoying much in getting

the girls to read good books. There has been a beginning made this year that may be carried on to much better advantage next year. We will scatter the good seed, and, if we are called away, it will still be watered, and will spring up and bear fruit to eternal life. Nothing done for Christ will be lost. How strange it is, that, knowing this, we do not seek to do more for him!"

To the same, on hearing of the accidental injury of her right hand, she writes: —

"*February* 3. — Has your right hand forgotten its cunning? Well, it is not because you have forgotten Jerusalem, for still you remember her above your chief joy. It is that you may better know that the Lord's right hand leads you, and makes you to dwell in safety. If I were with you I would take the Concordance, and look out all the 'right hands' of the Bible, and read them to you. This was once my work, when for three weeks my right hand rested. How well I remember those days of suffering, and the nights when the dear Nestorian girls watched by me till the morning light! When I fell, I was intent on what I thought was a good work, but I could not well have lost the lessons I learned while obliged to rest."

To the same: —

"15. — You have heard that God is surely in this place. We have seen his power, have felt his love, and our hearts are too full for utterance. A week ago last night I met thirty old scholars who were not Christians. There was quiet solemnity in the meeting, but I sat with them to weep; for I found not one in earnest for eternal life. A sleepless night followed. I had not strength for more than a single word of petition, 'Mercy!' Last night I could not sleep, but it was to thank the Lord for 'mercy' given to at least nineteen of those precious souls. There are others, new scholars, who have, as they and we hope, chosen Christ for their portion, so that we can believe that not less than thirty have made their peace with God during the last week. . . . Do you wonder that our eyes run down with tears? Do you wonder that we cling to Jesus more lovingly than ever? Dear friend, I wish you were with us. No, I do not. I think you may keep your eye right on Jesus better where you are than you could here; that is, *to pray*. And now keep praying for us 'till all are Christ's."

A few days later she wrote to a friend in Newburyport: —

"18. — The teachers were moved to much prayer, finding time every day to come into my room to pray, and two weeks ago last Tuesday evening, they came in at a late hour to talk of what could be done for the precious souls under our care. It was decided that we all engage in direct labor for Christians. We were constrained to do this, for many of the impenitent utterly refused to be spoken with. A week of this labor passed, but we saw no one deeply anxious among those not Christians. On Tuesday of last week Dr. K. came here on business. He preached that evening to the whole school. They were very solemn, as also on Thursday morning, when he again addressed them, and immediately left. He returned Friday afternoon, and that evening preached from 'Choose ye this day whom ye will serve.' Now the

Spirit was abundantly poured out. Many hearts were moved, and forty stayed to converse with him after the meeting. Many of these had passed through several revivals, and some of them had been here three years.

"The inquiry meeting on Saturday night was thronged, and those indulging hope filled a large room. Finding a still larger room necessary to accommodate all who had this year begun to hope, they were invited to the lecture-room, where, until now, the meetings for the impenitent had been held every Sabbath evening, there being, when the school opened, one hundred and nine of this class. You can imagine better than I can describe our feelings on finding seventy of that number present. We sang, 'Why was I made to hear his voice?' and after going back in our thoughts to the beginning of the year, the names of those who were at the first meeting of the impenitent were read, with the request that each, if now present, should rise as her name was called. It was a scene of melting tenderness. We wept tears for Jesus to wipe away. After a season of prayer and communion with the Saviour, we sang, 'Lord, I am thine, entirely thine.' I have been in my room much of the time the last two weeks; but with care and rest I have been able to go to several meetings, and there point souls to Christ; and three times I have met the whole school. In such days of waiting on the Lord strength has been renewed. The season has seemed much like some of those precious revivals of old. I have felt anew how delightful it is to work *with* the Spirit of God."

In a letter to another friend, alluding to that meeting of young converts, she says: "There were more than thirty names to which there was no response. I cannot describe to you the deep solemnity there was during the reading of those names. We seemed to be carried forward to another day when the Lord himself shall call for us. At one point four names were called, and no one rose. The solemnity that rested on us all was awful, as we seemed to realize what it is to be 'shut out.'"

Again she writes: —

"22.—The young Christians met together Saturday evening, and also last evening. There were eighty-one present. . . . There are now twenty-three without hope. All but ten of these have classed themselves with inquirers during the week. Feeling that I must see those ten, I asked them privately to come to my room before tea last night. Eight came, and four of them manifested much feeling before leaving. Two afterwards went to an inquiry meeting. We hope for still further blessings this week."

In a letter of later date she says: "Three, who were in my little meeting of the impenitent last Sunday evening, now hope they are Christians. I told them in that meeting that I should probably not ask one of them to answer another question about her soul till she wished me to do so, and added, 'but if any one of your number would have prayer offered for herself, she may come to my room at eight o'clock to-morrow evening.' One who had stoutly resisted every influence was the first to come in; and yesterday morning she came to tell me that she hoped she was Christ's. Two others who came in that night are beginning to entertain the same hope."

To a friend in Monson, she writes: —

"29.—Thursday, the day for prayer for literary institutions, was a day of deep interest here. The solemn quiet, the earnest prayers, and the wish to have the day longer, were affecting. I think I never attended prayer-meetings where there seemed more of heaven. We had seven prayer-meetings in the lecture-room, and there were many little meetings. Over two hundred requests for prayer were sent into those meetings. There are still about twenty who are without hope, but some of them seem very near the kingdom, while others are very far away."

"*March* 11.—It seems certain that I cannot go to Oroomiah this spring. I do not doubt my Father's wisdom in not giving me the health for it, but it is hard for the friends there. When I see you I will tell you about it. I have been very thankful to be here and see the harvest gathered in. I do not expect to remain here during the summer."

"25.—Most of the teachers and young ladies have left. I have lingered because I wanted to see these precious children to the end; and now I am taking away everything, so as to feel that my home is not to be here at all for the summer. Each passing day makes me feel more and more how great the blessing God has given us. I met the dear young Christians Monday night, and they pledged themselves to remember, each the others, at the hour of sunset. You will sometimes, at that hour, ask God to keep them from the evil that is in the world. Last night, even in the midst of the carrying out of the baggage, we had a prayer-meeting, at which more than two hundred were present. It was one of the most delightful seasons of prayer in which I ever participated. A great company left about five o'clock this morning; but they did not go till they had held a prayer-meeting in the reception-room. When the second company were ready to leave, we went to the library and had three prayers before we separated. There were about seventy in the meeting. They were all ready to go; but we continued praying till the 'long bell' told us that the carriages were at the door. It seemed so much like other years; just like that Eastern home."

CHAPTER XXVII.

LAST SICKNESS — DEATH — FUNERAL.

Before the term closed at South Hadley, Miss Fiske became convinced that she must abandon all hope of returning to Persia this year; and also that she could not prudently remain at the seminary during the summer. Entire rest and freedom from care seemed indispensable, and she accordingly went to her Shelburne home, hoping so far to recover her health as to be able, in a few weeks, to resume the writing of "Recollections of Mary Lyon."

Her plan at first was to spend the summer months by the sea-shore; and repeatedly the day was fixed for going to Newburyport, but her strength each time proved unequal to the journey. For weeks her trunk was packed, while she waited for some favorable change, and it remained packed to the last, but no change came for the better, until the great change which released her from all mortal suffering and bore her away to the rest and the rewards of heaven.

The following extracts from letters will be read with tender interest, and will indicate the progress made by the disease, until at length it silenced the pen that had for many years been so eloquent in the Master's service: —

TO MISS H. M. L.

"SHELBURNE, March 31, 1864.

"You ask me to write you a short letter, telling, first of all, of my health. I never like to talk or write of that. Yet I will do so now, for how can I do otherwise after all your kind inquiries? For several weeks I have not been nearly as well as usual, and so I shall not try to do anything more at South Hadley for the present. I do not know why I cannot do more, but I cannot. I think I shall feel better soon, — at least I hope so, and I know of nothing so good for me as quiet."

TO MISS RICE.

"SHELBURNE, April 1, 1864.

"MY DEAR SISTER: — My heart's tenderest sympathies are with you, and I have shrunk from telling you that I cannot go to you this spring. It is only a few weeks since I gave it up; that is, so as to feel sure that I cannot go. I trust that my letters have led you to see that I am not staying here, as some of you feared, to do other work. I have always felt that it would be wrong for me to make plans for life here; and, whatever you may hear of my movements, remember that when I form a plan to remain here, I shall tell you of it first of all. For six weeks in January and February I kept my bed half the time. I am now feeling much better, but can make but little effort, either physical or mental."

TO MISS H. M. L.

"May 12, 1864.

"I cannot now make any effort without suffering, so I am very good in obeying medical advisers, and am really doing nothing. I am charged not to go to South Hadley, and so I shall 'pass by on the other side' when I go to Newburyport. Those scenes of last winter were too much for me, but I should love to go to heaven from them."

TO DR. WRIGHT, ON THE EVE OF HIS LEAVING AMERICA TO RETURN TO PERSIA.

"SHELBURNE, May 26, 1864.

"MY DEAR BROTHER:—I know that your heart and hands are full these last days before leaving; but I doubt not that you are strengthened, and walk in light and peace. You know that you bear to those dear friends in Oroomiah the love and deepest interest of my heart. They will ask, as they have often done, 'Why does she delay her coming?' and they will henceforth ask this very gently, if my letters have helped them to understand how I long to be with them. If a sea voyage would take me there, I should not be slow in deciding to go to them. If I could not work, I could look upon those dear children again, and ask them to hold in remembrance the one way to our 'home,' when I shall have gone from them. Those dear native friends, how my heart goes out toward them! May you be spared to meet them and bless them in the name of the Lord!

"I am thankful that you can see the pillar of cloud rising, which you are to follow. May it lead you to the land which we saw from afar, and then dwelt therein to find the promises of our God 'yea and amen.' We were blessed with the 'early rain,' and my prayer is that in the 'latter rain' you may find a yet richer blessing. So, Lord, bless thy servant, and all those named by his name.

"Yours affectionately,

"FIDELIA FISKE."

As the disease progressed her sufferings increased, especially at night. May 31st, she writes: —

"Last night was one of those nights of suffering which give me days of weariness. I can write easier than I can do anything else. I do not feel anxious about the future. I may be better soon; if I am not, I do not believe I shall be kept here a great while. The whole system seems to me to be too much affected to get good from local treatment; and the disease, if not checked, will, I think, work rapidly. I may be wrong; but, be that as it may, I know all will be well."

Allusions in the two following letters will be more readily understood, if it be here stated that they were written soon after a trying sickness in the Oxford Female Seminary, Ohio, which broke up the school for the term: —

TO MRS. P.

"SHELBURNE, June 2, 1864.

"MY DEAR. MRS P.: — The accompanying letter from Miss J—— was sent me last night. When I read it I was dumb. I could not speak of it even to those by my side. I went to my room to pass a sleepless night. My thoughts would go to dear Miss P., and then back to our own dear Miss Lyon, as she bowed under a similar trial in 1840. You remember those days, and will be able to write Miss P. a letter that will comfort her. I want to write her this afternoon, but must wait till to-morrow, for feeling consumes all my strength very soon. I have been entirely satisfied in being here, because I was sure the Lord Jesus bade me stay and rest, and that he came before me to stay with me. How easy to feel that all is right, when we can see or believe that the Lord orders all! This entire resting has not often been necessary for me, and I almost feel it to be a new experience. But how much of it has been yours! What blessed lessons you have learned in the school of suffering! You have thus done much good to others, and certainly to me, for which I have often thanked the Lord."

TO MISS E. J.

"June 6, 1864.

"MY DEAR MISS J.:—How much I thank you for remembering me in your letter to the seminary of May 23d. I received it just at night last Wednesday, but I could not trust myself to read it till the next afternoon. Then my heart went out to you in sympathy which I have not ventured to attempt to express. Dear Miss Peabody! I love her as never before, and I am sure that the Saviour's voice is heard in all this, saying, 'Whom I love I chasten.' We open not our mouths, because our God has done it. You know a similar trial came upon our dear Miss Lyon in 1840. She took the cup from her Father's hand and meekly drank it, even to the dregs. But while the spirit was willing the flesh was weak. She broke down under it, but rose to be more than ever like her divine Master. . . . I stayed too long at the seminary, but I thank my God even for those last weeks. They were weeks of suffering crowned with holy joy. . . . If I get home before you do, I do not think I shall forget that you are coming. May we both be prepared for an abundant entrance into the world of light!"

TO MRS. S.

"June 4, 1864.

"These shaking tabernacles try us; but taking them down is no unimportant part of our preparation for the 'house not made with hands.' It is not our Father's will that we stay in them always, and, while abiding in them, he sees that we need to be often pointed to the hour when he will give us a body all glorious. . . . I can usually feel very happy in leaving my future with Him who has dealt so kindly with me in all the past. When I left Oroomiah I felt, as did others, that I could not live long. But my Father has given me years of very comfortable health, and he will give me more, if he needs me to labor any more for him."

TO D. T. F.

"June 16, 1864.

"I have not found myself as well as I hoped to be this week. For two or three days I was not able to go out, but am better now, though not well enough to go to Newburyport. I want to make a little change as soon as I am strong enough, and independent enough; but I wait cheerfully my Father's time. He makes my way an easy one, and I know he will again give me health if it is best for me. The friends leave for Oroomiah on Saturday. '*Why* might I not go with them?' I can hardly ask but with tears, and a full heart. It would do me good to know that 'the Lord had need of me there; but shall I doubt the love that keeps me here?'"

TO MISS H. M. L.

"June 17, 1864.

"Physicians are not agreed in reference to my ailments. The last theory is that the absorbents of the system generally refuse to perform their duty. This, of course, is attended with many hours of intense suffering, while I have many other hours of comparative ease. My arms are much of the time so swollen that I cannot raise them to my head, while my shoulders, and the entire breast and chest are in full sympathy, and the lower limbs are beginning to be affected also.

"All this makes me very dependent; too much so to allow me to think of being a visitor anywhere. A few weeks ago there was a strong feeling that I must take a voyage. It was proposed that I go to England with Dr. Wright and Mr. Coan, on their way to Oroomiah. I did not object, but it was a relief to me to have it decided that it was not best. My physician thinks that my voyage home gave me a new lease of life. I am willing to rest awhile, believing such to be my Father's will. I cannot sew, or do anything of the kind; but I write, taking the paper in my lap; and I enjoy reading very much. I do not attempt to converse with any one long at a time, because it takes the suffering members so long to compose themselves afterwards. I am sometimes obliged to take opiates to keep pain within limits; but much of the time I can do without them, and do not suffer as much as I did a few weeks ago. I am very far from being 'troubled,' because I know who is caring for me. He will never keep me in the furnace one moment longer than is necessary for the good of his cause on earth and in heaven; and can I not, if he strengthens me, rejoice in this? I am not in the habit of writing so fully in regard to myself, and should be ashamed of having done so, had you not asked it."

TO MRS. S. D. S.

"June 22, 1864.

"I know that the Lord is hearing the requests of others for me. He is giving me blessings which I do not think to ask for myself. He is so good to keep me from anxious thoughts about the future! They do not seem to have any place within me; so I know it is of the Lord."

"*July* 3. — There is no reason why I should not be cheerful and happy; and I wish to be so. I am sure that the Lord gives me much peace in answer to the prayers of his children. But when I look at myself soberly, it seems to me that I have very little reason to suppose that I can ever be well. While I feel that I ought to do everything that can be done to restore health, I feel from day to day that disease is getting a stronger and stronger hold, and that there is little prospect of any change for the better. I do not say this, expressing a preference either to go or to stay; but as a common-sense view. I am so afraid that I shall not be patient under suffering! Do pray that I may not, in word or heart, complain. It seems to me so certain that my Father would have me suffer, that I ask for patience rather than that I may be free from suffering."

The disease, which at first was thought to be of a cancerous nature, proved to be a general inflammation of the lymphatic vessels. It made rapid progress, and was attended with intense suffering. Her arms became so much swollen, that, within a few days after the last date, she was obliged wholly to lay aside her pen. — *The letters of Fidelia Fiske are ended.*

To her most intimate friend, the friend of many years, both in Persia and America, whose presence was a great comfort to Miss Fiske during her last days, we are largely indebted for the means of continuing the record of her life to its closing scene.

On the arrival of this friend, July 9th, Miss Fiske was able to walk from her chamber into the hall and greet her with her usual pleasant smile. For two nights she had been obliged to sleep in her chair. The inflammation and swelling about the chest and arms were so great as to make a reclining posture extremely painful; and during the last three weeks of her life she could rest only in her chair.

July 11th, being a very warm day, she suffered extremely. Her distress was at times so great that she could not keep back the tears, nor help saying, "Why is it that I must suffer so?" "Can I bear it?" "Am I so wicked as to need such discipline?" Then she would weep still more bitterly at the thought that she had been impatient. She said it was evidently her Father's will that she should suffer, and she wished to bear it without a murmur.

Many times during those trying days, as her friend

kneeled by her side, endeavoring to soothe and comfort her with some Scriptural promise, or verse of a hymn, she would rest her head on her friend's shoulder, the tears flowing fast, and say, "God bless you my sister! Say it over and over; it does comfort me."

Her nervous system seemed to be entirely prostrated, and it was painful beyond expression to see one who had been a daughter of consolation to multitudes, thus overwhelmed. But the Saviour loved his child, and wished to give her a new experience of fellowship in his suffering.

Amid all her pains and nervous disturbance, her faith remained clear and strong. "I have not a doubt," she said, "of my final acceptance. I know I am the Lord's, and he will save me; but I want to bear his sufferings so as to honor him. I do not want to give way to my feelings. It would be hard to endure so much suffering, if I did not know that it is my heavenly Father who sends it all in love. Yes, I am sure he knows what is best for me. I will trust — *I will — I will.*"

Saturday night, July 16th, she had severe paroxysms of pain, attended with fainting, and a slight wandering of the mind. Her extreme feebleness the next morning compelled her physician to relinquish the hope of her recovery, which till then he had cherished.

Monday, July 18th, with perfect calmness she gave directions as to the disposition of her wardrobe and other articles. In the afternoon a dear friend from Boston spent an hour with her, and, in the course of her conversation, observed that she thought

"Christ was honored more by our suffering as weak mortals, than he could be by our suffering as perfect beings, and that we could not prevent our exclamations or our tears under excruciating pain unless we were more than mortal." This thought seemed greatly to comfort Miss Fiske. Hitherto her requests to her friends had been, "Pray that I may have patience to endure;" afterwards it was, "Pray that the will of the Lord may be wholly accomplished in me."

The same day she dictated her last message to the teachers and pupils of Mount Holyoke Seminary, as follows: —

"I cannot allow you to separate without blessing you once more in the name of the Lord. I want to thank you for those precious notes from you, which have come flocking to my room for the last few days. I should love to write you individually, but I cannot do it, nor even collectively, except by the hand of another. Your notes have been an exceeding comfort to me, and your repeated assurances of remembrance in your prayers have been more to me than any earthly good. Let me thank you for it all, and assure you that Jesus will not forget it. I have loved you tenderly, and have loved to labor with you; and could I be with you this morning to give you one parting word, it would not be a new one, but one which I would have you ever hold in remembrance. 'Live for Christ;' in so doing we shall all be blessed in time and in eternity.

"Ever yours in the Lord,

"FIDELIA FISKE."

The next morning, after a paroxysm of pain, she said, "I think the Saviour can honor himself just as much by forgiving any seeming impatience, as by keeping me from it." In the evening she inquired if the doctor thought she would recover. When told that he did not, she replied, "I am glad to hear it; that is my own conviction, and it is a relief to know that it is his also." The next morning she said, "It makes the way seem shorter and easier to feel that there is no hope of recovery." She had before remarked that it seemed a long way back to health, and that she dreaded the process of getting well; but she was very careful about expressing any positive wish to die. "My life," she said, "has been one of uninterrupted prosperity, and my heavenly Father sees that I am not prepared for heaven without suffering here, and he will lay upon me no more strokes than I need; just a few more, and then he will take me to himself." She had enjoyed life, even its most laborious duties, and now expressed herself as equally ready to depart, or to remain and take up life's work anew, as she had done twenty-four years before, when brought back from the borders of the grave.

Wednesday, July 20th, she conversed freely with her family friends about leaving them. To one who was bathing her arms she said, "You will never be sorry for all the care you have taken of these poor arms. They will serve Jesus the better for it in the other world." Again, after listening to a hymn in which "eternal rest" was mentioned, she said that the idea of heaven as a place of "rest" merely, was not pleasant to her. She delighted to think of the saints as active, and engaged, as far as possible, in those employments which they had most enjoyed on earth. She often spoke of the loved ones she hoped soon to meet, and of the joy she should have in talking with them about the friends left on earth, and the events which had occurred here.

The only relief she had from sitting in her chair was to be removed to the lounge, and there supported in the arms of some friends.

On Friday, she said, "As I grow weaker I think less of the pain, and feel more the Saviour's arms about me, and it is sweet to feel them." For several years she had felt a dread of the last conflict, in consequence of having witnessed instances of death, and among friends, which were peculiarly painful. On being asked if she still felt that dread, she replied, "I can leave it now, and look beyond."

Sabbath morning she asked to have a number of the tracts entitled "Immanuel's Land" laid upon her table, so that every person coming into her room might take one.

The muscles about the chest had now become so contracted that she could not straighten herself sufficiently to rest her head on the back of her chair, and could sleep only by having her head supported by one attendant, and her arms by another.

On Monday it became evident that the end was near. Toward evening she dictated the following message to her friends in Oroomiah:—

"FRIENDS, DEARLY BELOVED: — As I stand on the borders of eternity, there is no new truth on which to dwell. Those truths which have sustained us in our labors together sustain now. Our labors together on earth are finished, but I trust not in heaven.

You labor on yet a little longer, while the Master calls for me. It is not meet that I say unto you, 'Be faithful in labor;' but, if you are so, you will soon be found with crowns upon your heads, and harps in your hands, — made perfect in Christ's righteousness. God grant that I may meet you there, though I fee , to-night, that I am all sin and unrighteousness."

To her mother she said, "I must soon go; there are others to care for you, and when the Master calls for you, you will then be glad that I have gone before; for I shall be there waiting to meet you."

Monday night was to the dear sufferer a very distressful one, and a part of the time she was delirious.

The next morning, Tuesday, July 26th, about half-past eight o'clock, Rev. E. Y. Swift called to see her. She signified her wish that he should come to her room. As he entered the door, she put out her hand to welcome him, and, in reply to his salutation, she said feebly, "Will you pray?" These were her last words. During the first part of the prayer she was greatly distressed, but as the petition was uttered that God would grant her a speedy release from her sufferings, and an abundant entrance into his everlasting kingdom, the struggle ceased; and, at the close of the prayer, only a few gentle breathings were perceptible. A life of prayer had ended in prayer, and the spirit of Fidelia Fiske had entered into glory.

The funeral services were attended on Thursday. At the house, Rev. Theophilus Packard, who was for many years Miss Fiske's beloved pastor, offered prayer. The procession of mourners then moved to the church, which was filled with those whose hearts seemed bowed with one great sorrow. After the singing of the hymn, "'Tis finished; the conflict is past," Rev. R. S. Billings, the pastor of the church, read appropriate passages of Scripture, and made a brief address, concluding with a statement of the principal facts in Miss Fiske's life. Rev. Drs. Anderson and Kirk, of Boston, then, in touching words, paid a fitting tribute to the memory of one whom they so well knew, and whose rare Christian worth they so highly appreciated. A tender and fervent prayer by Dr. Kirk, and the singing of another hymn, closed the deeply affecting services. It was a great disappointment to all, whom the mournful occasion drew together, that the coffin could not be opened to allow them to gaze once more upon the face of their beloved friend.

From the church the procession wound its way to the retired little cemetery, where she had indicated her wish to be buried. And there, amid sad hearts and tearful eyes, was laid to rest all that was mortal of Fidelia Fiske. The hour and the scene touchingly harmonized with the occasion. The sun was sinking in the west; the summits of the hills, among which the sainted one was born, were bathed in light, while their shadow was thrown over the spot where her body was finding its last resting-place. And it was easier, at such a solemn and tranquil hour, and amid such surroundings, for those who felt that they were indeed under a great shadow, to leave that precious dust, "Until the day break and the shadows flee away;" and from the sunlight on the neighboring hills, to lift their thoughts to those "everlasting hills," where there is no night, and where the departed one was already walking in garments more radiant than the sun, and whiter than the flowers strown upon her grave.

In the accompanying view of the cemetery where Miss Fiske was buried, the shaft at the right indicates her grave.

CHAPTER XXVIII.

TESTIMONIALS.

From Hoshebo. — Sarra. — Sanum. — Dea. Yonan. — Miss Rice. — Rev. Mr. Rhea. — Rev. Dr. Perkins. — Rev. Dr. Kirk. — Rev. Dr. Laurie. — Rev. Dr. Anderson.

THOSE who have followed the narrative of Miss Fiske's labors in the preceding pages must, it is believed, have felt themselves in the presence of a rare Christian woman, — a skilful Christian teacher, — an eminently devoted and successful Christian missionary.

In order that the reader may be able to compare the impressions which this narrative has made upon his own mind, with the impression made by Miss Fiske upon the minds of those who were favored with an intimate personal acquaintance with her, these closing pages are devoted to a few of the testimonials, which have been kindly furnished since her death. Their variety and fulness will render it needless for the compiler of this volume to transcribe his own impressions of a character, whose leading traits they so clearly indicate, and to which they pay so ample a tribute.

When the tidings of Miss Fiske's death reached Persia, there was bitter disappointment and profound grief, not only in the missionary circle, but among all classes of the Nestorians. Many of her pupils wrote letters of sympathy and condolence to her mother and sister, from which the following extracts are taken: —

FROM HOSHEBO, OF SARALAN.

"There is not one of the women of our people who ever saw Miss Fiske, who does not remember her with deepest regret at her death. The summing up of her record is simply this: she was very Christ-like, having a strong resemblance to himself in all his traits, especially in his adaptation of his parables to the state of every person. . . . She used to go often to some of the large villages, visiting from house to house, especially to comfort the poor women. She would sit down by the wheel a few minutes, and show them that as the body has need of food and raiment, so also the soul has wants which must be met, needing for its clothing the garment of Christ's righteousness, and for its food the hidden manna. She would also sit at the looms of the boys and young men, and weave a little, drawing their thoughts upward by her excellent skill in many ways, and then she would pray with them. After her visits to the houses, she would not spare herself the melting heats of summer, but would go into the fields to the women weeding cotton, and converse with them there.

"One trait, in which she was remarkable above all others, was that of taking care of the sick. She possessed that skill and ability which could control one in bodily ailments as well as in spiritual. She used to talk very much to us about taking care of the sick, and taught us that it was a holy and acceptable service; as our Lord says, 'I was sick, and ye visited me.'

"But what can I leave, and what can I write? There is more than I have power to relate respecting the completeness of my mother, Miss Fiske, so adorned with lofty and good deeds. Oh, if it be not possible that all, would that one or two, at least, of her flock might resemble her, even as she resembled Miss Lyon, the founder of Mount Holyoke Seminary!"

FROM SARRA, WIFE OF OSHANA.

"She was very dear to me because she has done so much for me, — more than my own loved parents. . . . She taught us many lessons with all the enthusiasm of her heart. What she loved most, and took the greatest pains to make us understand, was the Holy Scriptures. Her prayers were very fervent. She always had a particular subject for prayer. Whatever work she had before her she would commence it with prayer, asking help from the Great Teacher. She prayed much with us individually. Her prayers were not only ardent, but mingled with burning love. If she saw a fault in us (which often happened), she did not reprove us suddenly and with severity, but, although very sad and in tears, she waited, meanwhile asking help of her Father in heaven, then, with words gentle, but penetrating and awakening, she talked with us till our hearts melted like wax; then, in the ardor of her love, she knelt with us, committing us to the counsel and guidance of God. There was no heart that would not melt before the fire of her love, unless it were one entirely overcome by Satan. . . . She spoke much of acts of kindness in visiting the sick. In this she greatly resembled her Master. She talked much about propriety, politeness, and courtesy to every one, with affection for each other and for all. She spoke much upon cleanliness and good order in the house, and said that these were outward signs of Christianity; also of diligence in business, that we should not be dependent on others for assistance, but on the might of our own hands."

FROM SANUM.

"What shall I say? How shall I take my sorrowful pen to note down my grief and anguish for the mother whom I so much loved! Is it true, that one like Miss Fiske, a guide adorned with every kind of talent, now sleeps in the ground? We consider that our consolation is dead; that the beautiful staff of our support is broken; that the mount against which we leaned is removed; that the chief strong pillar of our women is cast down. We are distressed by the tidings of her death. Our limbs are broken. We are cast down lower than the dust. She possessed fine and beautiful traits, not found except in a few rare mortals. One was a humble, tender, loving heart, and a spirit that had within it a seat of love for every mortal. She knew how to win the heart of every one,—those of all ranks and characters, and temporal and spiritual conditions,—by meekly bowing her noble self to every condition.

"Her first meeting with me was in the yard at Seir. She quickly drew my heart to her by her love and delightful counsels. My heart was so melted that very minute, that I pulled out the clove that was in my bored nose, and the silver rings that were in my ears, and from that day I longed to enter the seminary of Miss Fiske, until God, in his good providence brought me to realize this desire in 1846.

"Although she had so heavy a burden upon her, she was alive to everything. Like the gentle rays of the sun that descend and effect such great things, she in all quietness used to accomplish great things. Yet was she ever awake to every naughty sound, however low. She used to fill us with amazement many times, for almost always when we had been saying naughty things, or committing some fault in school, or in the rooms, or in the yard, we looked up, and lo! she was standing right over our heads. As if an angel prompted her, she reproved us sharply and deeply so as to produce a great effect upon us. But she had also this gift, that she could win and heal the wounded heart, and we loved her a thousand times more than ever. When there was displeasure among us, she would say, 'My dear girls, I can read many of your thoughts; they are written on your faces; such a one thinks so, and such a one so;' and she almost always understood our hearts.

"Very often, when we were angry, she would melt us down by prayer. One day she had reproved me for a fault, and I was angry, and said, 'I'll go home and read no more.' She counselled me to remain. I said, 'No; I will go.' She said, 'Very well; we will pray together, and afterwards, if you desire, go.' We kneeled down, and, before we had finished praying, my heart was completely melted, and I rose and begged her forgiveness.

"What can I say of her trust in her Saviour? Very

often she spoke of going to heaven, and said she should do so and so there; and she spoke of these things with such relish and enjoyment that we always said, 'Blessed is such confidence!' Oh, how she longed for one thing which she has now attained, — to be able to sing. She sorrowed greatly that she had not this gift; but would say, 'I shall soon go to heaven, and shall sing there.'

"How can I help mentioning, further, some of the blessed fruits of the Spirit in her life, — the fear of the Lord, love, clear hope, perfect faith, holy zeal, peace, patience without guile, forbearance, wonderful humility, and the most perfect propriety in all her walk, conversation, and instruction. She also determined in her heart that she would not allow a woman to enter her door and depart without praying with her; and, if she was herself very much hurried with some other business, she committed those who came to some of us. She also prayed privately with every girl in school repeatedly every year; and every girl who wished to pray with her always enjoyed that favor."

FROM DEACON YONAN.

"We considered her very remarkable for her learning and skill. We often carried to her passages of Scripture, and difficult questions that arose. She would explain them, or decide on them with such modesty and skill that all parties would be satisfied. Sometimes the bishop, Mar. Elias, would say of her, 'She is a real Deborah.' If there were consultations to be held about the superintendence of the work of the Lord in a given place, or a given village, we relied on her advice; and, when we were in straits, she would open for us a way, and did not err. Sometimes we used to go to her to get her to help us compose our sermons, and she was very happy to help us. One day she said, 'I have very great joy in Nestorian preachers; the sounds and character of this language are finely fitted for preaching.' The Nestorian preachers used to consider her so learned, that they prepared their sermons with a great deal more thought, care, and watchfulness when she was to be in the congregation.

"She was also very skilful in the general management of affairs. Often she conversed with the priests, deacons, and chiefs among the people with so much skill, and she understood the case of each one so well, that not one of them could depart from her without feeling her power. The first word they would say, on leaving, was, 'She is a very wonderful woman.'

"One day a preacher ascended the pulpit to preach. After singing, and reading the Scriptures, he looked steadily in the face of the congregation, but, from timidity, said not a word. He requested a priest present to pray, and another to pronounce the benediction; and so the congregation dispersed. After a little while, Miss Fiske sent for him, and said to him, 'I thank you very much for your good sermon; it made a great impression on me.' And then she comforted and encouraged him. So, in all becoming ways, she could help every one according to his necessity."

A peculiar value attaches to the following testimony of Miss Rice, who was for eleven years Miss Fiske's loved and efficient associate teacher in the female seminary at Oroomiah: —

"Her character stands before me in living beauty, and my unskilful hand will try to give a few outlines of the picture.

"Unselfishness, benevolence, gentleness, prayerfulness, remarkable executive power, adaptation to circumstances, versatility, excellent judgment, perseverance, and a wonderful power of influencing others, were some of the natural traits of her character, which grace strengthened and beautified with the fruits of the Spirit.

"Her *unselfishness* was a very prominent trait in her character. Even in her childhood she was ready to give to others a portion better than her own. She carried this disposition with her through life. She was always aiming to lighten the burdens of others, while meekly bearing her own. In the division of school labor she always insisted on taking the larger and heavier share. Like her blessed Master, she lived not to please herself; she sought the comfort and happiness of others, often at great expense of time and strength to herself; but her sacrifices were freewill offerings, cheerfully laid on God's altar.

"Miss Fiske gave herself to her work with a devotion, which, to a less benevolent heart, would have been impossible. The Master whom she served was pleased to give her an early harvest.

"Who can describe the pure joy that filled her heart, as one and another of these wild girls became new creatures in Christ Jesus? She delighted to train them for Christ's High School, by her own lovely example and priceless instructions. She 'allured to brighter worlds, and led the way.' She was far more than a *teacher* in her relations to our school. She gave a mother's love and care to our family, and many are the devoted Nestorian daughters who are ready to rise up and call her their *blessed mother*.

"Gentle herself, her constant aim was to teach her pupils to profit from the motto, 'Study to be quiet.' Sometimes one of the older girls slept in her room, and, whatever her habits may have been previously, she soon learned, under Miss Fiske's training, to sleep quietly, and quickly rouse from slumber. In order to appreciate this fact, one should know that the sleep of Orientals is generally very heavy and deep, owing in part, no doubt, to a habit of mental inactivity in their waking hours.

"She labored much to cultivate habits of industry and self-denial among her pupils. In her they saw a living exponent of the exhortation, 'not slothful in business, fervent in spirit, serving the Lord.' She endeavored most earnestly to make her pupils *conscientious*. Missionaries alone can understand the difficulty and the greatness of this work. There are many Abrahams and Sarahs and Jacobs and Rebeccas in this part of the world, even in the nineteenth century.

"Devotedly attached to her Alma Mater, she was so successful in making our school a miniature Holyoke, that, in four years, the pupils in their bearing reminded their newly arrived teacher, very forcibly, of the South Hadley sisters, whom she had recently left, as did their teacher, of our loved principal Miss Lyon.

"Miss Fiske, as a teacher, was enthusiastic, and

thorough. The bright and the dull scholar found in her a friend, ready to appreciate their respective merits. For want of text-books, during several years, she spent much time in giving oral instruction to eager listeners. Our Bible lessons have ever been the favorite study in school. Nothing would gratify a class more than to hear that Miss Fiske would teach them this or that book of the Scriptures. Even the younger girls learned to prize the hour in which the school were allowed to ask Bible questions, particularly at the close of the Sabbath. Sometimes questions were left unanswered, and it was pleasant to notice how carefully the Holy Word was searched to find the reply. Miss Fiske often trenched on her hours of sleep to prepare her Bible questions, and her pupils considered it a privilege to copy them for future use. But the amount of practical instruction imparted during their recitations was beyond their ability to write, and were treasures for memory's storehouse.

"The records of the last day alone can disclose the incalculable value of the study of God's Word, as Miss Fiske taught it and *lived* it. She aimed to have our pupils regard it as *the rule of duty.* 'To the law and to the testimony,' they must go to decide the question of right and wrong. Not a few of them could *see* that the principles of government in our family were drawn from Holy Writ. Still, Miss Fiske, in their eyes, was not Moses, the lawgiver, but a reflection of the glory of Him, whose love filled her heart and shone in her every-day life. She lived nearer Calvary than Sinai. The suffering Saviour was the magnet of her soul.

"Her prayerfulness was remarkable. Her communings with her Father in heaven were so frequent, that she ever lived in the light of his countenance. As one of her pupils remarked, she always said, '*When* I reach heaven;' not '*if* I reach heaven.'

"Who can estimate the untold blessings that have descended on our school, — on our whole field, — in answer to her intercessions? She labored, and prayed, and hoped for the conversion of our *whole* family; she wrestled with the angel of the covenant, and often did she prevail. Never can we forget the earnestness with which she often entreated that no soul, who had dwelt on the heights of our Zion, should sink into the regions of despair.

"In matters small as well as great she was accustomed to consult the 'Beloved of her soul.' If she was tried or perplexed, she carried the case to God, and listened to hear what God, the Lord, should speak. If things went wrong in school, if her discerning eye saw tokens of concealed wickedness, she sought help from above; and wonderful were the answers to her prayers.

"Miss Fiske was no ascetic. She greatly enjoyed social intercourse, and no one, more than she, prized a home in a missionary family. She was a true sister there, entering most heartily into all their joys and sorrows, often applying her skilful hand to the domestic routine, to lighten the burden of a weary or feeble missionary sister. No one, so easily as she, could make the necessary preparations for a missionary tour, or a long journey, and no one could make a more attractive retreat for guests. She was a true '*Aunt Fidelia*' to all the missionary children. It was a treat to her to leave school-cares for a little while, and have a play with the younger children. She had particular skill in soothing the little ones, as well as in interesting the older ones, and, in times of sickness, they clung to her as to their own mothers. She would carry them very gently in her arms back and forth, walking backwards herself, one length of the room, to save the child the unpleasant motion of turning. She was an unspeakable comfort in the sickness of little children, as many mothers can testify.

"Nowhere has Miss Fiske left a more tenderly grateful remembrance than in the sick-room. Deeply devoted as she was to her school, — reluctantly withdrawing from it, for a few hours only; yet there was *one* call that met a quick response from her sympathizing heart. When any missionary family was suffering from sickness they were sure to welcome this angel of mercy.

"Ophthalmia is a prevalent disease during the summer in Persia. Seldom does a year pass, in which some members of our missionary circle, especially the children, do not suffer from it. Miss Fiske's benevolence exerted itself in unwearied care at such times. She never hesitated to confine herself to the darkened room, to bathe the inflamed, painful eyes; and when it was necessary to apply leeches, she was *the* one to do it successfully.

"Miss Fiske was capable of exerting a wonderful influence over others. No doubt this was greatly owing to that *love* that permeated her whole being. When it was necessary to administer reproof, her words were 'sharp arrows of the mighty, with coals of juniper.' But there was no room for resentment in the heart of the reproved, for the kind acts that followed, proved so strongly that she desired nothing but the real benefit of all, that they were received as the 'dew of Hermon, and as the dew that descended upon the mountains of Zion; for there the Lord commanded the blessing.'

"In all the busy weeks and months of preparation for our school, Miss Fiske daily and earnestly prayed for a blessing, a spiritual blessing, to descend on the work of our hands. She was rearing a temple, in which, she entreated, that 'the glory that excelleth' should dwell. Hence, her listening ear was ready to catch the first sound of 'the going in the tops of the mulberry trees,' and quickly did she gird herself for the work of laboring for awakened souls. Her love and anxiety for perishing souls were intense.

"Her zeal for the improvement of her sex knew no bounds; it was a ruling passion with her. No obstacles were considered insuperable in the prosecution of the work so near her heart.

"She was our 'beloved Persis,' who 'labored much in the Lord;' in charity, our Dorcas; in counsel and action, our Deborah; in praying, our weeping Hannah, our Phebe 'the succorer of many,' and now, our sainted sister, 'Fidelia the Faithful.' Gentle, unassuming, affectionate, confiding, sympathizing, considerate, and self-sacrificing, she possessed a truly feminine character, though she was capable of putting forth masculine, masterly efforts.

"Is any one ready to ask, 'Was her character so beautifully rounded that no sharp corner was visible?' Her most intimate companion can recall only one, and that was her extreme unwillingness to subject any one to inconvenience on her account. She delighted to spend and to be spent for others; but it was very painful for her to receive like favors in return. She had a very elastic constitution; hence her remarkable power of endurance; but she was not strong, and rarely did a day pass without physical suffering. She was particularly averse to hearing inquiries for her health. She would allow the girls (who counted it a great privilege) to give her feet a warm bath, when she was suffering from a neuralgic headache, or was overcome with fatigue; but she invariably declined the attention of watchers, assuring us that she should need no care, and would probably 'be a great deal better in the morning.' Lovely as she ever was in health, she was more sweetly so in illness.

"Precious sister! We joy for her in her abundant entrance into the everlasting kingdom.

"Then farewell, pure spirit! and oh, that on all
Thy mantle of love and devotion might fall!
Like thee may we toil, that with thee we may rest,
With our Saviour above, in the home of the blest."

The following graceful tribute is from the pen of Rev. S. A. Rhea, of the Nestorian Mission: —

"A very partial acquaintance with our departed friend would convince any one that there were combinations in her character rendering her one of the most remarkable of Christian women.

"While she was distinguished for the solidity of her judgment, the soberness and maturity of her opinions, she was also gifted with a poetic temperament. Her imagination was rich, and she had great depth and sensitiveness of feeling. How could she have written with such fascination, with such graphic power, had she not felt so deeply? How her strong feeling, her vivid imagination, found at once the most fluent, rich, and expressive utterance! How remarkable, too, was her executive ability! She would undertake the most extensive repairs, in person superintending the masons and workmen; she would plan and prepare for a long journey; she would lay in the stores requisite for a family of forty; she would do such things most noiselessly and thoroughly; and yet, when was there ever a human heart strung with more delicate sensibilities? Who could touch like her a wounded spirit? Who could more feelingly enter into your grief? Who could minister more softly and wisely at the couch of the suffering? Who like her could put on the last touches to the dress of the little babe fallen asleep in Jesus? Her masculine executive power, and her feminine delicacy, were a rare combination. She did not seem to lean strongly on any human arm; but she had found a companion for her lone spirit, — an arm into which she entwined her own, — a bosom on which, in childlike faith, she rested her head; and this was the secret of her fortitude and self-sacrifice, of her exquisite tenderness and delicacy of feeling.

"She was a school-mistress, absorbed in lessons, rules, discipline, — a routine, perhaps, calculated to make the nature cold, one-sided, and angular; and yet how fresh she kept her social sympathies! With what heartiness she would welcome you to her home! Who would imagine that on her rested much of the care of forty Oriental pupils? She seemed to have, at the time, no other thought than for the happiness of her guests. There was magnetic power about her. Where did it lie? In the centre of her heart was a pure, unselfish love, and it flashed out over her face; it tuned her voice; it beamed in her eyes; yea, it ran through her fingers, as she would lay her hand on the head of the little trembling girl who entered the school for the first time, perfectly assuring her. She had a wonderful power over native men, as well as women, and the more refined and intelligent they were, the more gracefully they bowed to her sway. Who of us has not been struck with the reverential manner with which Deacon Isaac always treated her? It was not love alone that gave her magnetic power; but with it, strong sense, tact, discretion to say just the right word to a given individual, and at the right time. She was gifted with a rare knowledge of the human heart. She had herself a human heart, and her knowledge of our nature was intuitive. She touched its springs like a magician. She was master of it. With such a finely-balanced mind, such depth and delicacy of sensibility, such love, such intuitive knowledge, and such discretion, any one could predict her power. You could foreshadow to your own mind her life-work, and its fruits, as a simple necessity for such a spirit. She would have been anywhere a mighty power for good. Circumstances were at her bidding; she was never their creature. May her beautiful mantle rest on multitudes of Persian women! May her angel spirit ever linger about us, and her sanctified memory hallow our toil!"

After the intelligence of Miss Fiske's death reached Oroomiah, Rev. Dr. Perkins preached a funeral sermon from Prov. xxxi. 29, from which the following passages are selected: —

"Our departed sister was eminently social. No one, male or female, was ever connected with our mission, who has contributed more to the intimate brotherly and sisterly relations and intercourse of its members; who delighted more to have them often at her hospitable table, always spread with the nicest taste of a skilful house-keeper; or more enjoyed mingling freely in all the families of the mission. The atmosphere of love, redolent with kindness, which she thus diffused through our circle, and which has been well defined as being to the missionary work what oil is to machinery, can only be fully known and appreciated in its absence.

"Her sympathy with the sick and the afflicted in our circle was a living fountain, at once deep and overflowing, and, as is wont to be the case with a heart so sympathetic and benignant as hers, she possessed the rarest qualities of a skilful nurse.

"Among the many proofs of her intellectual superiority, of which we are personally cognizant, I may mention the following: —

"Her ability and skill in the acquisition of the language of the Nestorians. Few members of our mission ever mastered it more readily, or used it more effectively.

"The general success with which she met the lot and filled the sphere of an unmarried lady in the missionary service, — a lot always fraught with peculiar difficulties, which may wellbe said, as a rule, to try women's souls. That Miss Fiske should take the high stand she did here at the outset, in that difficult position, and hold on for fifteen years in the field, never, to my knowledge, committing an indiscretion, disconcerted by no embarrassment, and seriously depressed by no trial or discouragement, proves her to have possessed an intellect alike strong and well balanced.

"Her good judgment, and great practical and executive skill and tact in managing all the affairs of her school, whether pertaining to its financial and other business concerns, or to its internal regulation, were quite remarkable.

"Her judgment on general missionary subjects also was so accurate that members of the mission were accustomed to consult her in regard to them, and often with great advantage.

"Her discernment of character, discriminating and almost intuitive, I have very seldom known surpassed. It was perfectly natural that the Secretaries of our Board, after her return to America, should give her almost plenipotentiary power in the selection of teachers for other fields as well as the one in which she had labored.

"I have mentioned her executive tact; but the terms fail to express a certain something which she so largely possessed, enabling her to accomplish with comparative ease what would be quite impracticable, or very difficult, to others. Her ceaseless industry and tireless energy do not explain it. There was the quick comprehension, and the ready, plastic hand, which hardly ever made a failure, or put forth an inefficient exertion. Every stroke and every touch from her always told in every undertaking. Her manner was so elastic and facile that her labors and instructions seemed to cost her little or no effort. There was not the slightest air of bluster nor of pretension about her. On the contrary, her movements were so quiet and unostentatious as to be hardly observed, except by their marvellous results. We should be inclined to denominate that 'something,' *genius;* but it was unaccompanied, in her, by the least particle of that eccentricity (not to say folly), which reputed genius so generally betrays and, perhaps, emulates.

"The great influence which she early acquired over masses of the Nestorians, with whom she became acquainted, is further proof of her intellectual superiority. Long before her return to America they had been in the habit of going to her for counsel, — at first the friends and relatives of her pupils; afterwards, multitudes more, of men as well as women, in all their difficulties of whatever kind, — about as much as to any male member of the mission. As a rule, she discouraged such applications for advice from the men, but she could not prevent them.

"A few weeks before her departure from the field, Mar. Yohannan, who had known and revered the founder of Mount Holyoke Seminary, said to me: 'There is no one like her in America. She is equal to four of Miss Lyon, who was the greatest woman there. She has forty eyes, and knows everything about her.' Bating the Oriental extravagance of the terms of this eulogium, we readily perceive in it the very high estimate which a shrewd native judge formed of her ability; and few Nestorians, who knew her as well, would not accord to her as high a commendation.

"Her piety was eminently active and practical. She had no faith in dreams of joys springing from Christian hopes which do not prompt to earnest effort to obey Christ, and glorify him in unwearying toils to gain gems for his crown.

"Her piety was eminently self-sacrificing as well as active. Its emblems might well be given as the 'Cross and the Crown,' aptly indicated in the favorite hymn which she so often desired to be sung:—

"'Must Jesus bear the cross alone,' etc.

"Her piety, though it did not, of course, create her superior womanly qualities and intellectual powers, did doubtless expand, hallow, and beautify them all, crowning her remarkable character with that singular completeness and symmetry which left so little wanting, as viewed from a human standpoint, to render her one of the most perfect, or, we would rather say, least imperfect, of mortals.

"Sunny and hopeful in her temperament by nature, our sister was yet more so by grace, and she was a very happy Christian; not rapturous, but calmly and serenely joyful in the Lord.

"It was a principle with her never to shrink from duty, however self-denying, in small things as well as great. And duty, as duty, almost ceased to be *self-denying*, for she served her Redeemer, not as a slave, but in delightful obedience; the love of Christ constraining her.

"Another point worthy of notice in her labors was her yearning solicitude and earnest prayer for her school, especially during seasons of refreshing from the presence of the Lord. Always faithful, it might be said of her at such times, emphatically, that she '*watched* for souls,' as one that must give an account.

There was no disposition on her part to shift responsibility. Always grateful for help, she still felt that on her, first and chiefly, rested the burden of her dear pupils, and that burden often well-nigh crushed her, till she could roll it off at the foot of the cross in agonizing prayer and earnest labors, which God is wont to honor as his chosen instrumentalities for leading lost ones into his fold.

"Another point in Miss Fiske's labors in her school, which is worthy of remark, was her intense concentration of interest upon individual pupils, especially the sick. How have we seen her hang over the sick ones, when apparently going down to the grave, with a constancy and tenderness in nursing them, hardly surpassed by the bleeding heart of any mother over her own suffering child, unconscious of weariness until she saw that the crisis had passed, when she would often find herself, for the time, entirely prostrated!"

Brief extracts from Dr. Kirk's remarks, at the funeral of Miss Fiske, as reported by one present, will indicate his high estimate of her character: —

"I wish to speak carefully; but I am sure I can say I never saw one who came nearer to Jesus in self-sacrifice. If ever there should be an extension of the eleventh chapter of Hebrews, I think the name of Fidelia Fiske would stand there. That is a list of those who either had remarkable faith, or who suffered for the truth. She was a martyr. She had made the *greatest* sacrifice. *She had given up her will;* and when you have done that, the rest is easy. To burn at the stake for a while, to be torn on the rack, to be devoured by wild beasts, is as nothing when you have torn out your own will, and laid it upon God's altar.

"And so God sent her to benighted Persia, that those poor people might have there an image of Jesus, and learn what he was like, not by cold theories, but by a living example. He brought her back to us, that we might see what sanctified human nature can become, and might gain a new view of the power of his grace.

"She loved the Bible, and carefully studied it day by day; not that she might talk about it, or theorize from it, or teach it to others, but as an expression of her Father's will. Hence her wonderful power in teaching it. She carried those Nestorian women through the whole, from Genesis to Revelation, and made every lesson glow with a living light! As a minister of the gospel, willingly would I have sat at her feet to learn her way of teaching that blessed book. I asked her to tell me her method; but her modesty prevented. I thank God that he has raised up some one to show us how the Bible can be read, and taught, and lived.

"*Her love* was Christlike. It went forth to every one. She never asked if others loved her; never thought whether the thing to be done was for her own ease or not. Her own comfort never seemed to come up in her thoughts, but only what would please her heavenly Father. That love made her so beloved at South Hadley; that love took her to Persia. O sisters, do you know of Fidelia Fiske's toils, her privations? and have you read of what her sex there have become? of those lovely, self-denying Christians?

"I wish to speak of what she has done for South Hadley. When Mary Lyon gave up Miss Fiske to the missionary work, it was a great trial to her; but she did not hesitate. She gave of her best, though the beloved seminary seemed so to need this 'beautiful staff,' and Miss Lyon, in time, went to her reward. The tendency of everything earthly is to gravitate, and this is true even of a religious school. That seminary had experienced this downward tendency, and had not altogether resisted it, when, from her Eastern home, trained to that wonderful perfection (which is a part of the 'hundred-fold more' of the missionary reward), Fidelia Fiske came back, and, under God, restored the institution, bringing to it such a remarkable blessing, that this year, out of three hundred and forty-four scholars, only nineteen left it unconverted. The teachers will all say, and my fellow-trustees will agree with me in saying, that Miss Fiske would not have lived in vain, had her life-work been confined to what she has accomplished at Mount Holyoke."

The compiler of "Woman and her Saviour in Persia," Rev. T. Laurie, D. D., speaks, in the following letter, from an intimate personal acquaintance with Miss Fiske: —

"You ask for my impressions of Miss Fiske. It is pleasant to recall them, for there is not an unpleasant one among them all. The chief impression left on my mind is one of *most attractive loveliness.* I do not mean beauty of person, for in this respect she was not gifted above many of her sex, and, when in repose, her features seemed to betray a sense of pain, as if mental activity was needed to make her forget bodily distress. Nor was it that which we call fascination, depending on a rare combination of natural graces well cultivated, and used with consummate art; but, if I might use an old term that expresses the idea exactly, 'It was *lovingness;* not a mere fondness, but a holy love, guided by an unusually quick Christian intelligence.' She ever radiated happiness on all about her. The sight of her made us all glad, from the little child to the oldest one in the family. While she stayed, our joy in her was unmingled, and, after she had gone, memory found no occasion for criticism.

"Nor was this a higher state into which she rose now and then from a lower level. It was the steady outflow of her daily life; rather it was the outgrowth of Christ in her; for he abode in her and she in him. In her presence, Christ seemed not far off, and afterwards you felt like saying with some of old, 'Did not our hearts burn within us?' Yet, with all this, there was not the least affectation of superior goodness; no talk about eminent holiness, as though others did not know so much about it; but it was as if Christ's own love flamed from him through a human heart, that we might admire its beauty, and praise the Lord. It was a calm love, not calling attention to itself; but, like a fountain, ever flowing quietly out of and beyond itself. It was an eminently intelligent love, acting always in the right way, and with a discreetness and beautiful propriety, that suggested the guidance of a higher power. It was a uniform love, like the light that noiselessly supplies life to the flower and the tiny moss, to the tree that shelters both, and to the birds which sing among the branches.

"When first brought to Christ, she was led to sympathize with his love to the whole world; and, in her after life, that sympathy was very practical. It was as if the fulness of love to all was poured on each object of it within her reach.

"Her fellowship with Christ was such as made him not only almost sensibly present to herself, but also to those who recognized Christ in her.

"She was one of the very few, to whose leading you could commit yourself without fear of being led in any other direction than toward Christ and conformity to his will.

"I hardly expect to meet with another Miss Fiske on earth, but it seems as though my intercourse with her here gave me some delightful anticipations of the fellowship of the redeemed above."

We close these testimonials with a letter from Rev. R. Anderson, D. D., the venerable Secretary of the American Board, whose dispassionate judgment and well-known accurate estimate of character give great weight to his words: —

"Miss Fidelia Fiske, so long a beloved member of our mission to the Nestorians, was a very remarkable woman. Yet this was not owing to the predominance of any one quality, but rather to a combination of qualities, intellectual and emotional, surpassing anything I had ever seen in any other person. I remember enough of her uncle Pliny Fiske, one of the two pioneers in the Palestine mission, to believe that his strong hold on the popular interest was owing to a similar cause. Her emotional nature was wonderfully sanctified; and all her powers being well developed, and all nicely adjusted one to another, the whole worked with regularity and ease. Hence that singular accuracy of judgment, that never failing sense of propriety, and that easy flow of appropriate thought, for which she was distinguished. Hence the apparent absence of fatigue in her protracted conversations and conversational addresses, which was matter of surprise to those who looked only upon her delicate frame. Hence the habitual control of her sanctified affections over her intellectual powers, and her unfailing self-possession, so that she seemed ever ready at the moment for the call of duty, especially when it was to meet the claims of perishing souls around her. In the structure and working of her whole nature, she seemed to me the nearest approach I ever saw, in man or woman, to my ideal of our blessed Saviour, as he appeared in his walks on earth.

"Her usefulness was as extraordinary as her character. For her 'to live, was Christ.' It was as natural for her to speak of him, and for him, as it was to breathe, and her pious discourse seemed never out of place, as thousands in this country could testify. Her influence on the Nestorian character, especially upon that of the Nestorian women, is well set forth in the book, entitled 'Woman and her Saviour in Persia;' and, I doubt not, it would be the judgment of the mission, that few of their number exerted so great a formative influence on the Nestorian mind, as did this departed sister. I should certainly find it hard to name one, among the thousand and more who have gone forth into the missions of the Board during my official life, who has a brighter record of missionary service."

www.ingramcontent.com/pod-product-compliance
Lightning Source LLC
LaVergne TN
LVHW011150110826
845150LV00006B/1211

9781425546380